AA BOOK
2015

Architectural Association School of Architecture

Contents

Director's Introduction   4

Foundation Course   6
First Year Studio
Intermediate School   24
Diploma School   104
Complementary School   190
Graduate School   206
Visiting School   272

Hooke Park   288
Workshops
Research Clusters

Appendix   298

Spaces   305

Directors Introduction

This year's *AA Book* is both a printed compilation of a year in time and a mirror to the hundreds of spaces that make up the AA School – the rooms that constitute the buildings we occupy on Bedford Square, the structures on our rural campus at Hooke Park in Dorset and the studios and settings of more than 50 Visiting School programmes that take place across five continents throughout the year. One of the most unique parts of AA life is how these spaces are utilised by our community of students, tutors, staff and members to learn about contemporary architecture and culture in the highest resolution possible: by engaging with it first-hand, at 1:1 scale. Serving as a space in its own right, this book is an attempt to document the outcomes of these experiences, and so the following pages are filled with a vast array of work produced by this year's Intermediate and Diploma units as well as students in Foundation, First Year and our 11 graduate programmes. As much as anything, these projects reveal that the more we give to our spaces the more we get out of them, for even behind the solid brick facade of our Bloomsbury home our world and the way we see it is in a constant state of flux, and is so much better for it.

Since 2007 the annual *AA Book* has extended its content beyond the work of the school's units and programmes to include specially commissioned pages that in some way draw on this changing environment. Thanks to Eyal Amsili Giovannetti for his models and renders of the rooms that make up our home at 32–39 Bedford Square – found on section dividers throughout this volume. Their mysterious views up, down, inside and out perfectly capture the shifting nature of our environment. Thank you, too, as always to our Print Studio, for their ability to produce a book in real-time alongside the projects themselves, to AA members far and wide for their ongoing support and to the hundreds of students, teachers and staff for making this year so special.

Brett Steele, Director, AA School

The AA Foundation uses the disciplines of art, film, architecture and craft to teach students how to become conceptual and creative thinkers. Ideas and designs are explored through the processes of model-making, sketching, drawing, filmmaking and performance. Throughout the year students explore their own individual design sensibilities and approaches while collectively engaging with the rich educational, cultural and social life of the AA and London.

FOUNDATION

FIRST YEAR

First Year introduces students to architectural design, critical thinking and experimental ways of working. It comprises approximately 60 students who work individually and in groups in an open studio format under the guidance of six experienced and energetic design tutors. Here, students begin to form their own architectural identities and personalities through a range of design ideas, agendas and interests. In addition to the studio, students take courses in history, theory, media, technology and technical studies. Together these courses lead to a portfolio of the year's work, the basis for entry into the Intermediate School.

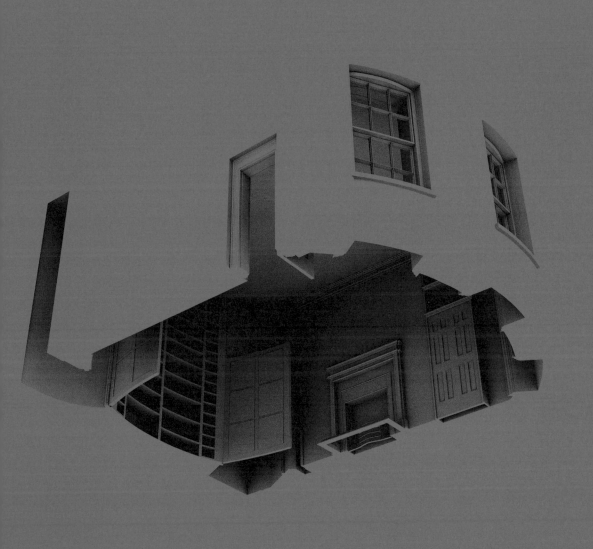

Foundation Course

Foundation Director
Saskia Lewis

Studio Masters
Umberto Bellardi-Ricci
Taneli Mansikkamaki

Many thanks to our
Consultants and Critics
Eduardo Andreu Gonzalez
Daniel Ayat
Sue Barr
Andre Baugh
Pascale Berthier
Mark Campbell
Barbara-Ann
  Campbell-Lange
Kleopatra Chelmi
Fenella Collingridge
Charlie Corry Wright
Georgie Corry Wright
Alison Crawshaw
Albane Duvillier
Trevor Flynn
Raluca Grada
Juliet Haysom
Antoni Malinovski
Clare Macdonald
Flora McLean
Sara Muzio
Francesco Neri
Joel Newman
Luca Nostri
Jessica Pappalardo
Christopher Pierce
Fearghus Raftery
Julian Roberts
Lewis Ronald
Matthew Rice
Heikki Salonen
Brett Steele
Terrence Taehyuk Kim
Sylvie Taher
Trys Smith
Vere Van Gool

The AA Foundation course is a one-year introduction to an art- and design-based education. It allows students to develop their conceptual ideas through experiments with a wide range of media and creative disciplines in an intimate studio-based environment. The course seeks to develop the intellectual and process-based abilities of each individual while simultaneously introducing each individual to themselves: their own interests, passions, aspirations and inspirations.

Sight to Site

We identified 1:1 sites across the school, made sketch surveys, drawings and models of complex junctions, cast them and extracted the fragments for further examination. We occupied modernist apartments in central London over periods of 24 hours, measured their volumes, made speculative filmic narratives about fictional events, documented views and bore witness to the shift of light across these volumes as night fell and in turn as darkness was consumed by dawn. In Lugo we found the Madonna and child suspended in the modernist grid of a reflected bank, and in Villa Saraceno we processed along axes, examined volume and material and documented how the building leaked light as it was consumed by the fall of a misty autumn night. We absorbed the architecture biennale and basked in the coloured facades of the island of Burano.

We carved out routes through London and identified buildings with intriguing histories. We knitted in Fitzrovian workhouses and explored histories of unrest in Brixton. We made physical both the horrors of war and pleasures of dance. We filmed in the footsteps of famous twentieth-century figures, recreating their shadows against walls that had regularly witnessed their wanderings. We made garments steeped with texts written in espresso and animated a ski trip across the hills of Hooke park. We cast bomb damage from the walls of buildings and explored the voids left by this violent energy bathed in white dust.

Students
Khaled Al-bashir
Anna Aleshkina
Nena Aru
Muqing Bai
Esther Brizard
Won Ho Chi
Luke Decker
Katarzyna Dobrowolska
Tera Elabboud
Jia Long Feng
Oussama Garti
Jeremy Gaunt
Philip Gharios
Theodora Giovanazzi
Amalia-Anastasia
  Gisca-Chitac
Kwang Yi Goh
Liam Hayes
Amaya Hernandez
Gaoqian Jiang
Lito Karamitsou
Jun Wei Koh
Katia Lechaczynski
Li Li
Leonard Liao-briere
Irina Elena Mania
Alexandru Mitea
Atiehsadat Naghavi
Dara Nerweyi
Jihane-may Slaoui
Shlok Soni
Zaina Sweidan
Maroussia Tasiaux
Ezgi Terzioglu
Taek Gyun Won
Sarochinee
  Wongchotsathit

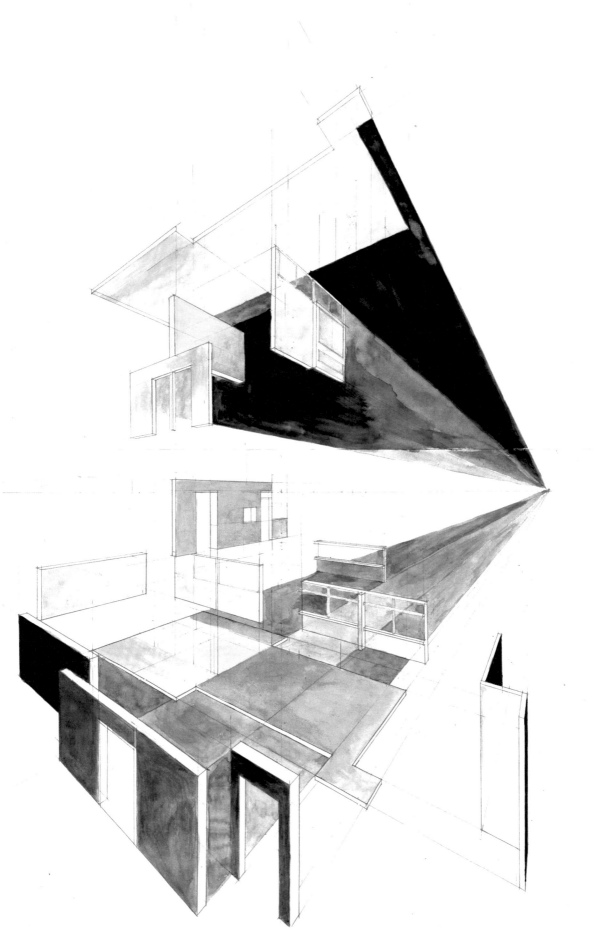

2

3

1. (previous page) Irina Mania — exploration of colour palette of 44 Great Arthur House Golden Lane Estate at dusk during 24-hour site survey

2. Nena Aru — leaking intimacy
3. Khalid Al-Bashir, study of a conversation reflected in a puddle — a transitory moment of circumstance, Lugo

4

5

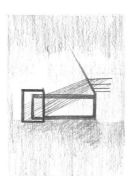

6

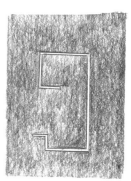

4. Irina Mania, study of a stair – form, material
and weathering, Lugo
5. Sarochinee Wongchotsathit – investigating
light through composition and refraction,
44 Great Arthur House, 24-hour survey

6. Lito Karamitsou – sketches of light and shadow
from a series of models

7

7. Zaina Sweidan – study of the reflection of a sill into
the perpendicular surface of a parked truck framed
through colour, Lugo

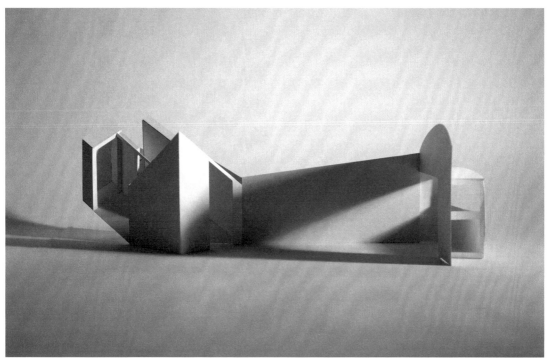

8

9

8. Kway Yi Goh – model of 351 Crescent House Golden Lane Estate subverted through perspective

9. Irina Mania – inhabitable 'eye' to act as *camera obscura* 1:1 exploration, Hooke Park

13

10

11

12

10. Atiehsadat Naghavi – structure and illumination
wrapping around a tree, 1:1 exploration and
investigation, Hooke Park
11. Ezgi Terzioglu – occupation of space, 44 Great
Arthur House Golden Lane Estate – 24-hour site survey

12. Won Ho Chi and Shlok Soni, in homage to *Easy Rider*
– 1:1 test installation, hybrid of a sledge and two tyres,
Hooke Park

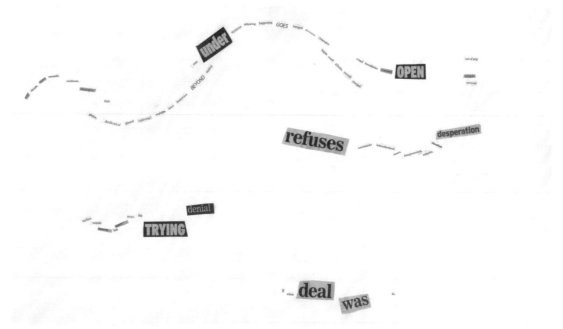

13

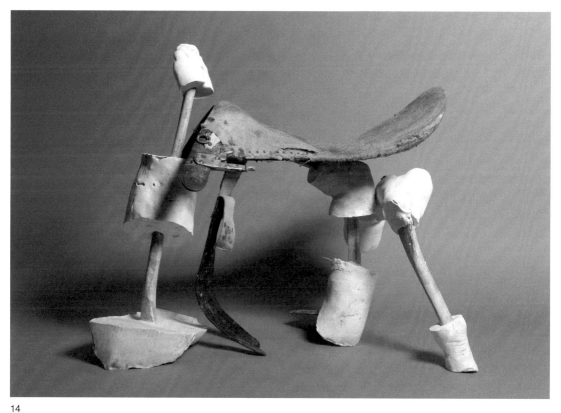

14

13. Sarochinee Wongchotsathit – exploring 'System' as a rhythmic pattern of time/emotion/function as it decomposes into disorder/chaos/anxiety, lateral text collage

14. Irina Mania, saddle, fallow deer bones and casts of human body parts – experiments in hybrid forms at 1:1, Hooke Park

First Year

Head of First Year
Monia De Marchi

Studio Staff
Fabrizio Ballabio
Shany Barath
Pol Esteve
Maria Shéhérazade
 Giudici
John Ng
Ryan Neiheiser

Visiting Tutors &
Workshops
Winston Hampel
Max Kahlen
Alex Kaiser
Ana Araujo
Sue Barr
Alessandro Bava
Davis Bestué
Marco Corazza
Ryan Dillon
Tommaso Franzolini
Ehud Freedman
Raluca Grada-Emandi
Guido Guidi
Stefan Jovanovic
Shaun Levin
Xavi Llarch
Oliviu Lugojan-Ghenciu
Juan Montiel
Francesco Neri
Joel Newman
Luca Nostri
Suzanne O'Connell
Jessica Pappalardo
Thomas Pearce
Edward Pepper
Alvaro Perez
Davide Sacconi
May Safwat
Ilona Sagar
Theo Spyropoulos
Catrina Stewart
Manijeh Verghese
Alexandra Vougia

Special thanks to Brett
Steele, Barbara-Ann
Campbell-Lange, Thomas
Weaver, the MS, HTS and
TS First Year tutors, our
guests and critics, the
admissions office and
maintenance staff.

Inhabiting Worlds, Muses vs Nemeses and Experiencing Now

The work from this year's explorations is collected into six words paired up as sentences across the following pages: Inhabiting Worlds, Muses vs Nemeses and Experiencing Now. 'Inhabiting Worlds' shows a series of projects that questioned what it means to be an inhabitant. We invented creatures and designed habitats with a series of installations and performances. Following the making of 1:1 inhabitations, we imagined tales for invented 'Worlds' with images and illustrations capturing near future environments. The second set of words combines two opposing explorations: 'Muses' collects reenactments of exemplary architecture projects and texts. We transformed past projects by challenging the permanence of designed spaces with novel temporalities and performative models. 'Nemeses' collects inventions and explorations on architecture form via its elements, language, timeframes and rhythms. The last two pages show different ways of engaging and exploring – 'Experiencing Now' gathers a series of searches into the present while directly experiencing its current conditions. On the left page, under the word 'Experiencing', we engaged with places and moments by crossing territories and by constructing projects within specific sensations where places, spaces and inhabitants are all seen as characters. Similarly, 'Now' collects translations of found stuff and information into distinct works that disclose our ways of looking, imagining and making in a spirit that is open and daringly vulnerable.

Students
Samir Abillama
Daria Aiatollahi Moussavi
Hasan Yehia Al-Rashid
Thanaporn
 Amornkasemwong
Selin Arisal
Sofiia Astrina
Julian Bachle
Aarohi Bakeri
Catinca Balinisteanu
Sofia Pia Belenky
Martina Bergamo
Maria Bessarabova
Alix Marie Biehler
Anna Brylka
Yoav Caspi
Max Celar
Gordon Hau Yan Chan
Kevin Ka Yu Chan
Lai Ka Annie Chan
Napat Chayochaichana
Ryan Mujung Chiu
Min Jung Cho
Clarissa Su Wen Chua
Jacopo Anthony Colarossi
Catalin-Ioan Crina
Leticia Dadalto Camara
Marion Delaporte
Hunter Doyle
Alia Durda
Shou Jian Eng
Karim Fouad Hefny

Shidi Fu
Georgia Hablutzel
Alma Margot Hawker
Jessica Hindradjaja
Erik Hoffmann Meyes
Zachariah Guan Poh
 Hong
Jou-Yu Huang
Chloe Louise Hudson
Wonyoung Jeong
Jae Whan Kim
Minju Kim
Alister Shung Hei Ko
Jasen Zi Xian Kok
Christopher Kokarev
Idil Ece Kucuk
Yana Kushpitovska
Hei Yeung Kwok
Ruby Silove Lanesman
Ye Jin Lee
Tanya Lee-Monteiro
Zineb Lemseffer
Chak Hin Leung
Roi Levin
Andy Tzu-hsiang Lin
Caterina Miralles
 Tagliabue
Molly Mummery
Moad Musbahi
Jaeseung Nam
Katayoun
 Nekourouymotlagh
Ananya Nevatia

Joyce Ng
Oluwafadekemi
 Ogunsanya
Joon Hyung Park
Jake Harrison Parkin
Anushri Patel
Natalia Pereverzina
Aoi Phillips Yamashita
Jonas Phillip Simon Popp
Ignatio Bhaskara Putra
Nathalie Reifschneider
Angelica Rimoldi
Simonpietro Salini
Zahra Sarbuland
Dor Schindler
Clara Julie Lea Schwarz
Esha Sikander
Younseo Song
Malgorzata Stanislawek
Aleksandar Stankovic
Oratai Taechamahaphant
Jocelyn Patricia Tang
Zi Ken Toh
Phillip Zhao Jie Tsang
Pranav Vakharia
Xuecheng Wang
Gigi Tsz Yan Wong
Sheng-Chin Wu
Yat Ching Marcus Yau
Xiaohan Yin
Hexuan Yu
Zhou Yu
Xinyi Zhang

16

2

3

4

1. (previous page) First Year works – accumulation of works, things and stuff that constantly transforms through modes of writing, designing and discussing.
2. Inhabiting the AA – constructing inhabitants, creatures and inhabitations in the AA

3. Inhabiting the First Year Studio with somatic release and group-building workshop – awakening in 5 stages
4. Inhabiting the AA with installations, performances and constructed experiences

5

6

7

5. Worlds – imagining tales for cities with a series
of illustrations and visual scenarios
6. Worlds – imagining tales for cities with a series
of translations from sound to visual

7. Worlds – constructing micro-worlds with a series
of interactive devices and installations

8

9

8. Muses – reimagining exemplary projects with temporary and permanent materials, programmes and sites

9. Muses – rebriefing the competition for Parc de la Villette with performative models and scenarios for a park for the twenty-first century

10

11

12

11. Nemeses – designing micro-worlds with models
while testing programmatic events and their effects
12. Nemeses – iterations of models discovering
different possibilities for elements, forms, spaces
and rhythms

10. Nemeses – inventing sequences of spaces
with organisational models for buildings types
and monsters

21

13

14

13. Experiencing the territory by capturing the shift from urban to landscape with the use of photography

14. Experiencing London with a series of time-based models and films

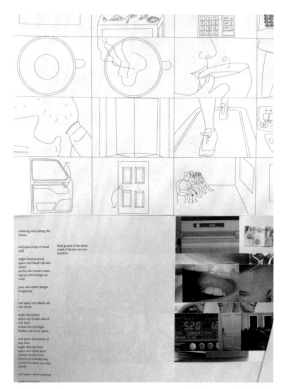

15

16

17

15. Now – constructing encounters in the city
with storyboards of spatial sequences
16. Now – capturing current conditions with film,
information, sounds and news

17. Now – a day in the First Year Studio capturing
the process of transforming material and stuff into
positions and projects

The Intermediate School gives Second and Third Year students the basis for development through experimentation within the structure of the unit system. Each year the Intermediate School offers a balance of units covering a diversity of questions and innovative approaches to material, craft and techniques of fabrication. Explorations of cultural and social issues are often set in inspiring places around the world. In parallel to the unit work, skills are developed through courses in history and theory, technical and media studies as well as professional practice.

INTERMEDIATE SCHOOL

Intermediate 1

Unit Staff
Mark Campbell
Stewart Dodd

With thanks
Miraj Ahmed
Ariadna Barthe
Cuatrecasas
Tyler Bollier
Barbara-Ann
  Campbell-Lange
Kate Davies
David Dunster
Nick Elias
Maria Fedorchenko
Murray Fraser
Vere van Gool
Carlos Jimenez
Saskia Lewis
Tyen Masten
Chris Matthews
Jongwon Na
Luke Pearson
Christopher Pierce
Takero Shimizaki
Steven Spier
Antoine Vaxelaire
Carlos Villanueva-Brandt
Kieran Thomas Wardle
Sarah Whiting

No Country

In many ways Texas defies description. Not only in terms of its scale, or the disconsolate vastness of the West Texan desert, but also as an idea. Larger than any European country, yet still only one of 50 states in the union, it illustrates both the exceptionalism and the latent absurdities of the democratic experiment of the United States. Governed by the harsh realities of petrochemical industries and internecine politics, Texas is a place where, as the writer Cormac McCarthy once suggested, we all come to be cured of our sentiments.

Our visit to the barren desert and petrochemical wastelands of Texas was the final stage of Intermediate 1's investigations into the beauties and paradoxes of the contemporary United States – an exploration that over the last five years has also taken in projects in the Borscht Belt, Detroit, Salton Sea and the Mississippi Delta. In each case, our work has sought to illustrate our fascination with the passing temporality of architecture and the residues of such failed utopias. Cinematic in scope, we viewed Texas through the lenses of Wim Wenders' *Paris, Texas* (1984) and the Coen brothers' *No Country for Old Men* (2007) as a precursor to questioning the architectural possibilities of the Lone Star State. Acting as 'archaeologists of the immediate future' (to paraphrase Reyner Banham), we sought to design a real, surreal or entirely speculative architectural intervention set in this vastness.

The resulting projects included: a glutted corporate city clustered around an oil tank; a hurricane defence; an evangelical campus; a middle school that fracks its own oil; a superhighway between Mexico and America; a rejuvenated landscape of cotton production; an Agave farming machine; a series of iconographic interventions across the Trans-Pecos desert; an obelisk and dam that mark Houston; a hybrid town and refinery; a reinvention of history; and an anti-battery of 264 identical buildings that consume 3 per cent of the world's energy.

Students
Lola Conte
Isotta Cornacchia Biasion
Liam Denhammer
Josh Harskamp
Chiyan Ho
Michael Ho
Lorenzo Lo Schiavo
Ana Nicolaescu
Sahir Patel
Shaan Patel
Rebecca Ploj
Andreea Vasilcin

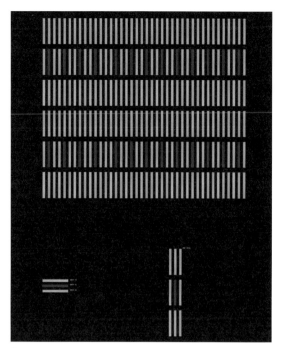

3

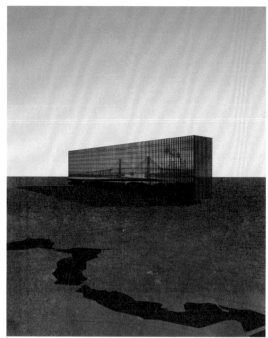

4

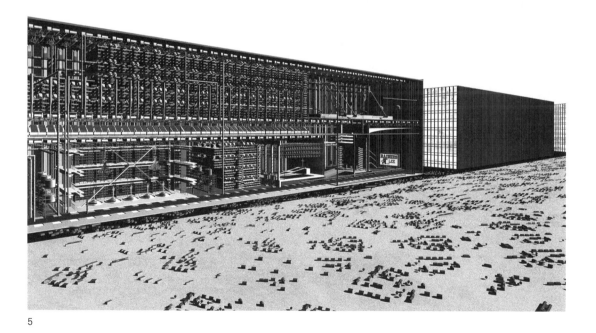

5

1. (previous page) Michael Ho, Manchester-Valero
Middle School & Oil Refinery, Manchester, Texas
2. (opposite) Chiyan Ho, interior, Dead Mall,
Baytown, Texas

3. Chiyan Ho, Organisational Grid of 264 mega-
structural buildings (208 residential units, 26 car
parking units and 26 freeway units), Baytown, Texas
4. Chiyan Ho, 1980s Mirror Glass Facade,
Baytown, Texas
5. Section, Anti-Battery, Baytown, Texas – the 264
buildings that form the project will consume 3 per cent
of the world's energy.

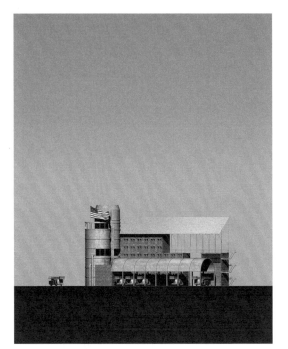

6

7

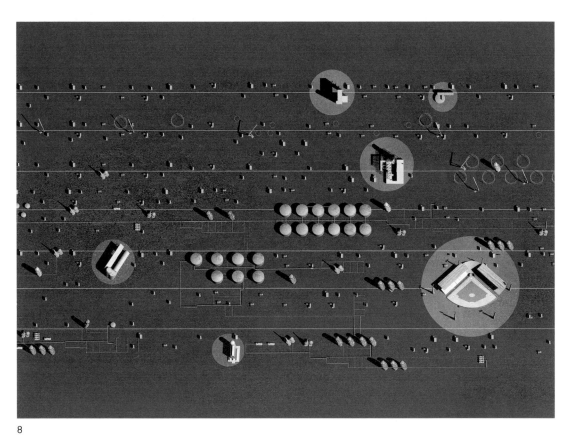

8

6. Michael Ho, Manchester-Valero Fire Station,
Manchester, Texas
7. Michael Ho, Manchester-Valero Hotel,
Manchester, Texas

8. Michael Ho, Valero refinery expansion sequence
2015–2035, Manchester, Texas
9. (opposite) Michael Ho, Apartment Building &
Refinery, Manchester, Texas

Intermediate 2

Tutors
Takero Shimazaki
Ana Araujo

A special thanks to those
who have supported us
All Inter 2 students from
2010–11 to 2014–15,
especially Patricia
Mato-Mora, Anton
Gorlenko and Alexandra
Savtchenko-Belskaia, for
helping us to further
develop the unit agenda

Willem de Bruijn
Antonino Cardillo
Miraj Ahmed
Marilyn Dyer
Barbara-Ann
   Campbell-Lange
Brett Steele

And to the AA tutors who
have provoked us
Maria Fedorchenko
Christopher Pierce
Stewart Dodd
Ricardo de Ostos
Carlos Villanueva Brandt
(for Lili Carr's
incredible project!)

A New Old Town: What is Your Vision?

Over our years of research, Intermediate Two has unearthed the poetics of tactile and sensual architecture, often through a careful study of the history of places.

This year's focus was the historic town of Aldermaston, Berkshire, and the Aldermaston Park, a vacant estate that sits in close proximity to the Atomic Weapons Establishment plant. We studied the buildings that occupy the town and estate as well as the landscape and garden walls. From here, strategies were devised to reimagine Aldermaston as a new town with a prominent role in today's British and international scene.

The average Aldermaston resident is approximately 50 years old. Based on this demographic we transformed the town into a pioneering resort for the ageing population. Learning from similarly visionary projects, such as the Royal Saltworks at Arc-et-Senans in France (1770s), we created an architectural setting to shape a new community and lifestyle.

Relying on memories and tradition, but also maintaining a forward-looking and innovative point of view, Intermediate Two works with the notion of the 'historical present', as defined by Italian architect Gio Ponti and refined by Italo-Brazilian architect Lina Bo Bardi. We are committed to understanding context in a complex manner by looking at its physical, temporal, social and nd political layers. Most importantly, we aim to contribute to the configuration of new contexts, dealing with our subjective and individual senses and emotions (psychological dimension) as members of a community (social dimension) and as agents of transformation (political dimension).

Students
Daria Belyakova
Anton Gorlenko
Juana Horcajo Rubi
Chung Kim
Li Zhi Loh
Paolo Emilio Pisano
Patricia Roig
Alexandra
   Savtchenko-Belskaia
Ke Bo Tsai
Yu-Hsiang Wang
Qinyang Zhu

2

3

1. (previous page) Yu-Hsiang Wang, Home for
Senior Citizens, Aldermaston Village

2 & 3. Anton Gorlenko, Chimney Skyline,
Aldermaston Park

4

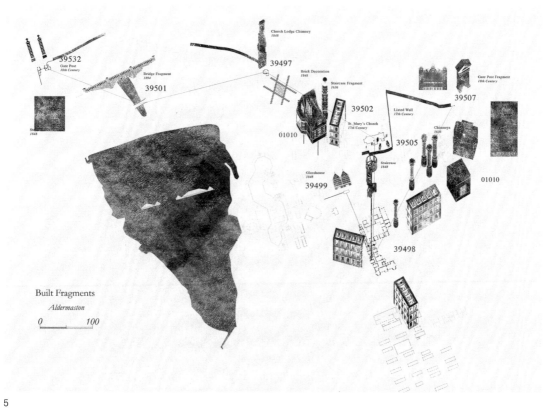

5

4. Li Zhi Loh, Alice's World

5. Paolo Pisano, Aldermaston Park (1815–2015)

6

7

8

6. Qinyang Zhu, Home for Children and the Elderly,
Aldermaston Park
7. Daria Belyakova, A Vision for Aldermaston Park

8. Ke Bo Tsai, Solar-Powered Bath House,
Aldermaston Park

9. Alexandra Savtchenko-Belskaia, Inhabiting the
Boundary, Aldermaston Village

Intermediate 3

Tutors
Nannette Jackowski
Ricardo de Ostos

Thank you to our
guest critics
Gian Luca Amadei
Ana Araujo
Kasper Ax
Giles Bruce
Nat Chard
James A Craig
Apostolos Despotidis
Oliver Domeisen
Maria Fedorchenko
Alvaro Fernandez
   Pulpeiro
Kostas Grigoriadis
Sarah Handelman
Daniel Kupfer
Alice Labourel
Samantha Lee
Abel Maciel
John Ng
Marco Poletti
Elke Presser
Caroline Rabourdin
Yael Reisner
Stefanos Roimpas
Jack Self
Theodore Spyropoulos
Brett Steele
Jeroen van Ameijde
Manijeh Verghese
Thomas Weaver
Ivana Wingham
Simon Withers
Yeena Yoon

Strange Land Mirage

What lies in the human unconscious that is released in dreams, forgotten by morning and manifests itself in myths? How are the archetypes of the human condition transferred to land in the form of memory and rituals? Set within our current context – an environment ruled by the commoditisation of property – Intermediate 3 searches for the idea of the mythical within land ownership, exploring architecture as a time-based occupation rather than a container of space.

We located these conditions during our travels to Sri Lanka, a country severed by 30 years of civil war, with a coastline washed away by the catastrophic 2004 tsunami and an urban economy of new large-scale developments bankrolled by foreign capital. In this multi-layered scenario the students investigated their own ideas of land archetypes – Promised Land, Cursed Land and Wonderland – working between large drawings and test prototypes. Drawings were initially used for investigations and as a way of evidencing intuition, clues, analyses and findings. Later they were used to comprehensively present the final proposal, which while utilising both approximation and precision was also always a rigorous exercise of the imagination.

By analysing the current postwar military condition Nicholas Zembashi proposed 'Insidious Colossus', a project where the human body is both a building and an ever-unfinished monument made of melted military machinery and filled with surprising urban functions. Both Assaf Kimmel and Nathan Su investigated the new investment boost in the capital of Colombo with the first proposing a radical alternative in the form of a hollow, mixed-ownership mountain and the second empowering citizens with a new system of participating in urban development utilising AR to influence the city fabric. In these projects and others the students of Intermediate 3 discovered new ways of looking at the status quo of ownership, using modern technologies, ancient myths and most important, people and their stories, to reveal the unwritten value of land.

Students
Yee Thong Chai
Jiehui (Avery) Chen
Dominika Demlova
Raphael Zwi Fogel
Assaf Kimmel
Christoph Lenhart
Yonathan Kevin Moore
Henry Si Yuan Ngo
Natalie Eugenia Ow
Susanna Steuerman-
   Kinston
Nathan Samuel
   Nap Tak Su
Nicholas Zembashi

1. Nathan Su, The Augury – a speculative future scenario in Slave Island, a contested site in Colombo, where local residents, government authorities and foreign investors are all vying for a piece of its increasingly valuable land. Constructed from real-time data sent directly from the phones of residents and investors, the Augury is an augmented reality projection of Slave Island's future, whose coherence and clarity directly reflects public sentiment. In front of a local land market, residents and investors gather to trade, encode and purchase 'totems' – augmented reality markers that confer ownership rights and the ability to encode futures into the Augury.

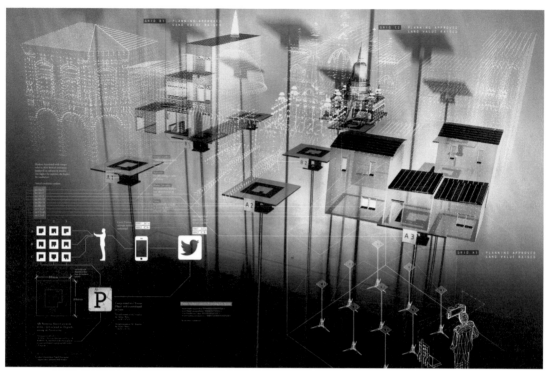

2

3

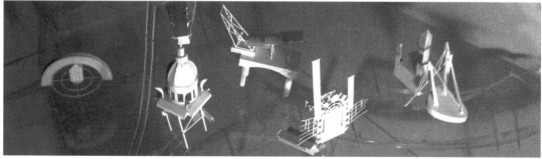

4

3. Natalie Eugenia Ow – in this speculation of an alternate timeline and a crossing of two communities, a synthesis of living is created as a refuge from the war. Essential traits and elements from each community are extracted, brought together and interweaved as a possible reinvention and adaptation of their hybridisation.

4. Natalie Eugenia Ow – paper model composed of fragments collected from mapping a route around London, embodying the way one first experiences a new and unfamiliar land. Through this collection of elements, the fragments piece themselves together to form bizarre hybrids recognisable only to the wanderer.

2. Nathan Su, Augmented Reality Prototype – introduces real-time user interaction to the augmentation process. The digital models are displayed on any markers that are detected in the webcam feed, allowing users to manipulate and visualise a digital environment in real time, in real space.

40

5

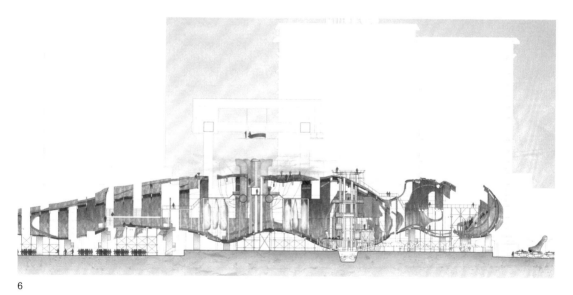

6

5. Nicholas Zembashi, Colossal Torso – the capital of Colombo hosts the microcosm of a nation within the contingent body of a growing colossus. Here lies the torso, the north central province of Anuradhapura (the biggest land parcel proportionate to the largest body part). Its cultural and geographic significance translates into the heart and soul of a giant. A shaft, not yet fully formed, becomes a supporting infrastructure for on-looking pilgrims while soldiers and military engineers lay skin plates in place.

6. Nicholas Zembashi, Insidious Colossus – the insides of the colossus, open to the public throughout the construction process, have become near-sacred spaces of national spectacle. Down the rabbit hole, a pilgrimage inside unveils a wonderland of shafts. Temples proportionate to religious territorial dominance are one of the first things encountered upon entry. Further in, an amphitheatre lies somewhere close to the scalp, tormenting voices inside its head.

7

8

7. Yonathan Moore – the war widows of north Sri Lanka come together to form a shared community under whose authority they reclaim land lost during the war and on which they build a new kind of farm. This house-farm has a polar arrangement of irrigation lines stemming from a water tank housed at its centre. As the house is open, the farm around it provides the enclosure, and the varied functions of the farm are aggregated to the zones created between its crop lines.

8. Yonathan Moore, Furnace Rover Prototype – exploring the notion of land demarcation in relation to the concept of no-man's-land. The rover is programmed to drive in these uncharted lands, leaving a trail of molten metal in its path and creating encryption patterns for future use. The result is a map drawn by borders on the land, and the tension between these forms the basis for a new law.

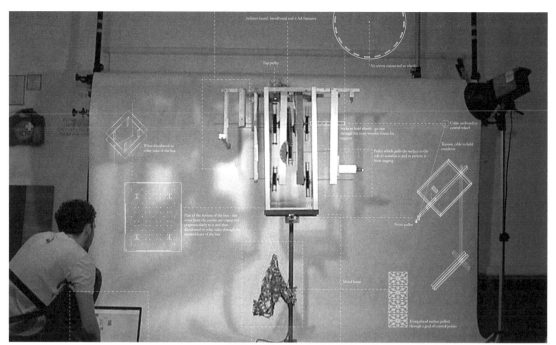

9

10

9. Assaf Kimmel, Lands of Cockaigne prototype – addresses the notion of the Promised Land and generates imaginary landscapes which are abundant in natural resources as an alternative to the limits of physical land. These are formed when natural resources are scarce. Activated by a live RSS feed from the New York Stock Exchange, the abstract landscape mutates to different forms of wild nature when stocks of companies that deal with natural resources go up. If landscape is a notion conceived by those living in the city, Promised Land exists in the minds of those living on exhausted land, emptied from its resources.

10. Assaf Kimmel, Colombo's Mountain – a project that responds to an expected expansion of Sri Lanka's capital city Colombo, which faces massive land reclamation projects through foreign investment. The project creates an alternative infrastructure for mixed-use housing and public leisure spaces, with the ambition to form a balance between market forces and the needs of its local population. Characterised both as a masterplan and a singular architectural undertaking, the project addresses the sweeping urbanisation of fast-growing cities, utilising building sequencing and spatial interdependency between the users.

Intermediate 4

Tutors
Michel da
  Costa Gonçalves
Nathalie Rozencwajg

Acknowledgements
Denis Lacej
Lara Belkind
Hao Wen Lim
Eugene Tan
Carolina Gismondi
Regina Kertapati
Hussam Dakak
Harikleia Karamali
Eulalia Moran
Peter Karl-Becher
Yechiam Karu
Daniel Leon
Barbara-Ann
  Campbell-Lange
Nuria Alvarez Lombardero
Carsten Wiewiorra
Brett Steele

Skyline

In today's emerging urban situation both the semantic and the cultural are perverted and dwarfed by the need for a global iconography. As cities struggle to achieve iconic status, local conditions have bent to the will of the global. Situating their prospective research in a moment of transience – between what was and what is to be – Intermediate 4 students looked to Paris, a city that defies change, in order to develop possible futures and alternative pasts for the twenty-first-century city.

'Skyline' was understood as a conceptual tool and revealing agent devised to read over-managed and augmented Singapore and tackle bi-polar Paris. Situating ourselves on their shared axis, the projects of Intermediate 4 exposed dualities between the ethereal image and the harsher self, studying the antagonistic relationship between the historical city and the segregated corporate district of La Défense. With the collective will of a nineteenth-century autocrat, our proposals invested an architectural no man's land where the Haussmannian mask disintegrates. We infiltrated world monuments from within and inhabited floating spaces around and above the city. Students suggested time-based strategies that played on a local psyche formed by paradoxical affinities for grandness, novelty and historical continuation. Alternative or derivative histories for a Paris redesigned through hypothetical changes produced a chain of events as an architectural project. Environmental and regulatory studies through parametric optimisation led to unexpected parallel cities, such as an inhabited urban cloud on stilts that mirrored its analogue essence.

Virtual verticality or erasure as a design technique revealed the collusion between form and social media-driven expectations. The interstitial gap between cultural and religious substance and the disincarnating action of monumentality engendered novel mapping and stealth projects in fleeting monuments.

A future Paris was made of many potential selves.

Students
Olukoyejo Olanrewaju
  Akinkugbe
So Jae An
Thanas Apilikitsmai
Raluca Beznea
Shu En Sarah Goh
Matthew Hepburn
Berkin Islam
Ioannis Kanakas
Fang Lee
Edward Zhiyi Li
Celine Elia Lea
  Lavinia Przedborski

2

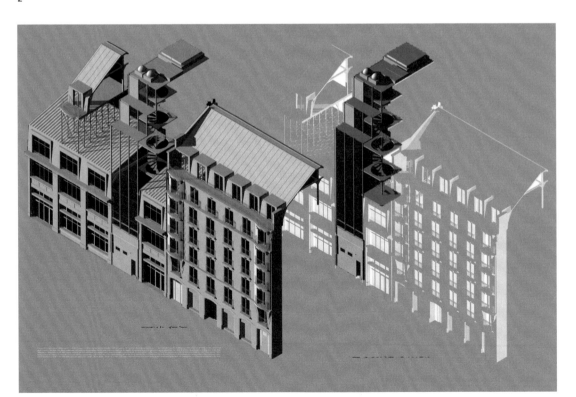

3

1. (previous page) Shu En Sarah Goh, The New Inserted Monument within – transforming the Palais Royal perception, allowing a fresh and invigorated perspective of the original monument

2. Ioannis Kanakas, Inhabited Dome – virtual verticality and the answer to the Parisian city through novel clouds of an ancient typology
3. Olukoyejo Akinkugbe – copy-paste as self-destruction of Paris through imposed homogenisation

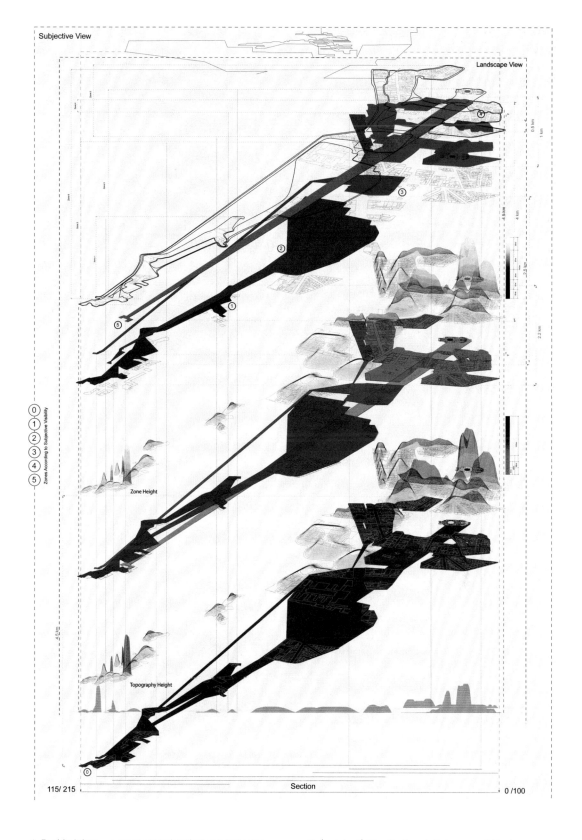

Subjective View

Landscape View

Zones According to Subjective Visibility

Section

115/ 215

0 /100

4. Berkin Islam – a vantage point that explores the cultural information hidden within the flat city-scape of Paris, expanding as a virtual monumentality that alters the landscape of the city

5. (overleaf) Shu En Sarah Goh – caught between politics and history, the architectural artefact Sainte Chapelle builds alternative futures as she reflects the power struggles of France

47

6

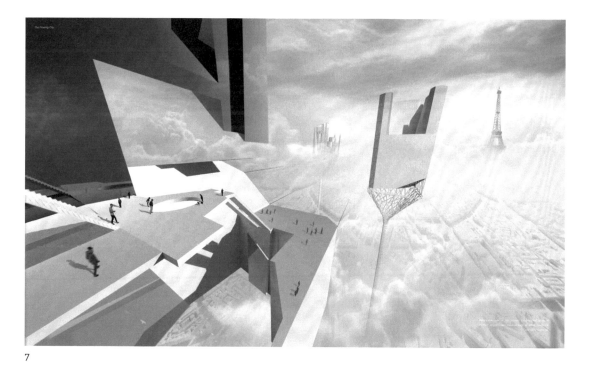

7

6 & 7. Berkin Islam – a series of monumental towers
disappearing above Paris, exploring a new typology
of an omnipresent and absent skyline

Intermediate 5

Unit Master
Ryan Dillon

Staff
Jorge X Méndez-Cáceres
Ralph Andrew Merkle

Friends
Ana Araujo
Charles Arsène-Henry
Maria Beyer Skydt
Valentin Bontjes
  van Beek
Barbara-Ann
  Campbell-Lange
Brendon Carlin
Mollie Claypool
Mark Cousins
Kate Davies
Kenneth Fraser
Gabriela García
  de Cortázar Galleguillos
Evan Greenberg
Kostas Grigoriadis
Samantha Hardingham
Nannette Jackowski
Costandis Kizis
Inigo Minns
Ricardo de Ostos
Jessica Reynolds
Natasha Sandmeier
Theodore Spyropolous
Emmanouil Stavrakakis
Brett Steele
Sylvie Taher
Thomas Weaver
Manja van de Worp
Jeroen van Armejide
Manijeh Verghese
Reiner Zettl

100,000,000,000,000 Rules[1]

01. Under the sovereignty of limitation, Architecture is liberated. Supra-canal; translation Along a VISIONARY nomadic stretch. This living highway breathes, igniting A revolution of the *human-powered*. 02. Decluttering is the solution for: living with maximum space given. Personal objects as ARCHITECTURAL constraint. Constant lives/Fixed waterway/Less Things/More emptiness: my Architecture 03. 'Living architecture' seldom encompasses waste; Restrained construction and ingestion, the INTERVENTIONS FOR(m) a mobile material. Abundant by the canal, they Navigate 'the system' like *excrement*. 04. || *Sampling* existing religious architectural ensemble | Composing transgression of busking law | Orchestrating reverberations of AN ALMOST-FUTURE | Resonating devices of diachronic movement | Emerging introspective culture of sounds || 05. *Ecologies* of building and living. Architectural bytes mobilise into space. ALONG AN artery constrained by: water – a new towpath connects: markets and stations with events. 06. *slowness*, as, a, new borough: architecture, mobilised, at, 1 m / 23 min, an, AQUEOS SLICE, elevates, from, underground – fitzcarraldo, slicing, through, London's efficiency. a, constraint, inhabited: operative delay – 07. Canal penetration, an institutional escape. Everyman's office objects dismantled, reused. WITHIN LONDON subvert office architecture. Liberate living through cathartic ritual. Stress, dismantle, build, travel, *Escape*! 08. Activating industry along the Viaduct, architectural devices are manufacture systems, OPTIMISTICALLY bridge residents; reshape living. Extracting condition of canal segment, as source of local *production*. 09. Hunt disused architectural edifices, cut Fragments soak in canal water Cook, serve, host ALTERING living To make a communal *meal* Add a dash of dialogue. 10. An arbitrary collection of pieces (fancifully constrained into architectural mobiles (shifting level of OUR PERCEPTION (putting ordinary life on standstill (transgressing any gap via *play*)))). 11. Canal conducts life and mobility. So does walking a step. All activities OF EVERYDAY are; not restricted when architecture does – what canal and *steps* do. 12. When solid atoms become liquid; provisional acts of mobility consolidate, through acts of everyday LIFE; then architecture reappropriates existing infrastructures; the *Hexatic* phase is to begin!

Students
Matteo Agnoletto
Kamila Natalia Imbir
Jinah Kim
Time Kitilimtrakul
Sandra Karolina Kolacz
Nabla Mohammed Yahya
Thao P Nguyen
Samuel Ramnek Petri
Jacek Rewinski
Palita Rompotiyoke
Tuan Anh Tran
Jane Wong

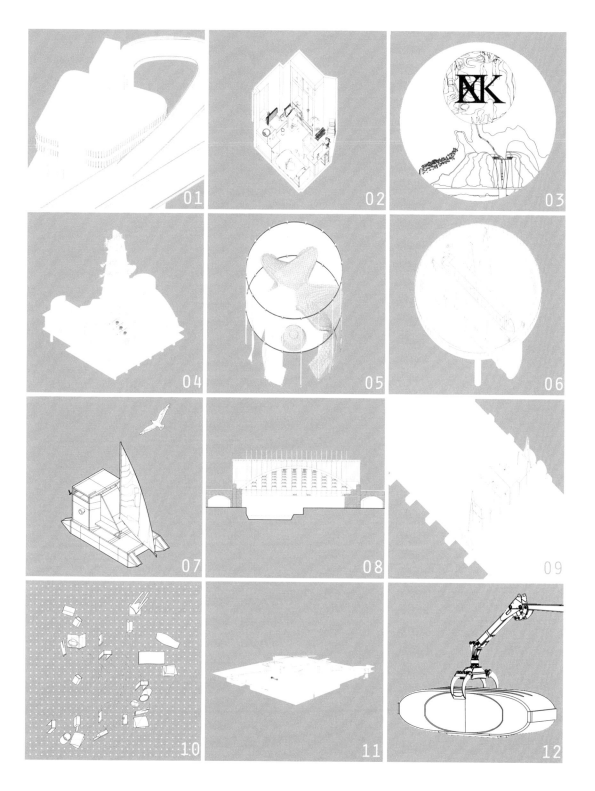

1. RULE 1 – 25 Words per student; RULE 2: Each segment is to contain five words. Each text is to be 25 words that total five segments: RULE 3: Collective Unit Statement, each student is to use one word given by their tutor that creates a vertical sentence within the text (in CAPS): RULE 4 – Sentences do not have to conclude with full stops: RULE 5 – Each student must use one word from the following: LIVING or MOBILITY, for the word that was NOT chosen, each student must select a synonym as its replacement – RULE 6: Each student must use one word from the following: CANAL or CONSTRAINT, for the word that was NOT chosen, each student must select a synonym as its replacement – RULE 7, each student is required to use the word: ARCHITECTURE – RULE 8, 12 Keywords (one starter or one conclusion) – RULE 9, words not to be used: site, typology, programme, function, context

2

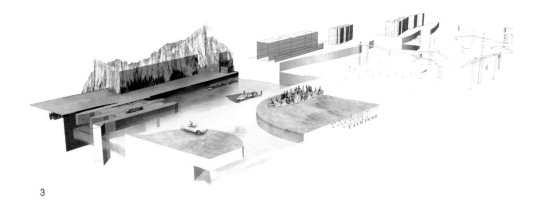

3

2. Jacek Rewinski, To make a communal *meal* Add a dash of dialogue

3. Jinah Kim, Canal conducts life and mobility. So does walking a *step*

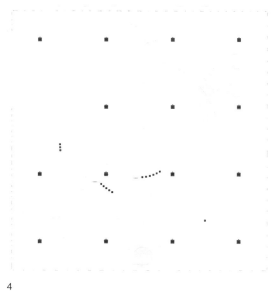

4

5

6

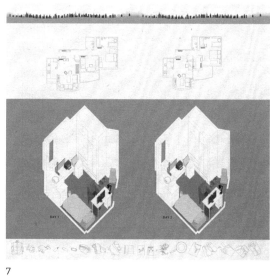

7

4. Jane Wong, *slowness*, as, a, new borough
5. Tuan Anh Tran, Extracting condition of canal segment, as source of local *production*

6. Sandra Karolina Kolacz, 'Living architecture' seldom encompasses *excrement*
7. Thao P Nguyen, *Decluttering* is the solution for: living

8

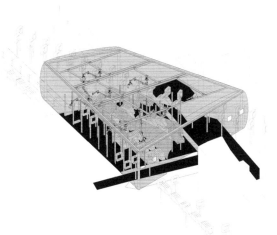

9

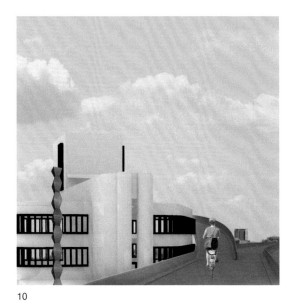

10

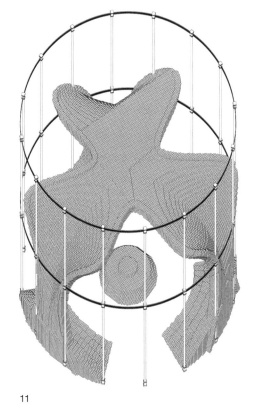

11

8. Kamila Natalia Imbir, Stress, dismantle, build, travel, *Escape!*
9. Matteo Agnoletto, the *Hexatic* phase is to begin!

10. Nabla Mohammed Yahya, A revolution of the *human-powered*
11. Time Kitilimtrakul, Architectural *modacubes* mobilise into space

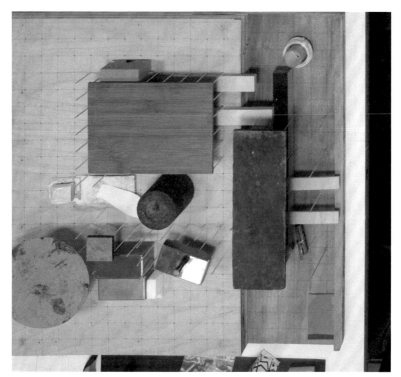

12

13

12. Samuel Ramnek Petri, (transgressing any gap via *play*))))

13. Palita Rompotiyoke, *Sampling* existing religious architectural ensemble

Intermediate 6

Unit Masters
Jeroen van Ameijde
Brendon Carlin

Unit Tutor
James Kwang-Ho Chung

Seminars
Doreen Bernath

Critios
Valentin Bontjes
  van Beek
Andrea Bugli
Ryan Dillon
Felix Fassbinder
Maria Fedorchenko
Tomasso Franzolini
Evan Greenberg
Soomeen Hahm
Manuel Jimenez Garcia
Alexandros Kallegias
Zaid Kashef Alghata
Angel Fernando
  Lara Moreira
Ricardo de Ostos
Christopher Pierce
Martin Self
Marco Vanucci
Manijeh Verghese
Michael Weinstock
Andrew Yau
Lara Yegenoglu
Qin Zhao

This year, Intermediate 6 has adopted the theme of 'deep planning' as a working method and ethos, applying an 'integral, time- and user-based approach' to architecture and urbanism. Based on this information-based mode of practice, the unit has embarked upon a detailed mapping of civic life in order to generate projects that can initiate progressive shifts within society. 'Deep planning' allowed us to further our understanding of the complex realities of the urban condition and to discuss the indirect role of the architect's interventions within a dynamic reading of human activities and other mechanisms of urban life.

In Term 1, students worked in teams of three on spatial analyses of particular parameters such as environment, programme, materiality and visibility. Using the former Festival of Britain site at London's South Bank, we produced a collective information model that was used as a laboratory to test enhancements that affected the vibrancy of public space. During our study trip to Shanghai and Tokyo, we documented a range of cultural phenomena taking place within the urban interiors of these hyper-cities. These observations demonstrated how evolving communities and three-dimensional urban planning create opportunities for enhanced cultural expression and interactions.

Throughout Terms 2 and 3, and supported by a programme of seminars, the unit students developed individual design proposals at the South Bank site, operating at both architectural and urban scales. Responding to the site's historic traces of ambitious experimentation, our projects question the role and materialisation of a national cultural centre within an increasingly commodifying urban territory. By proposing a variety of intensified urban spaces serving both consumption and non-commercial uses, students speculate on new types of architectural systems that apply a synergetic interweaving of private and public urban domains.

Students
Francesco Catemario
  di Quadri
Leong Nin (Alex) Chan
Michael Cheung
Marco Chui
Luca Gamberini
Mizue Katayama
Tsz Chun (David) Lam
Elizabeth Low
Natacha Pradere
Ao Tan
Xxx Yihong
Wenjun Zheng

1

2

1 & 2. Luca Gamberini – on analysing the social
dynamics of pocket spaces at the perimeter of urban
plazas, a series of new urban routes and courtyards
was created using variable types of edge conditions.
The different degrees of porosity of the perimeter
mediate between passers-by and commercial
programmes and provide resting spaces, separated
from the intensified public realm.

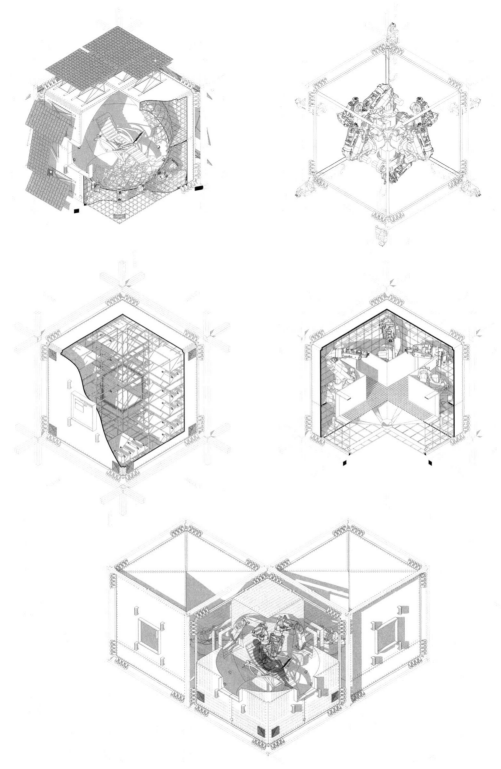

3. Francesco Catemario – a series of mobile pods that will inhabit the 'Anti-cultural Culture Monument', a machinic self-constructing mega-structure for voluntary exclusion from physical society. Inhabitants can fully concentrate on virtual social interaction in pods that contain media screens and infrastructures for life support. The colony of virtual citizens is serviced by specialised pods that deliver food and health-care and recycle human waste and remains.

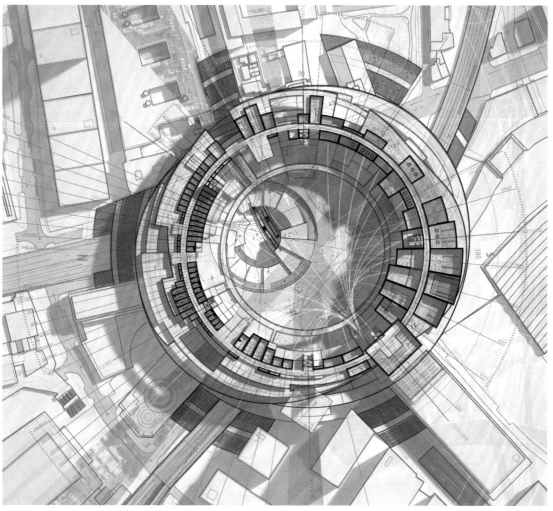

4

5

4 & 5. Alex Chan, London Zone Zero – investigating
a new centre for London by incorporating an extreme
concentration of commercial and cultural programmes.
The circular infrastructure promotes synergies
between programmes and visitor groups, creating
highly charged event spaces in the interior. Spiral
walkways form streets that extend up into the project,
allowing access to smaller-scale public spaces and
residential areas at higher levels of the ring.

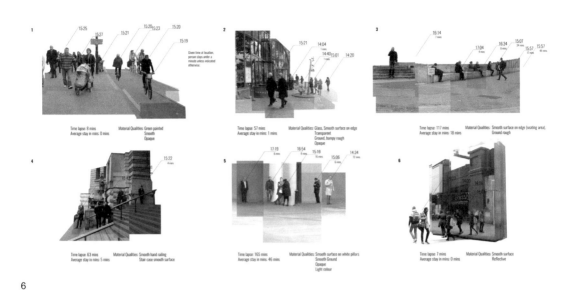

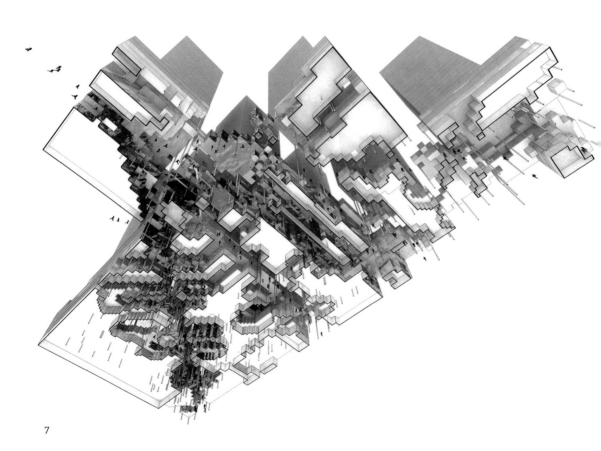

6. Alex Chan, Natacha Pradere and Xxx Yihong – mapping of human behaviour and the duration of activities in relation to the materiality and 'smoothness' of the surfaces of the city

7. Natacha Pradere – new urban fabric in between Waterloo Station and the Royal Festival Hall, featuring various degrees of 'friction' between people flows and interaction surfaces

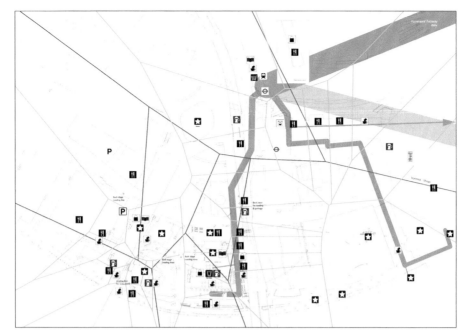

8

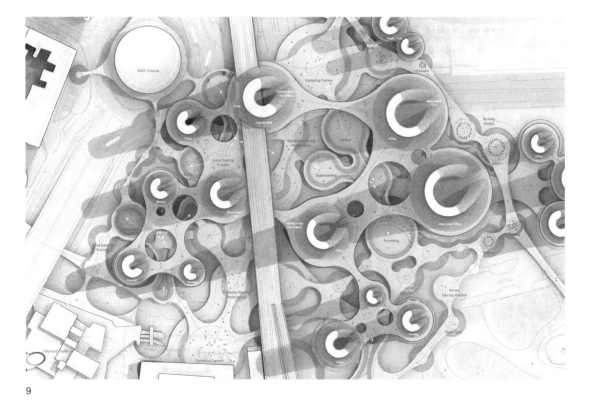

9

8 & 9. Mizue Katayama – mapping of existing facilities for cultural expression around London's South Bank, using spontaneous activities in public space as a measure of democratic success. Using specific diameters of group activities and networking strategies to provoke exchange, the project becomes a radical re-imagining of the site as an infrastructure for participatory development.

Intermediate 7

Unit Master
Maria Fedorchenko

Workshops
Magnus Casselbrant
Tommaso Franzolini
Jesper Henriksson
Gergely Kovacs
Lorenzo Perri
Antoine Vaxelaire

Thanks to
Barbara-Ann
   Campbell-Lange
Miraj Ahmed
Ana Araujo
Roz Barr
Lawrence Barth
Matthew Butcher
Mark Campbell
Brendon Carlin
Kristof Crolla
Ricardo de Ostos
Steward Dodd
Kenneth Fraser
Kostas Grigoriadis
Maria Shéhérazade
   Giudici
Winston Hampel
Brian Hatton
Francesca Hughes
Sam Jacoby
Katya Larina
Dirk Lellau
Jonas Lundberg
Nuria Lombardero
Tyen Masten
Inigo Minns
Vanessa Norwood
Chris Pierce
Manolis Stavrakakis
Brett Steele
Jeroen van Armeijde
Manijeh Verghese
Carlos Villanueva Brandt
Ivana Wingham
Former Inter 7 students
Marina Lathouri and
   HCT students
All of our critics
   and guests

Architecture Culture: Sites of Exchange

Let's admit it: we are all fascinated by the architectural culture – that fiery web of interconnections between ideas and sites, figures and contexts – but when it comes to its impact on how and what kinds of architecture we are to produce, there are difficulties. This year the unit focused on those links and loops of production and reproduction to inform new sites of exchange. Most projects were developed on two levels: initially charting cross-flows between the institution and the city and then relating creative processes and spaces.

With Berlin as the ideal architectural game-board, we tested interfaces between built and imaginary cities. From pragmatic solutions for catalytic expos and exhibition battlegrounds, to speculations on the uncanny dream cities of morphologies, all projects asked: what happens to architecture as it is bought or stolen, violated or released back into the city? Out of this questioning, our 'memory palaces' and laboratories amassed both curatorial and industrial machines to reduce or augment the samples, to test hybrids or chimeras and ultimately, to provoke alternative preservation and renewal. However, hosting extended life cycles of architecture in our experimental institutions also forced us to re-examine the processes of production and the infrastructures that support them. Thus, we sought thick yet fluid frameworks for our 'culture factories'. Whether we condensed disparate platforms into clusters – from cine-city studios to towers of knowledge – or splintered cultural cores to blur the lines between live/work/show, the extended scenario for 'diffused condensers' was always our common concern.

Multiplying levels and scales of work, we developed our visionary projects for urban exchanges as both theoretical provocations and practical demonstrations. Letting cultural and spatial pursuits inform each other, we exposed our design thinking to even larger feedback loops that define social and spatial orders, systems of production and products.

Students
Kosha Ahmadi
Alexander Christian
   Foss Ball
Alvaro Calle Moreno
Kenneth Chow
Mads Bjørn Christiansen
Adolfo Del Valle Neira
Alessandro Magliani
Anna Martsenko
Zsuzsa Peter
Gleb Sheykin
Sebastian Tiew
Gabriel Wulf

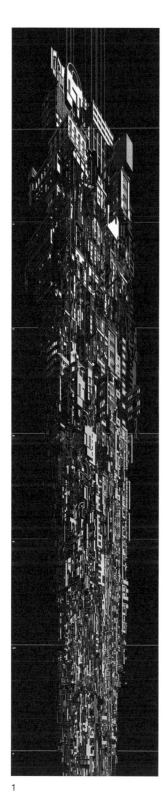

1. Sebastian Tiew, Memory Palace – tackling cycles of construction, destruction and reconstruction, an alternative Stadtschloss is colonised by cultural and material machines that devour, process and eject architectural fragments and provisional assemblages – ready to engage new memorial sites.

2. Gleb Sheykin, River of Facades – following a series of anti-preservation heists, stolen facades are delaminated, hybridised or cloned as they pass through a vast cultural depository, poised between a theoretical speculation and a practical experiment on the renewable image of the city.

3

4

5

3–5. Gleb Sheykin, River of Facades

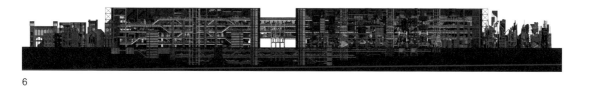

6

7

8

6–8. Sebastian Tiew, Memory Palace

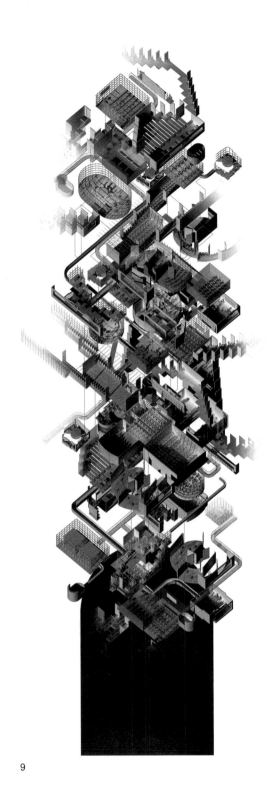

9

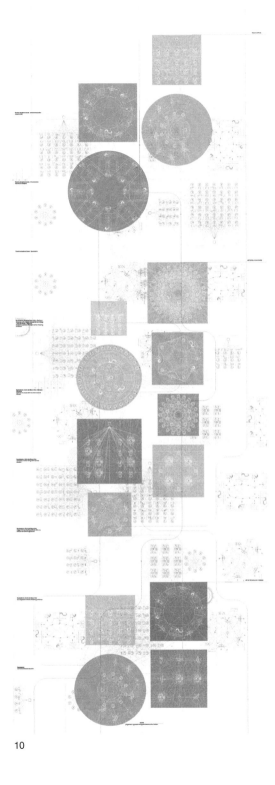

10

9 & 10. Zsuzsa Peter, Imaginist BauAkademie – testing a future educational institution that embraces diversity and rejects boundaries, the project collapses the traits of various architectural schools across space and time. An evolving 'tower of knowledge' is a nexus of emerging theoretical approaches, design methods and typological elements.

11 (opposite) Alessandro Magliani, Dream-City of Morphologies – a real Berlin coexists with the uncanny disciplinary city: a platform for experimentation with morphological 'themes' (from interruption to remix) as seen in exaggerated blocks and anomalous urban structures.

Intermediate 8

Unit Staff
Francisco González
  de Canales
Nuria Álvarez Lombardero

Workshop tutors
Hao Wen Lim
Stavros Papavassiliou

Special thanks
Pedro Alonso and Jose
Rosas Vera, Pontificia
Universidad Católica
  de Chile
Mauricio Puente,
Pontificia Universidad
Católica de Valparaiso

Thanks to our Critics
Gabriela García
  de Cortázar
Hernan Pitto Bellochio
Catalina Pollack
Elif Erdine
Pierandrea Angius
Yota Adilenidou
Pol Esteve
Adam Kaasa
Barbara-Ann
  Campbell-Lange
Ryan Dillon
Kasper Ax
Israel Nagore
Rob Stuart Smith
Marie Isabel
  de Monseignat
Naiara Vegara
Beth Hughes
Javier Castañón
Lara Belkind
Jerry Tate
Fabrizio Ballabio
Kenneth Fraser
Brett Steele
Alvaro Arancibia
Francisco Chateau
Edgar Gonzalez
Maria Shéhérazade
  Giudici
Miraj Ahmed
Ryan Neiheiser
Max Kahlen
Brendon Carlin
Denis Lacej
Loreto Flores
Ciriaco Castro

Politics of the Neoliberal Block Santiago de Chile Colonial Grid

'On October 12, 1492, America discovered capitalism.'
Eduardo Galeano

Following the unit's research in Buenos Aires and São Paulo, this year Intermediate 8 completed its three-year exploration of the large urban block in the South American metropolis. This year's city of focus, Santiago de Chile, has offered an incredible opportunity for investigating how political, urban and architectural consequences are intertwined today.

Supported by seminars, readings, trips and debates, conversation has revolved around how neoliberal policy-making in Chile has altered not only the ways in which the city of Santiago has been shaped, but also the most basic spaces in which its citizens' everyday life unfolds. In Santiago, everything that was ever part of the welfare state – housing, education, health, transportation, culture, sports – has undergone a radical process of privatisation that spans from urban planning to domestic life. By confronting, bypassing and even co-opting these processes, students have investigated alternatives to this current state of affairs, seriously considering all possible consequences of their design proposals, from the urban scale to individual, material experience.

All projects have been placed within the 120m^2 colonial grid of Santiago's city centre, a prototypical area in decay since the Pinochet era and the neoliberal push of urban development to the periphery. The different block proposals made within this grid not only offer individual sparks against the darkest night of social equality, but also portray a coherent argument for rethinking the city as a whole.

Students
Amar Piyush Mehta
Antonin Hautefort
Elias Michael Tamer
Hana Shokr
Jeanne Sophie
  Charlotte Clerc
Mikolaj Karczewski
Patricia de Osma Arena
Olimpia Presutti
Raya Shaban
Shira Rotem
Sophia Alami Gouraftei
Yasmina Abou Jaoude

1

2

1. Shira Rotem – evolving scheme for a housing proposal based on variable and dynamic sharing

2. Patricia de Osma – emergency block for earthquake aftermaths bridging across the Mapocho River

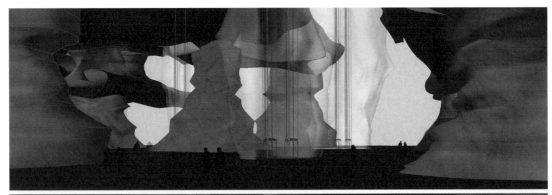

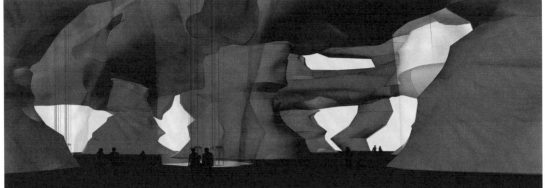

3

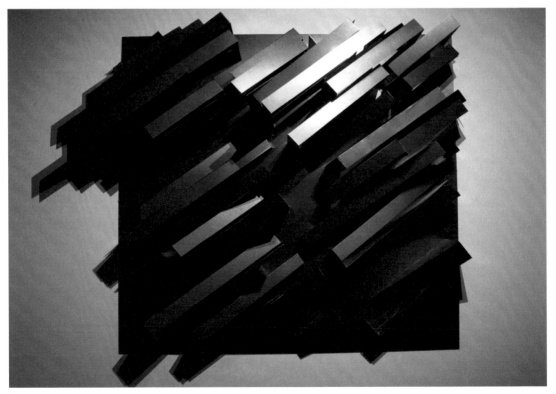

4

3. Mikolaj Karczewski – formal explorations on the possibilities of inhabiting vertical and horizontal voids carved on a solid block

4. Shira Rotem – formal exploration on public/ private ambiguity by manipulating space, shadow and reflection

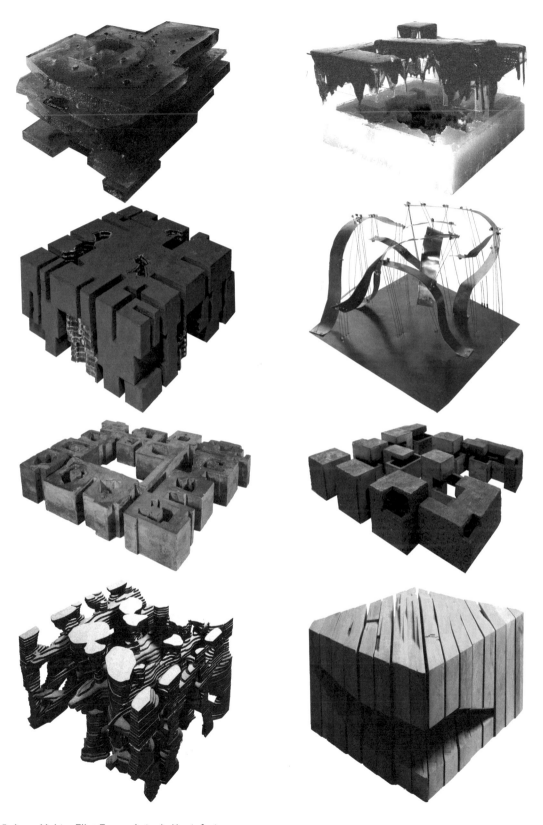

5. Amar Mehta, Elias Tamer, Antonin Hautefort, Yasmina Abou Jaoude, Raya Shaban, Hana Shokr, Mikolaj Karczewski and Patricia de Osma – an archipelago of urban blocks for Santiago city centre

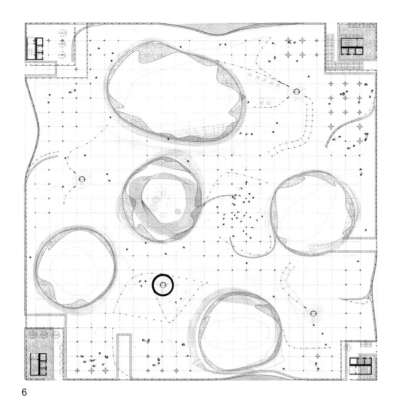

6

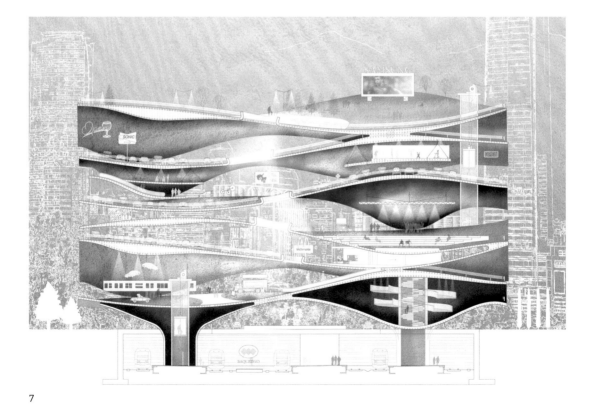

7

6. Antonin Hautefort – plan explorations for a Mapuche health and ritual centre in Santiago city centre

7. Amar Mehta – considering car parking as an opportunity for defining a new public space typology in Plaza Italia

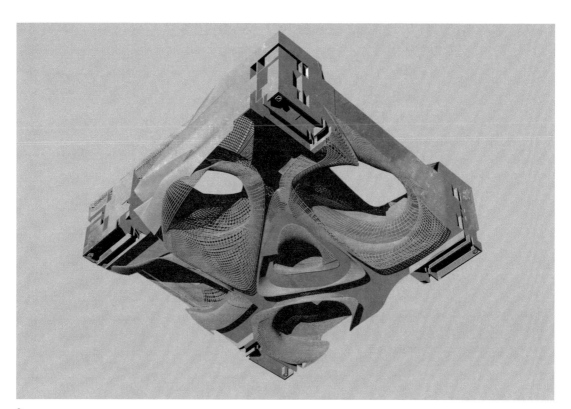

8

9

8. Antonin Hautefort – dialogue between two formal and material entities in a bilingual approach to the urban city block

9. Patricia de Osma – infrastructural development of an urban block for housing communities in an earthquake emergency

Intermediate 9

Tutors
Christopher Pierce
Christopher Matthews
Charlotte Moe

Acknowledgements

Denmark:
Daniel Christensen
Mark Hermansen
Arielle Johnson
Jørgen Jørgensen
Niels Pedersen
Tøger Nis Thomsen

UK:
Miraj Ahmed
Flavie Audi
Ariadna Barthe
Valentin Bontjes
  van Beek
Carlos Villanueva Brandt
Maria Brewster
Giles Bruce
Barbara-Ann
  Campbell-Lange
Kate Davies
Stewart Dodd
Eleanor Dodman
Pol Esteve
Maria Fedorchenko
Kenneth Fraser
Wolfgang Frese
Winston Hampel
Francesca Hughes
Lily Jencks
Basmah Kaki
Amandine Kastler
Mark Kelly
Monia De Marchi
Giles Martin
Ian O'Brien
John Outram
Igor Pantic
Ananth Ramaswamy
Benjamin Reynolds
Umberto Bellardi Ricci
Natasha Sandmeier
Takero Shimazaki
Brett Steele
Rachel Edwards Stuart
Hugh Todd
Emmanuel Vercruysse
Manijeh Verghese
Madelon Vriesendorp
Matthew Wells
Gareth Wilkins
Solomia Zoumaras

Spain:
Ricardo Bofill
Natalia Chiner
Toni Cumella
Guillem Cumella
Jesper Thorup Jensen
Teresa Ventura

Sponsors
Ceràmica Cumella

Super Tasters

Who could possibly have guessed that from a slowly dehydrated leek, desiccated pomegranate, pared papaya, forensically sliced pepper, deconstructed beechnut, magnified coconut or fermented mangosteen you could construct an array of architectural projects? Ingredients such as these were the starting point for all our drawings and 3D work this year – a pantry of references that represented quite a departure from our usual modus operandi. Over the last few years our shtick has been to revisit, and in the process attempt to reinvent, the B-side of modernism's golden generation, usually settling on an overweight and over-indulged figure like Stirling, Aalto or as we intended this year Jørn Utzon. However, having spent much of October on a fleet of sturdy bikes scouring and scraping the little of what's left of the barrel of Utzon's legacy in and around his Danish hometown, we changed tack and dropped in on a not insignificant upstart in Scandinavian culture – star chef René Redzepi's restaurant Noma – in the process transposing the model of the overstuffed and overfed onto ourselves.

For the uninitiated, over the last dozen years a bunch of jumped-up 'seal fuckers', as Redzepi and his fellow chefs were once termed, have foraged their region in assembling plates of unparalleled deliciousness for Copenhagen's midday and evening diners. We joined them in sampling this fare, but on a following morning, when we visited the Noma kitchens, the chefs spoke of an architectural imposition they were currently battling – a proposal to build a bridge from the city's mainland København quarter to their own, fiercely independent, dockland Christianshavn Island. And so responding to their anguish, we set the unit the task of using the same urban ingredients to produce a more palatable solution for the city's disconnected harbour.

Among the 11 new projects we produced, many obliterated the offending bridge, a couple of others crowded out its failures with multiple other bridges, at least one relocated the restaurant to the adjacent Papirøen Island, a few more turned it into a 'church of the poisoned mind' or 'yellow brick road', and one French student who, having had more than enough of what she considered a bunch of 'arrogant, self-obsessed, celebrity chefs', realigned the city and its cuisine along more appropriate Francophile lines by drowning the whole thing in sauce.

Students
Caroline Esclapez
Dalia Matsuura Frontini
Ronghua Lei
Kevin Leung
Cheryl Lim
Vasilisa Lucic
Beatrice Melli
Bodo Neuss
Nabil Randeree
Ines Tazi
Brandon Whitwell-Mak

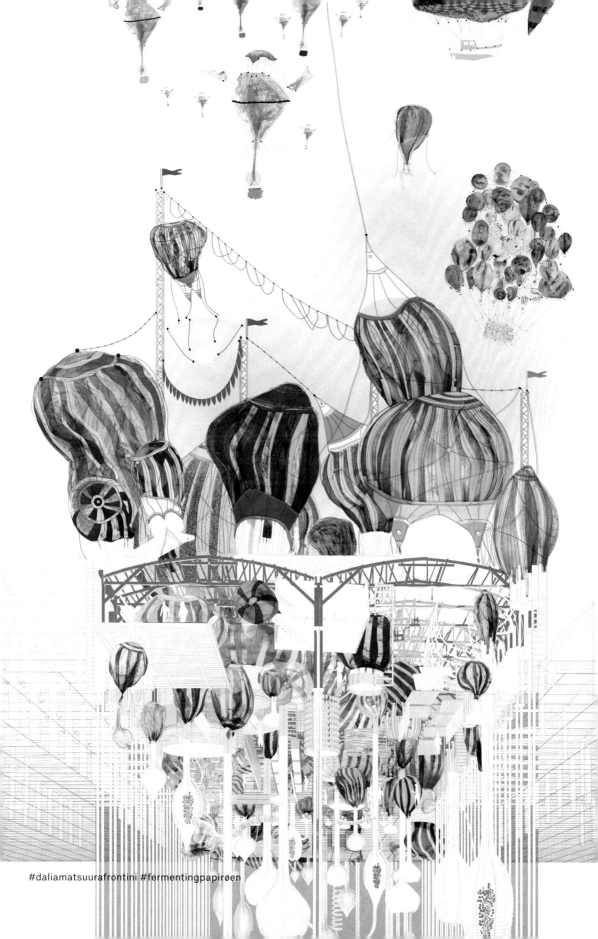

#daliamatsuurafrontini #fermentingpapirøen

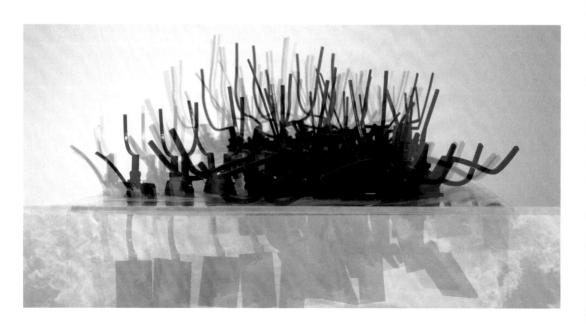

#beatricemelli #inderhavnreanimated

#bodoneuss #templeofcompost

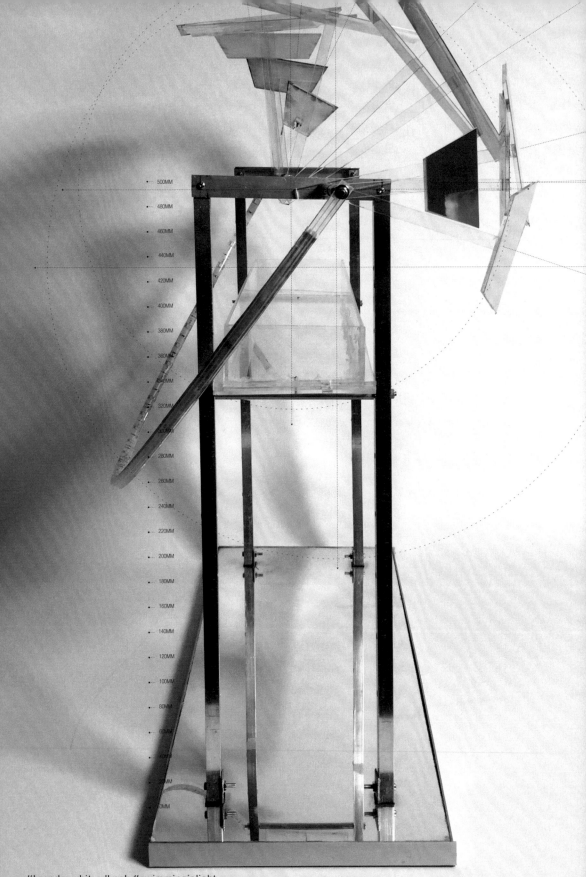

500MM
480MM
460MM
440MM
420MM
400MM
380MM
360MM
340MM
320MM
300MM
280MM
260MM
240MM
220MM
200MM
180MM
160MM
140MM
120MM
100MM
80MM
60MM
40MM
20MM
0MM

#brandonwhitwellmak #swimminginlight

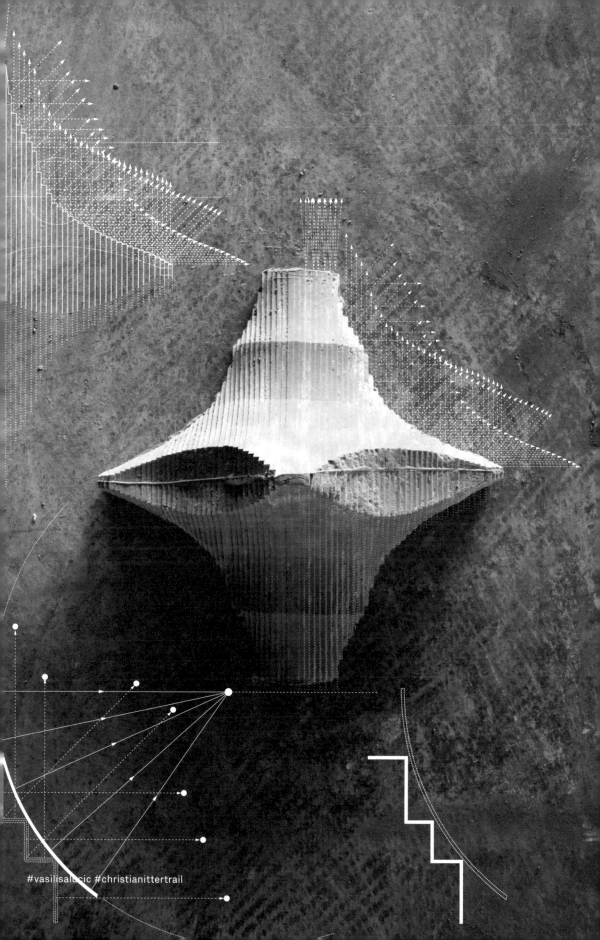

#vasilisalucic #christianittertrail

Intermediate 10

Unit Master
Valentin Bontjes
  van Beek

Thanks and gratitude
go out to the unit's
supporters and visiting
critics
AA Maintenance
  Department
Fabrizio Ballabio
Lawrence Barth
Sue Barr
Umberto Bellardi Ricci
Florian Busch
Barbara-Ann
  Campbell-Lange
Brendon Carlin
Michel Da Costa
  Gonçalves
Kate Davies
Ryan Dillon
Shin Egashira
Belinda Flaherty
Kenneth Fraser
Francisco Gonzalez
  de Canales
Sarah Handelman
Tom Heneghan
Hugo Hinsley
Alex Hurst
Kanto Iwamura
Max Kahlen
Taebeom Kim
Olaf Kneer
Taneli Manskkamaki
Marianne Mueller
Tyen Masten
Vanessa Norwood
Jessica Reynolds
Wataru Sawada
Rory Sherlock
Hiroe Shigemitsu
Juri Shigemitsu
Shutoko Metropolitan
  Expressway Company
Brett Steele
Sylvie Taher
Jorgen Tandberg
Jeroen van Ameijde
Manijeh Verghese
Carlos Villanueva Brandt
Thomas Weaver
Yuichi-ro Yamanaka
Junko Yanagisawa

Intermediate 10 continued to explore design as a process of addition through the practice of insertion, multiplication and cancellation on multiple scales by focusing on the term *addendum*, understood in its broadest sense. The resulting additions were to be both practical and conceptual, exploring things as much as ideas, and a tool for generating a new part of London's seemingly ever-expanding urban fabric.

The year began with a ten-day design competition for a new studio space constructed on top of the Morwell Street terrace and using only the leftover plywood from the AA's 2014 Maison Dom-ino project. Over Christmas the unit then conducted a two-week study visit to Tokyo, another rapidly growing city, visiting a range of buildings, offices and sites, which all in their particular ways touched upon different aspects of addendum. These included Kenzo Tange's St Mary's Cathedral and Yoyogi National Gymnasium; the control centre, Ohashi junction and Yamate tunnel of the Shutoko Metropolitan Expressway Company; the Ichida Family House, Denchu Hirakashi House and atelier in the Nesu area; a freezing boat trip along the Kanada Gawa canal; and a series of works by Florian Busch, SOY Labo, Toyo Ito, SANAA and seemingly every Tokyo 7-11, department store, metro station, police station and street corner.

Back in London, the consequence of these explorations took the form of yearlong projects that ranged from a vertical market in Camden and a memorial at Hyde Park Corner, to the transformation of the London terrace house into a Tokyo-style block and an artificial 300m high mountain spanning the length of Oxford Street. In their wilfulness, all of these proposals demonstrated an engaging set of opposing forces – respectful of history, yet utterly fantastical; civic-minded and serious, but also whimsical; conscious that architecture is a collective pursuit, but also obsessive and single-minded. Yet what remained inviolable throughout was an adherence to form – in every instance, the architecture presented was about building, and the articulation of ideas was always made accessible through models, images and drawings, so that in the end, the addendum we displayed was really only ever about the stuff of good form.

Students
Janos Bergab-Sawicz
Caroline Bongartz
Daria Gavrilova
Veronika Janovcova
Adi Krainer
Kyung Kuk Kang (Steve)
Hye Rim Lee
Buster Rönngren
Timothy O'Hare
Arefeh Sanaei
Tommaso Sordon
Jiahui Yuan

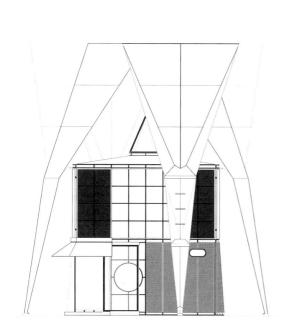

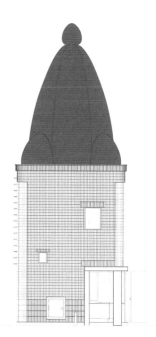

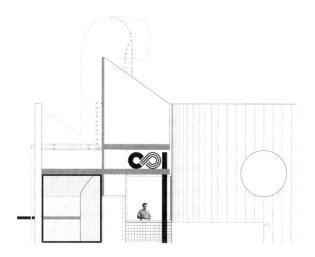

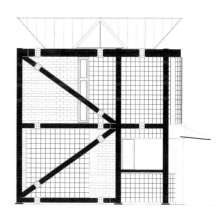

1. (above) Buster Rönngren, In Elevation: Three Tokyo Koban, one London Centre for Public Integrity – in Japan police stations, or Koban, are state property. Having observed, measured and documented their presence, the project claims the right to revise the public building; rather than being in service of the citizens, it signifies what is essentially civic.

2. (overleaf, left) Tommaso Sordon, The Telegraph Post-Tokyo – the pole can be reduced to two aspects: the concrete pole, or the 'Addition' to the city, and the different elements affixed to it – the 'Added Value' to the city. It works as an enduring structure, which over time can host variations and refinements to improve the functioning of the city based on need.

3. (overleaf, right) Arefeh Sanaei, The Impossible Occurrence Of The Mountain – Bruno Taut moved his city into the mountains to escape the rationalism and materialism of the world below. Here, the mountain is brought into the city, bringing London one step closer to utopia.

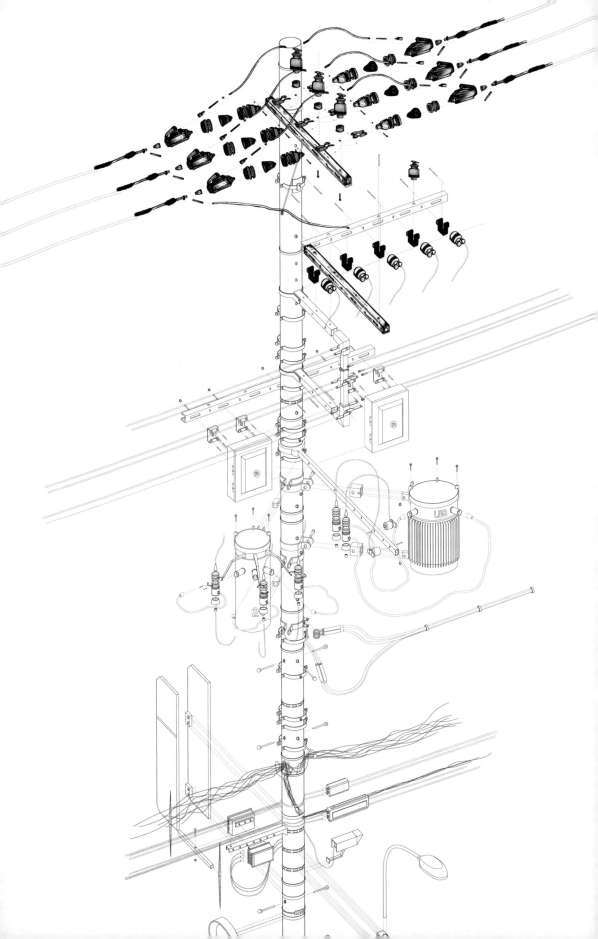

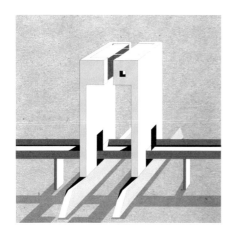
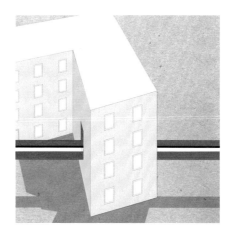
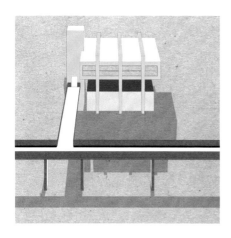
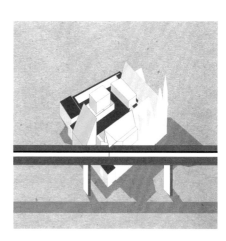

4. (opposite) Timothy O'Hare – responding to the looming Shell Centre redevelopment that now threatens public spaces of the Southbank, the project proposes an under- and over-ground railway station to activate a dormant sense of publicness. At the singular point of the station, different infrastructural systems collide and produce a large void, a pocket of low pressure resilient to privatisation and development.

5. (above) Daria Gavrilova – generating a cross-grid system over the existing undeveloped area, a new walkway forms, introducing direct movement over the site and highlighting neglected features of Kensal Town.

Intermediate 11

Unit Staff
Nacho Martín Asunción
Manuel Collado Arpia
Manijeh Verghese

Acknowledgements
BQ 3D-printer CESSION
Lotocoho
Fernando Gomez
Tessa Katz
Catarina Sampaio Cruz
Andreas Stylianou
Reem Nasir
Agata Pilarska
Nobrow Press
Devin Herd
Samantha Bendzulla
Robert Weinek
Monique Schiess
Andrew Fleming
All of our critics
   and collaborators

Sub-Saharan Spaceships: Nomadic Structures for a Techno-Tribal Community

There's a global belief that technology has become a controlling force over privacy – that it monitors our activities and stores all our data. But there are communities of techno-activists that are using technology to spark new forms of creativity, experimentation and mobility. This year Cape Town offered a fertile context for such activism. Within the fragile ecosystem of post-apartheid South Africa, we designed lightweight temporary structures to integrate factions of society and bridge historically segregated infrastructural boundaries to create a stronger, more united urban reality.

We began by designing jewellery with digital sensory effects, creating a relationship to the body by redefining its limits and connecting with the traditional craft of the country. Moving up in scale, we then designed nomadic techno-architecture that cultivated a relationship to these new wearable pieces in order to define new channels for social exchange.

Emily's survival collar for both festival-goers and displaced populations extended into a series of pneumatic dwellings, storage and supply units for both the Afrika Burn Festival (a satellite of Burning Man) and Cape Town's migrant communities. Micko's psychedelic laser totems reinvented the simultaneity of a global event, creating a party through non-verbal communication at every scale. Shereen blurred the boundaries between physical, virtual and augmented realities to connect the socially and geographically disparate. Ali's modified piercing gave us superpowers to share tastes, and his various plug-in architectures resolved the issue of taste scarcity in South Africa. Edmund chose to reinvent the monument, no longer creating structures to remind us of the past but to dissolve boundaries between social groups of the present. And Jakob created an arsenal of endangered plant-related strategies for the shack-dweller to ensure the permanence of township communities.

Students
Ali Mirzaei
Anatolios Stathiou
Edmund Lam
Emily Hayden
Gian Andrea Diana
Jakob Sköte
Milivoje Sestovic
Petro El Hage
Sadia Rahman
Shereen Doummar
Vidhi Goel
Yang Yang Chen

86

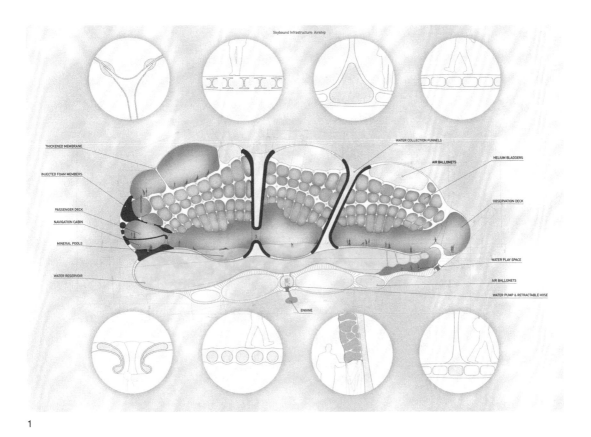

1

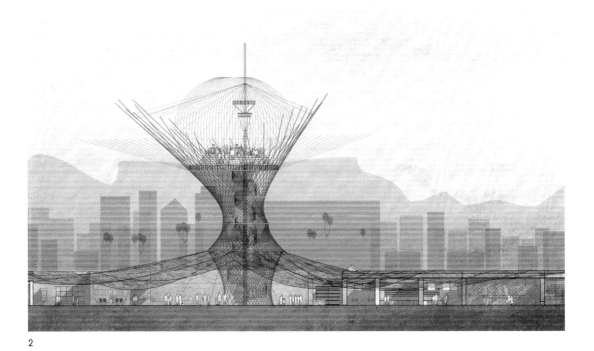

2

1. Emily Hayden – a pneumatic airship that uses air, water and expandable foam to construct a series of surface textures for a hybrid festival and survival programme

2. Yang Yang Chen – a mental health satellite integrated into an informal village in Cape Town with a social space below and a meditation/treatment area above

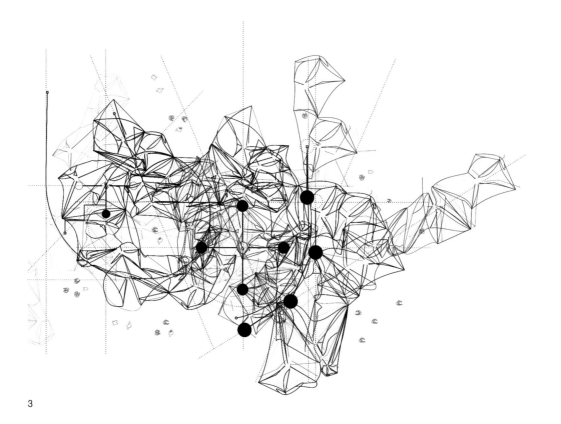

3

4

3. Petro El Hage – the choreographic score of a pressure-responsive tent that houses a series of dance performances as it traverses the city

4. Ali Mirzaei – a new market for taste experience questioning how we smell, hear, see, feel, digitally taste and share local flavours

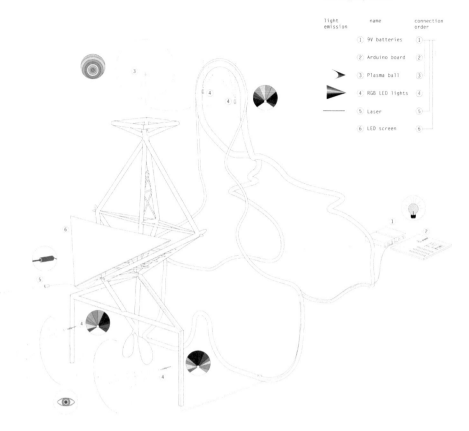

Technology organisation

light emission		name	connection order
	(1)	9V batteries	(1)
	(2)	Arduino board	(2)
	(3)	Plasma ball	(3)
	(4)	RGB LED lights	(4)
	(5)	Laser	(5)
	(6)	LED screen	(6)

5

5. Milivoje Sestovic – space goggles for a new type of
social communication of emotions that simultaneously
functions as a small-scale party infrastructure and
wearable ornamentation

6

7

6. Gian Andrea Diana – a mapping of the invisible
communication networks between sea platform,
surfer, marine life and drones

7. Anatolios Stathiou – using a system of artificial
clouds, messages sourced from digital data are
projected allowing communication between Cape
Town's neighbouring segregated areas.

8

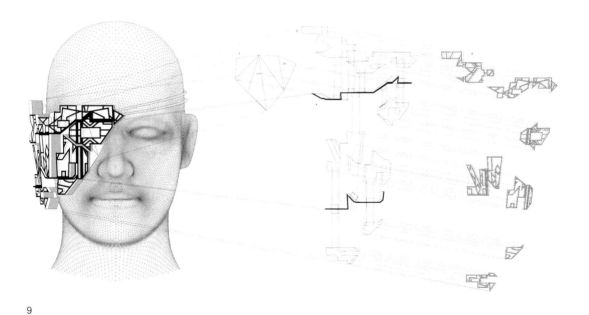

9

8. Jakob Sköte – the humble shack is transformed into tools for a new subversive community that uses endangered plants to ensure the permanence of informal settlements.

9. Shereen Doummar – a mask that both hides and celebrates identity as it seams together physical, virtual and augmented realities

Intermediate 12

Unit Staff
Tyen Masten
Inigo Minns

Workshop Collaborators
Nick Brooks
Maud Sanciaume
  and Johannes Schick
Josef Hargrave,
  Arup Foresight

Additional thanks to
Flavie Audi
Fabrizio Ballabio
Shany Barath
Kate Davies
Barbara-Ann
  Campbell-Lange
Mark Campbell
Magnus Casselbrant
Aleks Catina
Ryan Dillon
Shin Egashira
Sarah Featherstone
Maria Fedorchenko
Chia Ferrari
Kostas Grigoriadis
Francesca Hughes
Takako Hasegawa
Pablo Leon De La Barra
Xavi Llarch-Font
Sarah Manning
Monia de Marchi
John Ng
Luis Ortega
Ricardo de Ostos
Christopher Pierce
Catalina Pollak
Jose Arturo Revilla
Ben Reynolds
Takero Shimazaki
Caroline Sohie
Ricardo Sosa Mejia
Carlos Villanueva-Brandt

**And special thanks to
everyone in Mexico City**
Daniela and Valeria Torres
Jorge Ambrosi
Rodolfo Diaz Cervantes
Carmen Cordera
Gabriella Etchegaray
Ricardo Fernandez
Luis Flores
Lety Lozano
Cesar Lopez-Negrete
Alberto Lopez Monzon
Carlos Hernandez Matos
Ingrid Moye
Alejandra Guerrero Ruiz
Surella Segu Marcos
Christoph Zeller

Happening Architecture – Love Will Tear Us Apart

Intermediate 12 has looked at the role of events in the production of architecture, focusing on the 'moment' as a trigger for something far larger and more impactful. We have explored the ephemeral manifestations of architecture and how they help define the experiences central to our cultural environments.

Set in the context of the politically fraught Mexico City, the projects act as a trigger or stage allowing actions to occur. They speculate on the future possibilities of the life and legacy of a proposal far beyond the architect. As such the focus of the work is less on the architectural object, instead emphasising the crafting of the actions that the architecture is there to support. We have considered the contingent in architecture and tested the idea of agency beyond the profession by asking how the audience and user can inform the production of spaces and cities. To do this we have treated events as design elements with specific temporality, shifting the emphasis away from the purely spatial and onto the activities and users themselves.

The unit is design and research-driven, using representational drawings and design techniques from a range of alternative disciplines. We have queried whether the finite nature of traditional architectural models and drawings are suitable ways of expressing unfolding social and cultural events. Instead the shifting and pulsing of these events over time was choreographed through an architectural score that became both a record and instruction for proposals. As a final outcome the students produced a number of 2D and 3D objects that reflect their constructed events.

Whether addressing political activism, engaging with the performative properties of mass entertainment, supporting traditional cultures or exploring innovative construction techniques, we have questioned the role of the architectural project and considered it less as a fixed solution and more as a designed continuation of experiences, moments, journeys and trajectories over time.

Students
Arya Arabshahi
Jocelyn Arnold
Iris Gramegna
Omer Hadar
Eva Ibañez
Oskar Johanson
Mingyi Lim
Ioana Man
Patricia Moericke Prieto
Patricia de Souza Leão
  Müller
Russell Royer
Alexandra Shatalova

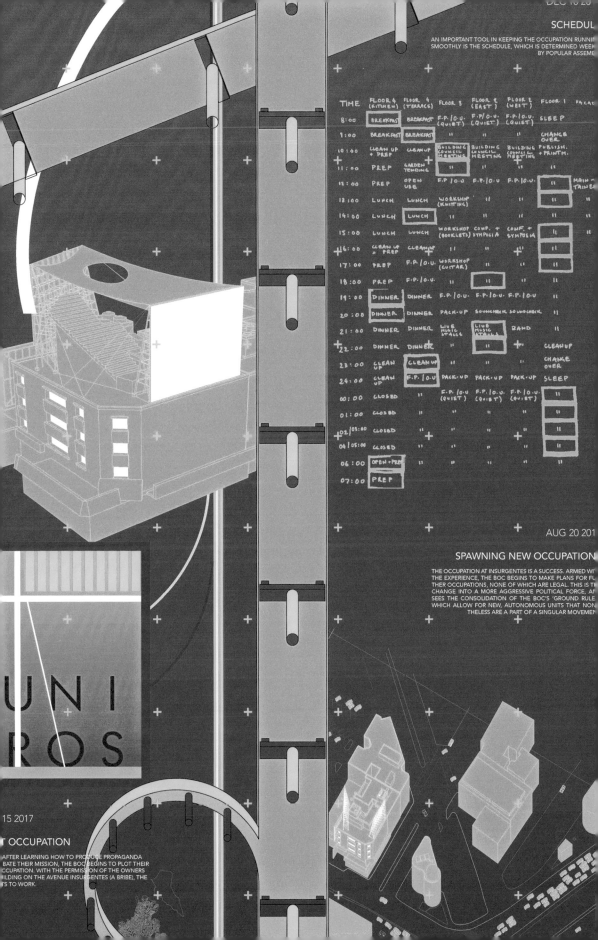

TIME	FLOOR 4 (KITCHEN)	FLOOR 4 (TERRACE)	FLOOR 3	FLOOR 2 (EAST)	FLOOR 2 (WEST)	FLOOR 1	FACAI
8:00	BREAKFAST	BREAKFAST	F.P./O.U. (QUIET)	F.P./O.U. (QUIET)	F.P./O.U. (QUIET)	SLEEP	
9:00	BREAKFAST	BREAKFAST	"	"	"	CHANGE OVER	
10:00	CLEAN UP + PREP	CLEAN UP	BUILDING COUNCIL MEETING	BUILDING COUNCIL MEETING	BUILDING COUNCIL MEETING	PUBLISH. + PRINTM.	
11:00	PREP	GARDEN TENDING	"	"	"	"	
12:00	PREP	OPEN USE	F.P./O.U.	F.P./O.U.	F.P./O.U.		MAIN-TAINER
13:00	LUNCH	LUNCH	WORKSHOP (KNITTING)	"	"	"	
14:00	LUNCH	LUNCH					
15:00	LUNCH	LUNCH	WORKSHOP (BOOKLETS)	CONF. + SYMPOSIA	CONF. + SYMPOSIA	"	
16:00	CLEAN UP + PREP	CLEANUP	"	"	"	"	
17:00	PREP	F.P./O.U.	WORKSHOP (GUITAR)	"	"		
18:00	PREP	F.P./O.U.	"	"			
19:00	DINNER	DINNER	F.P./O.U.	F.P./O.U.	F.P./O.U.		
20:00	DINNER	DINNER	PACK-UP	SOUNDCHECK	SOUNDCHECK		
21:00	DINNER	DINNER	LIVE MUSIC STALLS	LIVE MUSIC STALLS	BAND	"	
22:00	DINNER	DINNER	"	"	"	CLEANUP	
23:00	CLEAN UP	CLEAN UP	"	"	"	CHANGE OVER	
24:00	CLEAN UP	F.P./O.U	PACK-UP	PACK-UP	PACK-UP	SLEEP	
00:00	CLOSED	"	F.P./O.U (QUIET)	F.P./O.U (QUIET)	F.P./O.U (QUIET)	"	
01:00	CLOSED	"	"	"	"	"	
02/03:00	CLOSED	"	"	"	"	"	
04/05:00	CLOSED	"	"	"	"	"	
06:00	OPEN + PREP	"					
07:00	PREP						

AUG 20 201

SPAWNING NEW OCCUPATION

THE OCCUPATION AT INSURGENTES IS A SUCCESS. ARMED WIT
THE EXPERIENCE, THE BOC BEGINS TO MAKE PLANS FOR FU
THER OCCUPATIONS, NONE OF WHICH ARE LEGAL. THIS IS TH
CHANGE INTO A MORE AGGRESSIVE POLITICAL FORCE, AN
SEES THE CONSOLIDATION OF THE BOC'S 'GROUND RULE
WHICH ALLOW FOR NEW, AUTONOMOUS UNITS THAT NON
THELESS ARE A PART OF A SINGULAR MOVEMEN

UNI
ROS

15 2017

T OCCUPATION

AFTER LEARNING HOW TO PRODUCE PROPAGANDA
BATE THEIR MISSION, THE BOC BEGINS TO PLOT THEIR
CCUPATION. WITH THE PERMISSION OF THE OWNERS
ILDING ON THE AVENUE INSURGENTES (A BRIBE), THE
S TO WORK.

2

3

1. (previous page) Oskar Johanson, Billboard
Occupation Council 30-year plan – score for a strategy
to unite disparate leftist factions using architecture
and media to realise a common goal of political reform
2. Iris Gramegna, Sugar Components Melt Away with
the Rainy Season of Mexico – an investigation into
constructing Intangible Heritage while questioning
the paradox of materialising the invisible

3. Ioana Man, The Route of Piety – a new pilgrimage
footpath in Guadalupe, which enables mutual hijacking
between church, tourists and residents, triggering a
new hosting-based vernacular
4. (opposite) Arya Arabshahi, Extremes of Error – using
street-view mapping as an interface to explore the
tension between the graphical and physical production
of space

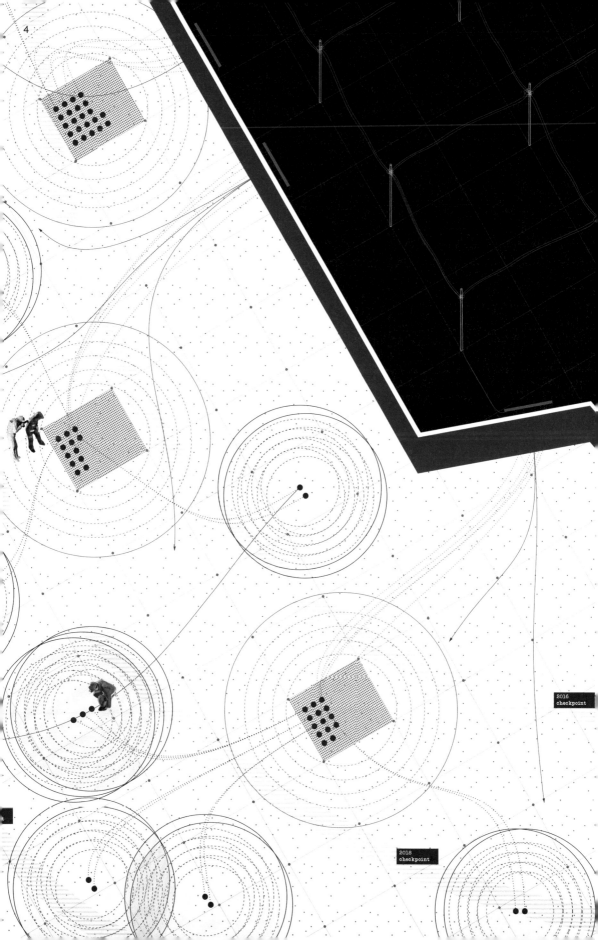

4

2016
checkpoint

2018
checkpoint

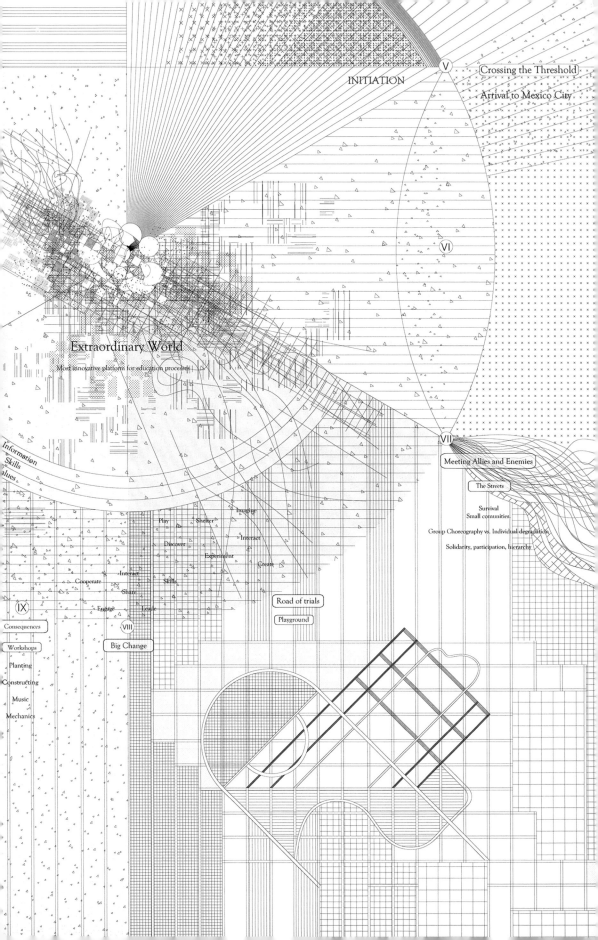

INITIATION

V

Crossing the Threshold

Arrival to Mexico City

VI

Extraordinary World

Most innovative platform for education processes

VII

Meeting Allies and Enemies

The Streets

Survival
Small comunities.

Group Choreography vs. Individual degradation

Solidarity, participation, hierarchy

Information
Skills
Values

Imagine

Play   Shelter

Interact

Discover

Experiment

Create

Interact

Cooperate   Skills

Share

IX   Engage   Leade   Road of trials

Consequences   Playground

Workshops   VIII

Planting   Big Change

Constructing

Music

Mechanics

6

7

5. (opposite) Eva Ibañez, Hero's Journey Score –
a pedagogic programme enabling self-authored
development for under-privileged children in
Mexico City
6. Jocelyn Arnold, Contemporary Votive Image –
a strategy to archive the true identity of the
marginalised Tepito neighbourhood in Mexico
City as it undergoes gentrification

7. Alexandra Shatalova, Architecture as Expression
of Female Power – an institution for women to form a
resistance against gender-based violence in Mexico

Intermediate 13

Tutors
Jessica Reynolds
Lily Jencks
Tatiana von Preussen

Acknowledgements
Brett Steele
Barbara-Ann
  Campbell-Lange
Ryan Dillon
Ryan Neiheiser
Manijeh Verghese
Mark Cousins
Stuart Dodd
Takero Shimazaki
Ana Araujo
Natasha Sandmeier
Miraj Ahmed
Valentin Bontjes
  van Beek
Tyen Masten
Stuart Dodd
Justin Desyllas
Catherine Pease
Tomas Klassnik
Alex Whitby-Scott
Fabrizio Ballabio
Nick Hornby
Megan Burke
Tessa Katz
Shumi Bose
Graham Baldwin
Shi Yuan
Eva Eylers
Carolina Lopez Blanco
Diego Teixeira Seisdedos
Mark Campbell
John Ng
Alison Crawshaw
Marco Vanucci
Shin Egashira

Sick City Rehab : Toxicity and Health in the Twenty-First Century
Our unit imagines new health institutions for London. Through an exploration of health conditions, students reinvent the institution as a site of participation, criticism, social responsibility and historical awareness. The year consists of
five stages:

1   SYMPTOMS: students create a prosthetic that responds to a chosen health condition
2   TESTS: students examine a history of architectural typologies of health
3   DIAGNOSIS: students assess the urban condition of London to locate their individual sites
4   TREATMENT: students prescribe new institutions for the city
5   AFTERCARE: students review the long-term side effects of their proposals.

Ema exhaustively bores OCD patients of their own symptoms in repetitive and radiating structures of order and disorder in Piccadilly Circus. Infertile couples are invited to artificially procreate in Choi's monumental feminist fabric-lined womb. Roman's planted bee highways are punctuated with immunisation towers made of honeycomb that offer respite for hay fever sufferers. Irene casts phantom shadows of demolished industrial architecture in Canning Town. Ali celebrates insomnia by awakening derelict tube stations. The booms and busts of the global economic market are registered in Maryam's atmospheric canopy hovering over Canary Wharf. Andrew helps London to articulate itself by extruding walls around private space, and amplifying the sound of public discourse. Rufus combats global epidemics through a transformative roofscape that quarantines the infected until eventually the remaining healthy population must seek refuge inside it. Andrea deconstructs London's narcissistic epidemic by proposing new Cathedrals of Self Worship in the City. Mona creates a gradient of care for dementia patients between the community and the hospital. Lydia inserts an architectural soundscape on the roof of St Pancras hospital. Raphael tackles seasonal affective disorder by recreating light conditions from different biomes.
    These proposals provocatively challenge both the norms of perception through experimental representation, and traditional institutional structures through a renewed relationship to the body.

Students
Maryam Alfalasi   Roman Lovegrove
Seungah Choi   Raphael Iruzun Martins
Ali El-Hashimi   Andrea Nuccetelli
Mona Hadar   Rufus Shen
Ema Hana Kacar   Irene Squilloni
Lydia Liu   Andrew Yuen

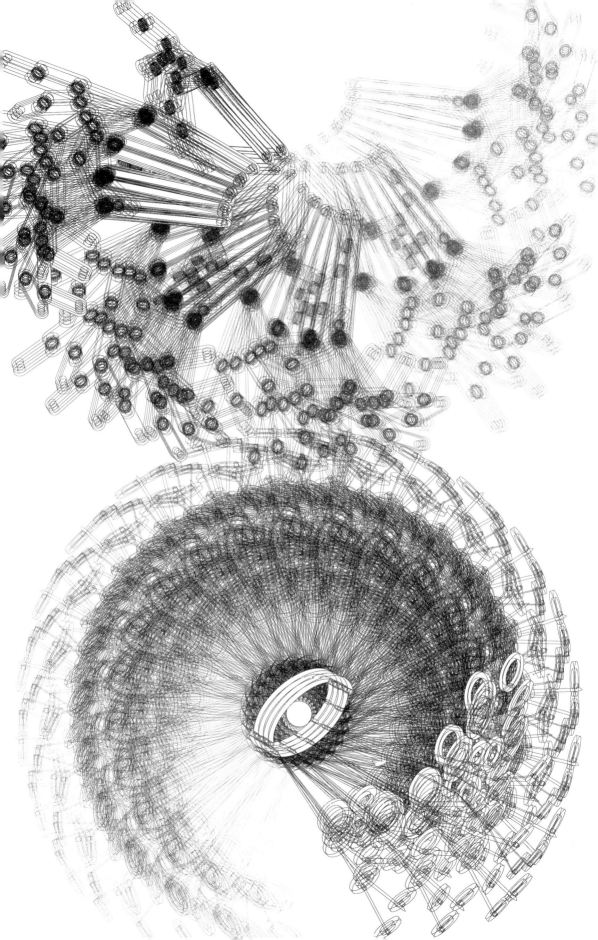

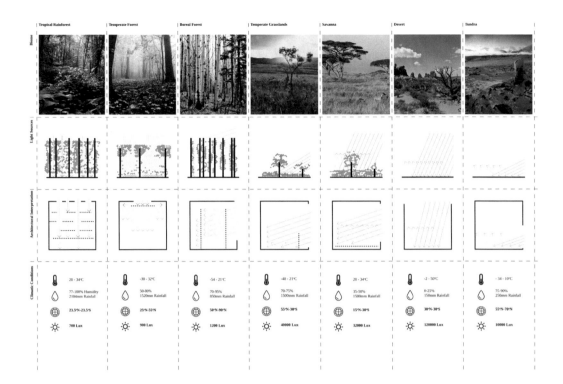

	Tropical Rainforest	Temperate Forest	Boreal Forest	Temperate Grasslands	Savanna	Desert	Tundra
Climatic Conditions							
🌡 Temperature	20 - 34°C	-30 - 32°C	-54 - 21°C	-40 - 21°C	20 - 34°C	-2 - 50°C	- 34 - 10°C
💧 Humidity / Rainfall	77-100% Humidity, 2104mm Rainfall	50-80%, 1520mm Rainfall	70-95%, 850mm Rainfall	70-75%, 1500mm Rainfall	35-50%, 1500mm Rainfall	0-25%, 150mm Rainfall	75-90%, 250mm Rainfall
🌐 Latitude	23.5°N-23.5°S	25°N-55°N	50°N-90°N	55°N-30°S	15°N-30°S	30°N-30°S	55°N-70°N
☀ Light	700 Lux	900 Lux	1200 Lux	40000 Lux	32000 Lux	120000 Lux	10000 Lux

2

3

1. (previous page) Ema Hana Kacar, Prosthetics for Obsessive Compulsive Disorder patients – two devices for hands to prohibit or to exaggerate a repetitive act

2. Raphael Iruzun Martins, Research into Seasonal Affective Disorder – light analysis of the seven biomes

3. Roman Lovegrove, Urban Plans for Allergy Sufferers – colour-coded bee-highways and wax towers connecting London's parks

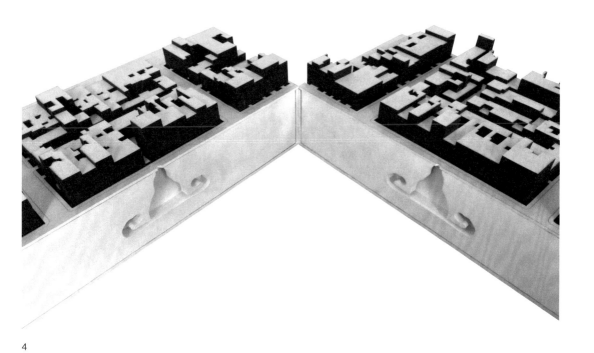

4

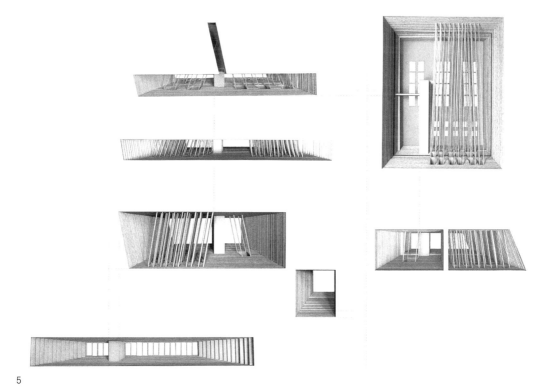

5

4. Seungah Choi, Centre for Infertility –
a monumental womb for the city

5. Irene Squilloni, Rehabilitation Centre –
built of shadows and phantoms' limbs

6

7

6. Lydia Liu, Sound Therapy Hospital – rooftop acoustic interventions to connect the patients, public and context

7. Ema Hana Kacar, Halo – radiating and repetitive structures that re-order Piccadilly Circus

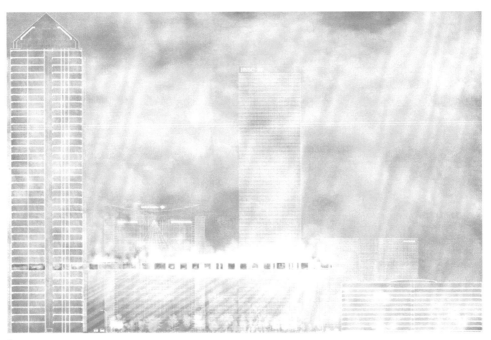

8

9

8. Maryam Alfalasi, Cocaine Addiction Canopy –
steaming or raining paths provide a counterbalance
to the booms and busts of the global market

9. Andrew Yuen, Speech Therapy Centre –
articulating walls and amplifying movement

The Diploma School is part of the AA's famed unit system of teaching and offers opportunities for architectural experimentation and consolidation. With a broad range of interests and teaching methods, the aim is to marry drawing and technical proficiency to form complex intellectual agendas in an atmosphere of lively and informed debate. Students work in a close-knit yet open environment that fosters the development of their own creative independence and intelligence. They learn to hone their research skills and refine proposals into high-level design portfolios at the end of the year. They begin to define their voices as designers and to articulate individual academic agendas that will carry them into their future professional careers.

DIPLOMA SCHOOL

Diploma 1

Staff
Miraj Ahmed
Martin Jameson

Thanks to
Ashmolean Museum,
  Oxford
Blake Society
Adriana Diaz-Enciso
Tim Heath
Peabody Estates Ltd
Ken Baikie
Clare Bennie
Paul Fowler
Dan Hill
Pierre d'Avoine
Barbara-Ann
  Campbell-Lange
Kevin Cash
Javier Castañón
Shin Egashira
Sam Jacob
Conrad Koslowsky
Jon Lopez
Jane McAllister
Hikaru Nissanke
Cecilie Ohlsen
Elena Palacios Carral
Gregory Ross
Davide Sacconi
Cecilie Sachs Olsen
Francisco Sanin
Irénée Scalbert
Colette Sheddick
Takero Shimazaki
Brett Steele
Patrick Usborne
Manijeh Verghese
Paul Warner

Golgonooza

'The town is not really like a natural phenomenon. It is an artefact – an artefact of a curious kind, compounded of willed and random elements, imperfectly controlled, if it is related to physiology at all, it is more like a dream than anything else.' Joseph Rykwert, *The Idea of a Town*

Golgonooza, William Blake's 'other' London describes the city as an 'ever building, ever falling' process that perpetually tends towards the ideal but is accepting of its flaws and imperfections. Much likes Rykwert's notion of the city as a dream, Blake conceived the real city as a place of imagination: a construct of the mind. As such he placed particular emphasis on the role of the artist as a visionary, someone capable of unshackling the 'mind-forged manacles' of daily existence in order to access the eternal and real.

Thamesmead, the 1960s suburban new town was probably the last of the 'visionary' building projects of London. The designers of the Greater London Council (GLC) imagined a contemporary city of 50,000 people set within a picturesque landscape of lakes and canals. This city was never realised: lack of money and poor management left a half-built estate without a centre – to many a paradigm of inherent limitations of large-scale city planning. After years of neglect, Peabody has acquired the estate and a process of change and development is now underway.

But what of the original vision: can it be reframed? The 'Golden Builders' of Diploma 1 have conceived three potential approaches. The first embraces the cycle of destruction and reconstruction and locates the eternal in the cosmic axes of the city and the urban grid – the staircase to the universal. The second approach uncovers the ancient myths of Thamesmead – the arcadian landscape, the ancient Quincunx – and posits these as the 'willed elements' of Rykwertian conjecture. The last goes further and examines the potential of alchemical transformation of urban base matter into the sublime: a gilded 'city crown'.

Students
Madiha Ahmad
Andrew Bardzik
Asad Bazraa
Hyunwoo Chung
Maria José Concha
Yasser Dahhan
Fatemeh Ghasemei
Ada Keco
Yu Hin Kwok
Regina Shi Qi Ng
Marie-Louise Raue
Helene Solvay
Cliff Tan
Nuria Romo Torres

1. Regina Shi Qi Ng, The Hall of Air above the Crossness
sewage treatment plant – massive columns manifest
the alchemical transformation of base sewage from
sludge tanks to the gilded crown hall.

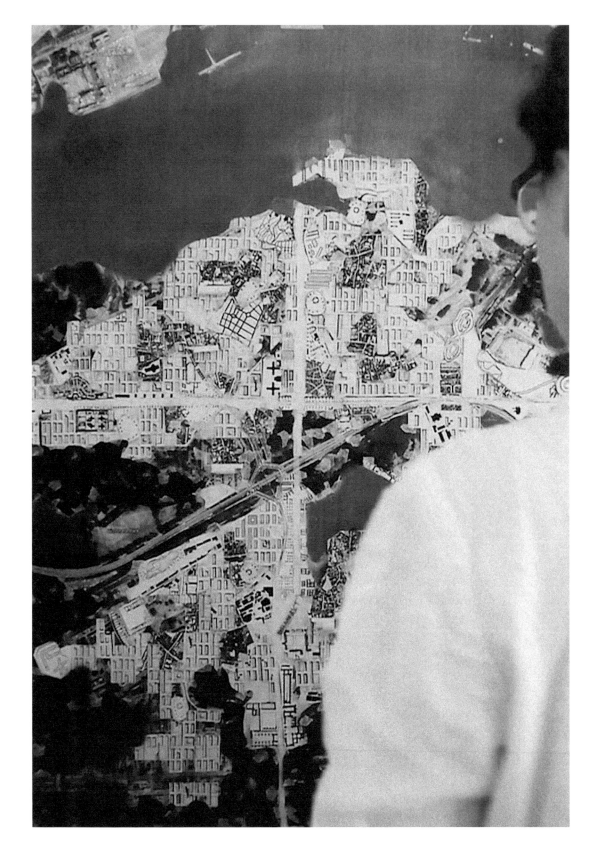

2. Marie-Louise Raue, Eternal Thamesmead:
Ever Building, Ever Falling

3. Andrew Bardzik, Thamesmead island people's
palace – the bestowment of a venerable heart

4

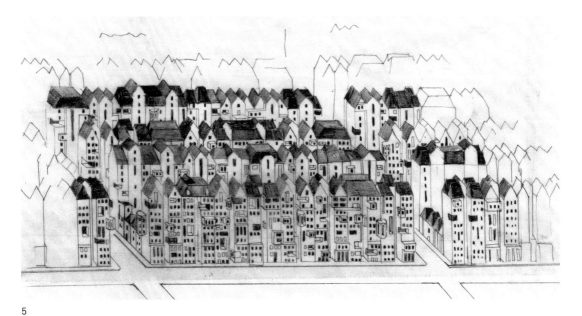

5

4 & 5. Helene Solvay, The Quest For Jerusalem's
Chamber: An Unofficial Appendix of Delight to
the London Housing Guide

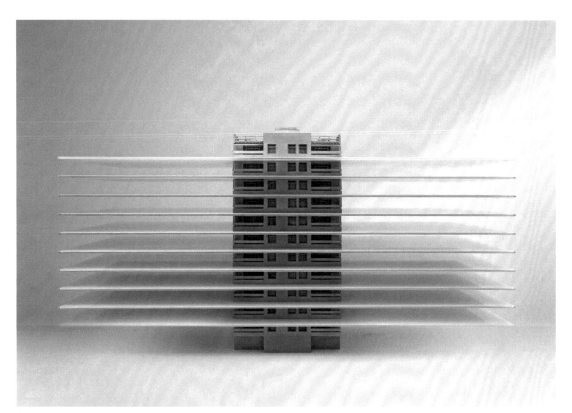

6

7

6 & 7. Cliff Tan, ModelMead: Re-imagining the
Historic Modernist City

Diploma 2

Staff
Didier Faustino
Kostas Grigoriadis

Thanks To
Miraj Ahmed
Carlos Villanueva Brandt
Ryan Dillon
Marie-Hélène Fabre
Felix Fassbinder
Maria Fedorchenko
Kenneth Fraser
Manuel Jimenez Garcia
Evan Greenberg
David Greene
Karsten Huneck
Barbara-Ann
  Campbell-Lange
Theo Lalis
Hander Lara
Tyen Masten
Ricardo de Ostos
Dakis Panagiotou
Brent Patterson
Chris Pierce
Ben Reynolds
Simon Rowe
Yoandry 'Chapo' Sapoten
Gisell Soto
Theodore Spyropoulos
Marco Vanucci
Andrew Yau
John Zhang

Over the course of four years Diploma 2 has explored the idea of self-governance, this year researching how such an insular condition affects the notion of domesticity. The site for exploring these ideas was Cuba, a country whose historical autonomy is effectively becoming more interdependent and complex as its economy gradually opens up to the world. The aim then has been to uncover hidden tendencies or areas of opportunity and to nest our partially or fully self-governed proposals within their already autonomous, albeit volatile, context.

Housing is a main issue that has been explored from various perspectives. Jing proposed a prototypical building that can be replicated in disused urban sites and consists of an openly occupied lower space and private market development. For Nicolas, political and social changes have typically resulted in cul-de-sac-like domestic spaces that are now designed to absorb change through flexibility. Michael rethought the conventional housing typology by proposing a purposefully complex domestic layout to respond to life's contingencies. Duc proposed an open, short- and long-term stay framework designed with minimal private and abundant public space. Eleonora's project questioned UNESCO's facade-centric approach to restoration and proposed that domestic spaces also need to be preserved as relics of days gone by. For Rachel, utilising the renowned Cuban health system to treat patients with infectious diseases resulted in a new type of urbanism of isolation. Bozar explored the theme of the 'state of the exception', proposing a building where this state could be managed and ideas of monumentality and symbolism could be explored. Lastly, Li's proposal for a socialist factory that systematises and opens up the current model of informal goods bartering was a move towards addressing the inequalities engendered by an imminent open-market takeover.

Students
Paul Challis
Nicolas Chung
Sam Esses
Eleonora Hadjigeorgiou
Rachel Khalil
Duc Minh Le
Costas Lemos
Jing Liang
Michael Westerlund
Jonathan Wong
Bozar Ben Zeev
Li Zhang

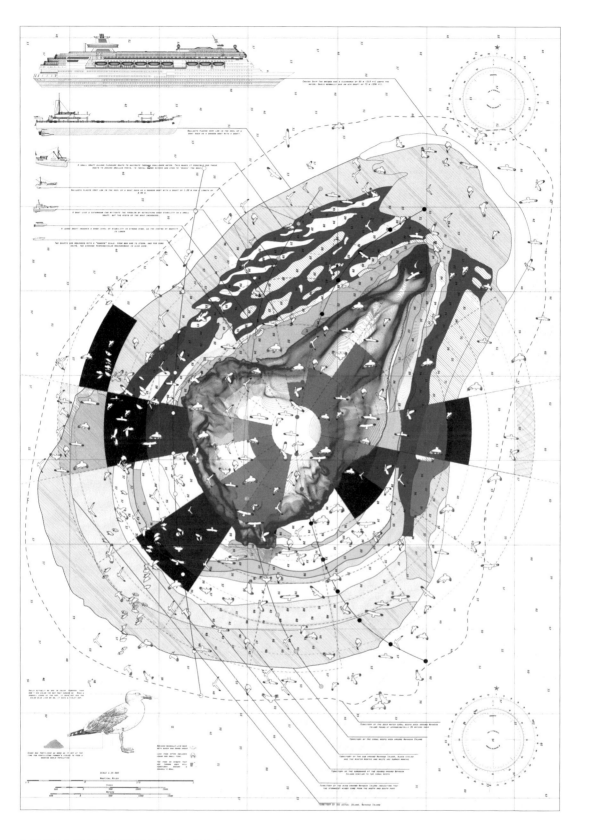

1. Costas Lemos, An Island Is Land – in order to expand
Cuban territorial and financial interests, a new island
landscape is terra-formed in an artificially accelerated
geological process.

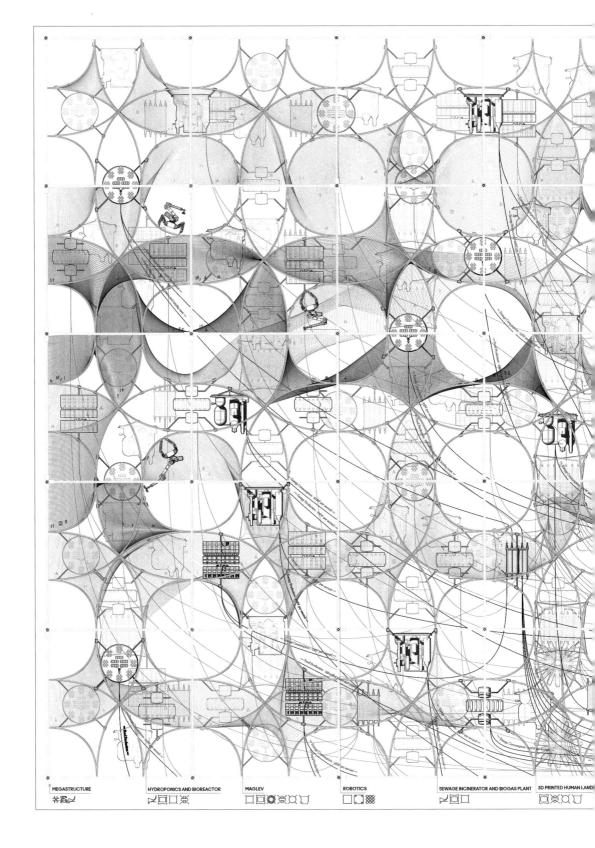

MEGASTRUCTURE HYDROPONICS AND BIOREACTOR MAGLEV ROBOTICS SEWAGE INCINERATOR AND BIOGAS PLANT 3D PRINTED HUMAN LAND[...]

2. Paul Challis, Algocene – a new layer is added to
the earth's crust to form the latest geological epoch
wherein human and algorithm symbiosis is achieved.

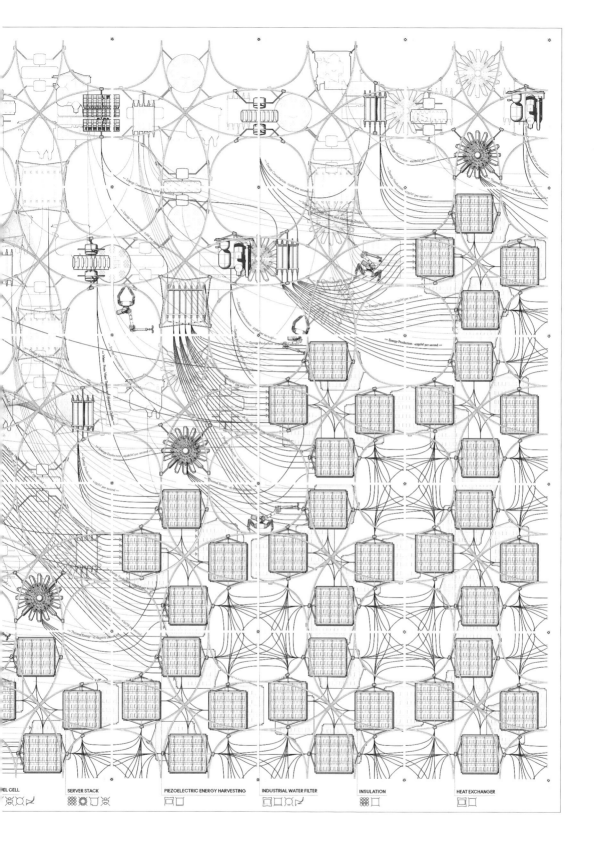

EL CELL   SERVER STACK   PIEZOELECTRIC ENERGY HARVESTING   INDUSTRIAL WATER FILTER   INSULATION   HEAT EXCHANGER

115

3. Sam Esses, Event City – an extreme festivalisation of Havana exploits culture as a device to manufacture authentic experiences and market itself as a must-go destination.

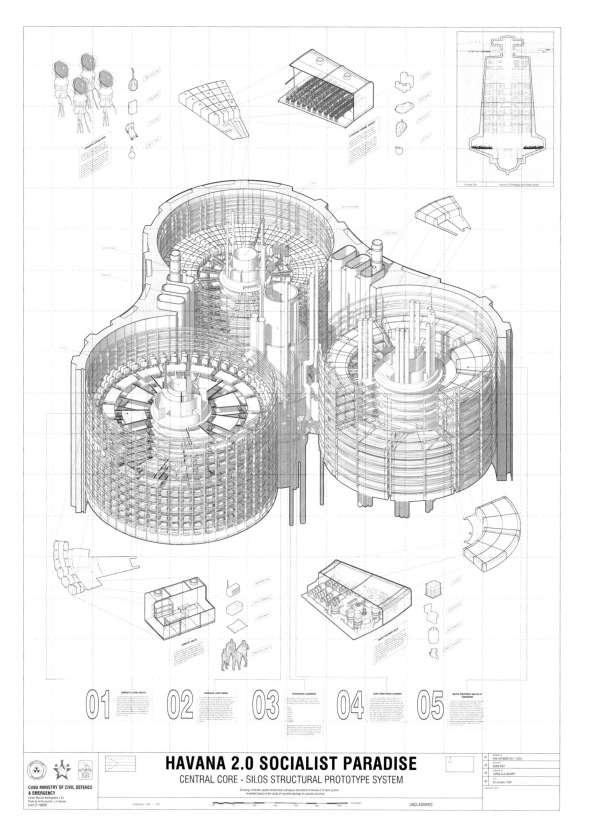

4. Jonathan Wong, Havana 2.0: the Socialist Paradise Prototype – an underground silo is controlled and operated through a centralised core that houses an extreme new domesticity.

Diploma 3

Unit Masters
Daniel Bosia
Marco Vanucci
Adiam Sertzu

Special thanks
Albert W Taylor
Angel Lara-Moreira
Barbara-Ann
  Campbell-Lange
Brett Steele
Bruce Davidson
Carol Patterson
Ciro Najle
Charlie Corry-Wright
DaeWha Kang
Daniel Bergsagel
Evan Greenberg
Filippo Innocenti
Hanif Kara
Javier Castañón
Jens Pedersen
Jeroen Janssen
Jessica In
Jessica Reynolds
John Bell
Jordi Pages Ramon
Kostas Grigoriadis
Luis Viu Rebes
Manja van de Worp
Matt Chan
Mehran Gharleghi
Mei Chan
Nacho Marti
Natasha Sandmeier
Robin Adams
Tommaso Franzolini
Valeria Segovia
Yasaman Mousavi
Zaid Kashef Alghata

This year Diploma 3 focused its research on 'the contemporary factory'. Often overlooked by architects, the increasing complexity of the modern factory and warehouse offers the opportunity to establish a new dialogue on the relationship between industry, technology, engineering and architecture. In particular, we investigated the functional, structural and environmental demands of large technological envelopes. We studied the organisation of the contemporary space of production: the flows of matter, humans and machines; the production lines and their spatial requirements; the programmatic proximities and the strategies of the compartmentalisation of functions. We built and studied prototypes as a means for understanding the relationship between structure, material systems, spatial qualities and organisation. We considered recycling and car plants, body-parts factories, natural stone extraction and manufacturing plants as well as agricultural factories. For these, we developed material, geometrical and structural systems by means of computational protocols and material craft: prefabricated performative flooring/facade/partitioning panels for a plant that can be disassembled and relocated; recycled masonry systems; adjustable moulds for a customised discretisation of the envelope; lamellae to allow natural ventilation and sun shading; fully fitted composite panels for a grey-collar factory.

Furthermore, the unit travelled to Turin where we visited and studied some of the most inspiring examples of twentieth-century industrial architecture.

Students
Alexander Streatfeild
Anna Muzychak
Dionysis Tzakis
Gulsah Unal
Heon Woo Park
Naz Atalay
Yiran Guo
YongPeng Liu

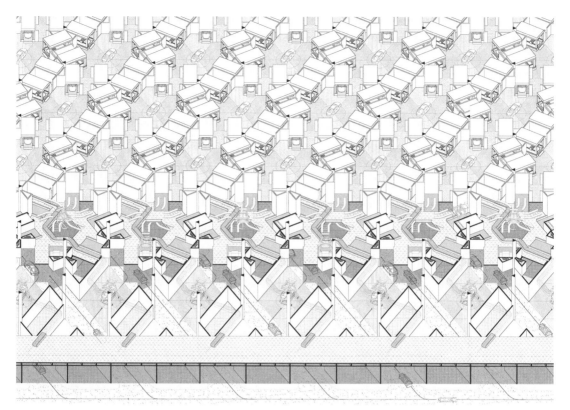

2

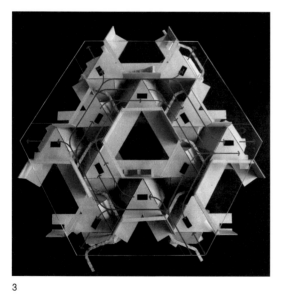

3

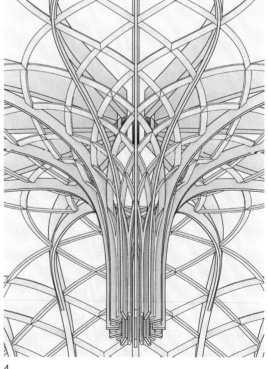

4

1. (previous page) YongPeng Liu, 3D-printing car manufacturing plant – designed as a kit of parts that can be assembled into independent units
2. YongPeng Liu, Aggregation factory
3. YongPeng Liu, Micro-factory model

4. Alex Streatfeild, Bike factory, column detail – a new bicycle factory in west London studying the articulation of the envelope as a circulatory artery

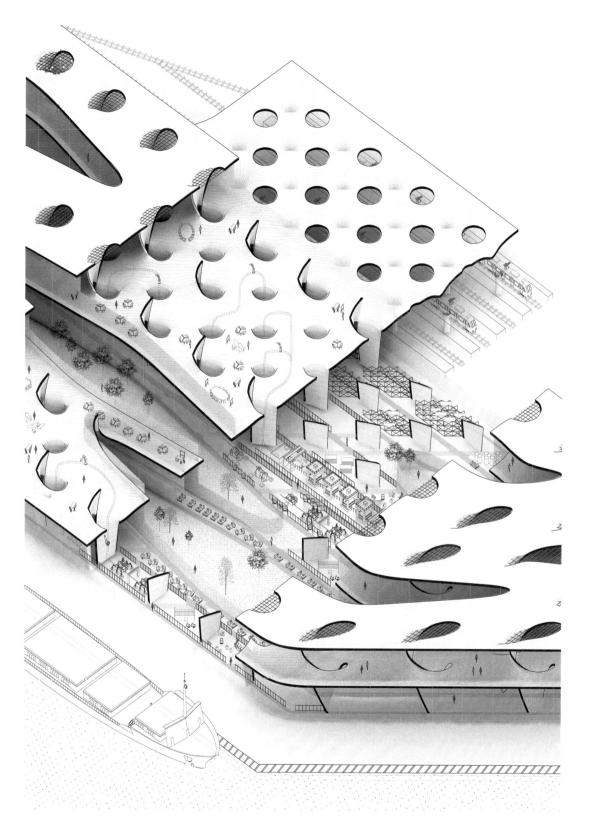

5. Dionysis Tzakis, Grey collar factory, axonometric view – the project addresses the contemporary shift in manufacturing industry: the introduction of robotic arms and cad/cam technology requires a new kind of workforce.

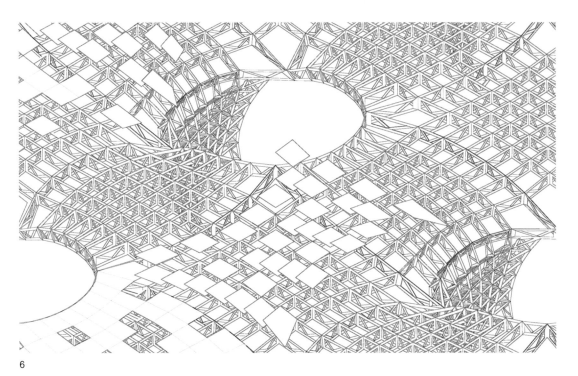

6

7

6. Dionysis Tzakis, Grey collar factory, roof structure
– the project is composed of fully fitted composite
panels that can be assembled to form a visually porous,
modular envelope.
7. Anna Muzychak, Body-part manufacturing campus,
axonometric view – development of a body-part
manufacturing campus on the outskirts of Stuttgart

8. (opposite) Naz Atalay – recycling factory in
Amsterdam articulated around a set of conveyor
belts which transport materials to dismantling,
sorting and re-use facilities

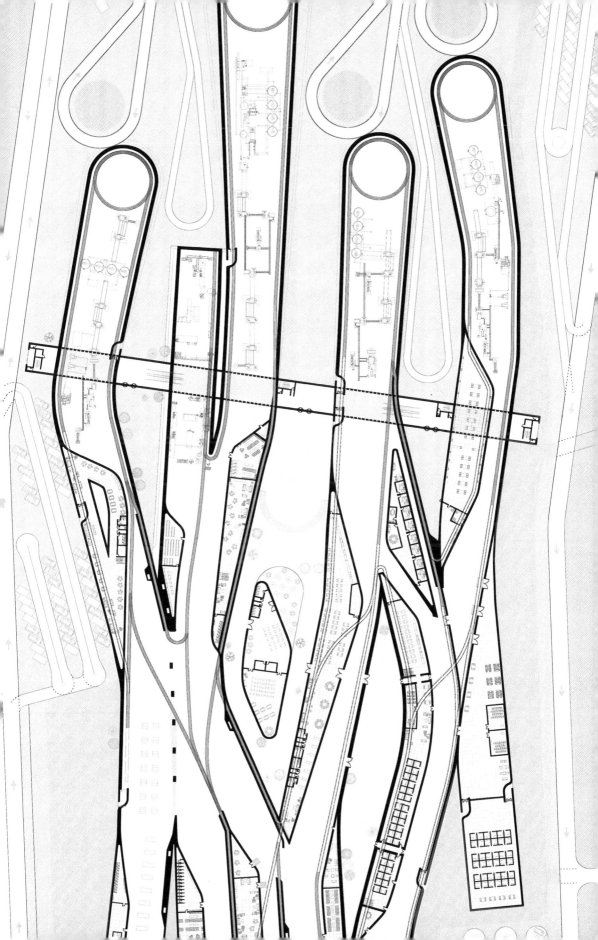

Diploma 4

Unit Masters
John Palmesino
Ann-Sofi Rönnskog

Thanks to
Andy Lowe
Lindsey Bremner
Bruno Latour
Barbara-Ann
  Campbell-Lange
Kelly Shannon
Javier Castañón
Didier Madoc Jones
Haus der Kulturen
  der Welt HKW, Berlin
Digital Humanities
  Laboratory EPFL
  Lausanne
UNOSAT
United Nations
World Trade
  Organization (WTO)
CERN
British Geological
  Survey (BGS)
Jan Zalasiewicz
Colin Waters
Carlos Villanueva Brandt
Tobias Klein
Tom Fox
Stavros Papavassiliou
Roland Shaw
Graham Smith
Yi-Jen Chen

The Coast of Europe – Polity and Space

The European project is a vast re-moulding of the interconnections between the organisation of material spaces and the institutional structures that organise life. As it unfolds over time, across a variety of spaces, it shapes a new architecture in which construction processes and the forming of human environments are torqued by a multitude of forces. A study of the material characterisation of urbanisation processes in the Anthropocene asked what are the material movements, their consolidation, dispersal, accumulation and stratification that shape Europe today?

Eleni investigates the Qatari extractive processes as a wide and fragile global architecture operating both at the margins and in the very heart of Europe. Maria traces the elusive works of a global commodity-trading corporation to discover the complex making of an architecture of secrecy and violence. Minh analyses new forms of financial regulation to realign London to wider circulations of sea economies. Leander studies the implications of a transcontinental electricity grid on the energy transition, visualising electro-magnetic fields of contemporary life. Konstantina unfolds a series of control and surveillance perimeters to balance the pervasive biometric spaces of a unified European airspace. Aikaterini explores withdrawal as a potential to reshape Greek mountainous environments as sites for technological and political experimentation. Susan intersects academic instrumental knowledge in postcolonial Hong Kong. Camille investigates the transformation and re-articulation of maintenance processes in metropolitan London. Nicole rediscovers connections between European climatic architecture and contemporary Chinese efforts to tackle urban and economic change. Hao Wen follows the Nordic model of economic development across contemporary financialised territories. Svetlana envisions a political technology disassembling multiple borderlines fracturing the territories of Ukraine. Angelina thinks British landscapes through the half-life of radioactive nuclear waste. Rula re-invents the Mesopotamian system as entangled spaces with shadows of violence always looming.

Students
Leander Adrian
Angelina Bennison
Camille Corthouts
Svetlana Demchenko
Konstantina Koulouri
Susan Li
Hao Wen Lim
Van Phung Hieu Minh
Maria Radjenovic
Rula Sayegh
Aikaterini Laoura
  Tsitouridou
Eleni Tzavellou Gavalla
Xinyue Nicole Zhang

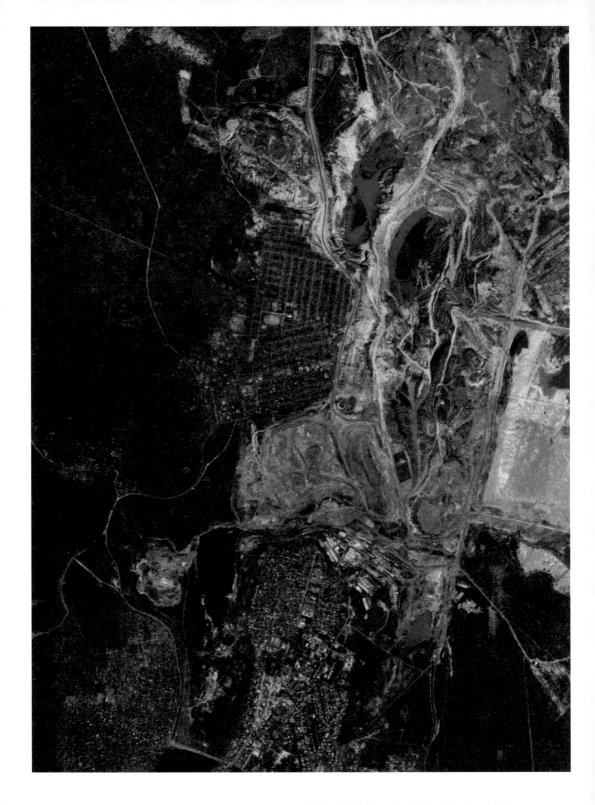

1. (previous page) Territorial Agency formed a delegation of current and former Diploma 4 students to represent oil kept in the ground at the climate change negotiation simulation of COP21 Make it Work! in Paris organised by Bruno Latour and Sciences Po. Photo COP21MIW

2. Maria Radjenovic, The Architecture of Secrecy – a ten-year transformation image of the Kolwezi Katanga mining operations in the DRCongo
3. (opposite) Van Phung Hieu Minh, Between Land and Sea – shadows of the millenary extraterritorial polities of the City of London intersecting contemporary high-frequency trading.

4. Eleni Tzavellou Gavalla, Territories Generated by Extraction – a material characterisation of the architectural transformations of Qatar

5. (opposite) Leander Adrian, Elektropolis: Networks of Power – one hundred years of material transformation in the heart of Berlin as a counterpart to the establishment of the electricity grid

Diploma 5

Unit Staff
Cristina Díaz Moreno
Efrén García Grinda
Benjamin Reynolds

Guests
Miraj Ahmed
Katie Albertucci
Pier Vittorio Aureli
Paul Bailey
Fabrizio Ballabio
Shany Barath
Alessandro Bava
Daniel Bossia
Ed Bottoms
Barbara-Ann
   Campbell-Lange
Magnus Casselbrant
Javier Castañon
James Kwang-ho Chung
Oliver Domeisen
Shin Egashira
Maria Fedorchenko
Kostas Grigoriadis
Valle Medina
Samantha McLean
Song Jie Lim
John Ng
John Palmesino
Oscar Santillan
Adiam Sertzu
Theodore Spyropoulos
Brett Steele
Rob Stuart-Smith
Dora Sweijd
Robert Taylor
Dries van de Velde
Marco Vanucci
Carlos Villanueva-Brandt
Michael Weinstock
Ivana Wingham
Andrew Yau

Thanks to
Diane and
   Mike Weinstock
Sayaka Namba
Pei-Yao Wu

Rare New Species

Today, when a simple term entered into a search engine displays a universe of possible connections to other words, documents and images, the goal of any cultural practice should involve making new meanings through the qualities of these very links. But how does a practice produce novelty – that refreshed way of understanding the same problems, situations and conflicts – so that it remains connected to the world while also taking on a new kind of critical position?

This year the so-called Consortium of Fantastic Ideas dived into the sea of typological creativity, producing a family of oddities, evolutionary experiments and organisational and linguistic exceptions in the form of medium-scale buildings. Exploring the potential of the exceptional and specific in a world that is more homogeneous, monocultural and predictable than ever, the members of the Consortium worked within the field of the collective, exploring mundane and ordinary human daily activities to articulate new and weird species of environments and forms of togetherness. Behind the apparent familiarity of our surroundings are cultural, productive, social and political emerging realities of an extraordinary and hidden nature.

A flat landscape defining an elevated horizon hovering over Sheik Zayed Road for the disparate communities and religions that coexist in the UAE; eight generations of video games which take the form of a renewed physical reincarnation of a multifocal area; a dark and hyper-traditional polygamous community that hides in a monumental piece of art-based real-estate in Marfa, Texas; and a mythical device that constantly records the shifting boundaries of a coral island and discusses the territorial fights in the South China Sea are just some of the endeavours of the projects presented. Their common ambition is to address the relevance and validity of not only spatial models and inherited languages, but also the productive, technological and social systems from which they emerge.

Fourth Year Students
Norine Chu Yin Lok
Guanlian Gordon Gn
Erez Ezra
Reem Nasir
Maria Olmos Zunica
Frederique Paraskevas
Lorenzo Perri
Qin (Lexie) Zhao

Fifth Year Students
Laura Jane Lim Sam
Fortuné Penniman
Vidhya Pushpanathan
Christopher Yah
   Chuen Shen

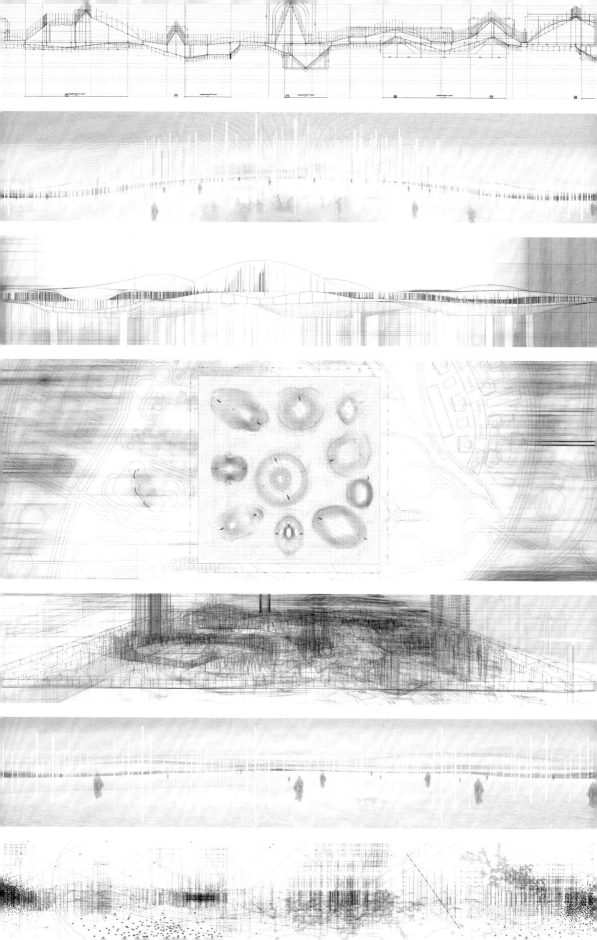

1. (previous page) Fortuné Penniman, Temple Mall
– Dubai is a sanitised city of place-less and mono-cultural interiors, where public space as we know it does not exist. The shopping-mall, the terminal, the lobby; to be in Dubai, is to be both everywhere and nowhere. The Temple Mall is a space of cultural concentration that temporarily suspends social hierarchies between different 'local' occupants of Dubai. Through a controlled distribution of light, wind and views, normal mechanisms for orientations are taken away, creating an experience of public-ness that is common to all. The Mall is a mirador that internalises the elemental world of the desert. What we observe is not nature itself, but nature exposed to our common methods of observation – a horizon-field, where climate and perception induce social relationships that would not otherwise exist.

2. Vidhya Pushpanathan, Genesis X: The First Settlers
– Genesis X is an intentional commune for the exiled polygamous Islamic community, the Obedient Wives. An external image constructed with exaggerated scales of impenetrable American Puritanism forms, shielding settlers from America's ever-growing Islamophobia. An internal system with gradients of different ornamental lattice densities transitions between American and Islamic motifs underlining an overlay of different existing cultures trying to co-exist. Interstitial spaces are carved into the interiors that envelop the tension between the comfort of the known and discomfort of the unknown when the public meet the first settlers in a rare new formal space for a rare new community.

3. Christopher Yah Chuen Shen, Gaming Oubliette: the Spectacle of Infinite Dimensions – 'level up' as reality is reconstructed into an immersive, augmented video gaming experience where both the audio-visual language and the interaction processes associated with them connect players and their bodies to the physical plane, even if their minds are overwhelmingly allured during playtime in virtual space. With the spread of online role-playing games, this hybrid space transcends traditional gaming experiences, allowing players to live out new dimensions and alternate characters without limits. The project is situated at the beginning of spaces that emerge from the superimposition of the physical and the virtual, which constitute themselves through the convergence of 'technology', 'space' and 'community'.

4. Lorenzo Perri, The Dogmatic Garden: Coranic Academy in Baghdad – the phenomenon of Isis forces us to reconsider how in the Islamic world religion intersects with politics and education. How does a religious dogma play an active role in society, providing an imposed direction for Muslim life and influencing the whole understanding of human behaviours? The Coranic Academy offers an alternative in which dogmatism is pursued through education and its different methodologies. Through institutional rigour the original identity of Islam – one based on unity and tolerance – is restored. Internalising the symbolic and typological features of the Islamic Paradise and the Kullyesi, the Academy is conceived as a synthetic garden, formed only by water and architectural elements. The Iconoclast abstraction is pushed to the extreme, informing the spatial features and creating a built metaphor of a dogma.

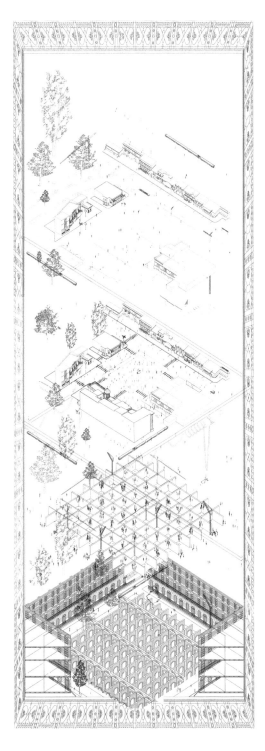

5. Erez Ezra, Transient London, Public Domesticity
– within a city's continuous renewal and decay,
a new condition of public living is being forged in
which lives are compartmentalised and transient.
The private house is the new public space, unfolding
worlds that create fluidity in matter and in programme.
Constructed through a series of interlocking rooms,
the public domain is infinite and the consumption
and accumulation of objects left behind reform the
structure, its behaviour and its functions. Through
the movements and positioning of bodies in space
the experience of a post-cinematic phenomenon
is created and divided into environments – detached
from one another; over-crowded; constantly
reinventing; existing in a continuous flux of renewal
and decay; fragmented and changing – where all
memory is lost within the structure and reconstructed
as a shared experience.

Diploma 6

Unit Masters
Liam Young
Kate Davies

Special Forces
Oliviu Lugojan-Ghenciu,
  Motion Designer
Tim Maughan,
  Screenwriter
Dave Ferner, Animator
Carlos Casas, Filmmaker
Aneek Thapar,
  Sound Designer
Toby Smith,
  Photographer
Alonso Barros, Lawyer
The indigenous
  communities of Peine
  in the Atacama and
  Santa Rosa in the
  Amazon
ALMA Radio Telescope
  Observatory
Rockwood Lithium Mine
San Cristobal Silver Mine
The capable drivers of
  Imbex Bolivian 4WD
The petrol-fuelled
  daredevils of the
  Dakar Rally

The Unknown Fields Division: Lithium Dreams

Diploma 6 – the 'Unknown Fields Division' – is a nomadic design studio that ventures out on annual expeditions to the ends of the earth to explore peripheral landscapes, industrial ecologies and precarious wilderness.

This year we travelled from rain-soaked forests to parched flat earth, through the energy rich landscapes of the Bolivian Amazon and the Atacama Desert. Here the ground is charged with potential, for below the mirror-like surface of the world's largest salt flat, Salar De Uyuni, is a grey gold called Lithium, a material which epitomises a burgeoning new era of electric fuel.

Unknown Fields chronicled these resource landscapes, investigating the infrastructures that serve as energy conduits, translating matter like a luminous language – from a hole in the ground to the glow of our phones – to trace a wild journey of electrons from the radiant gizmos of our familiar city deep into landscapes far, far away.

In the bright white light of the salt flats, Eleanore of our Mythic Industries Department has initiated a carnival of adorned mining machines and decorative gas masks to celebrate a new alliance between Lithium companies and indigenous landowners, while Natali's Intentional Fossils Lab has preserved the violence of a Dakar Rally crash with a 10,000-year-old monument to our petrochemical fetish. As part of our Invisible Territories Division Mikhaila encoded a new cultural territory in the derelict bandwidth of the electromagnetic spectrum, and Addison traced one of Paris Hilton's instagram posts about a new handbag all the way to the national park it created in the Bolivian Amazon. Jason, of our Accident Design Bureau, has choreographed the collapse of 'the mountain that eats men' and instigated its eternal rebuilding as a macabre tourist attraction. Lara of the Centre for Floral Mining has researched the flower species that bloom in the presence of metals to reimagine mine sites as exotic gardens. In our Department of Speculative Energy Nicholas takes us on a journey along Elon Musk's Gigaloop to witness a future in which batteries have become the scarce resource. Meanwhile Kassandra has dreamt up history's largest solar farm, a modern-day Eldorado that sacrifices all of Chile to power our entire planet.

Students
Eleonore Audi
Lara Behmoaram
  de Toledo
Mikhaila Fam
Cheng Feng Men
Yufei Li
Kassandra Lim
Natali Markantonatou
Alexey Marfin
Nicholas Masterton
Patrick Morris
Richard Seymour
Jonathan Skerritt
Addison Yick

1. Richard Seymour, the Corporation of Nature – the great Incan god Viracocha created the universe, sun, moon, stars and time by instructing the sun to move across the sky. Tears descend as rain from his eyes. In the twenty-first century the great acts of creation and tragedy are gauged by their impact on the FTSE. Water, a substance of mythology and creation is also a finite resource. For the past ten years out of ten, water stocks have outperformed those of gold on financial markets. In 2010 Bolivia became the first nation to give legal personhood to its landscape to protect it. Richard Seymour of Unknown Field's Markets and Mountains Bureau has formed the Corporation of Nature and imagines Bolivia floating a 49 per cent share of its water assets. Here landscape is a person, and water is a company. An act of legal wit lifted from the corporate world designed to protect and profit from one of the world's most diverse ecologies. Told through the format of an annual audit report, lakes, lagoons, glaciers, flora, and fauna, are quantified and valued for their water content. The landscape is re-engineered to trap water like gold in vaults and manipulate flows like trades across the market. Year on year. Ice on ice. Silt on silt. An act of design based in the realm of law, to offer an alternative to a system in which the financial landscape has superseded the real landscape from which its value is derived.

2. Alexey Marfin, Everyday Extraordinary – our experiences of places and cities are riddled with the ghosts of internet memes, youtube phantoms, and daydream projections. Where we are is not important anymore as virtual landscapes flood domestic interiors and exotic worlds shimmer like mirages at the end of everyday streets. In our Department of Digital Imaginaries Alexey captures the banalities of a daily commute through a city of infinitely variable virtual fabrications, constructing a world where everyday spaces are designed to function as vessels for the extraordinary. This is a city where online extremes and digital distractions become manifested as experiential constructs; inhabitable and tangible, disposable and single-serving. We drift through an electric reality of a million animated movies cast in place through the eyes of machine vision systems. They construct a media sea of constant extremes, fantasies and the extraordinary. Flying cat videos, tinder profiles, people being hit by lightning, televised decapitation, intimate celebrity breakdowns and the world's fastest car have all left the screen to furnish the augmented realities of our daily world. We explore the collisions between the everyday and disposable extraordinary in a single breath as every minute a new impossible or imaginary is uploaded to the internet to become just one of hundreds of extraordinary events to be consumed that day. The extraordinary is the new normal and we swipe right, refresh, scroll down and continue on our way.

3. Yufei Li, The Atlas of Vanishing Landscapes – a weeping glacier sits patiently in your bathroom waiting for you to return from work, you feel a pang of guilt as you've not thought about it for a while. A giant iceberg materialises in the financial district – is it a harbinger, a signal or a ghost? There are economic risks concealed in this calving digital glacier, but who will tend it? By creating a parallel reality, Yufei of our Department of Ghost Cartographies has reconstructed a fragile nature, translating the live city data-scape into a set of digital landscape apparitions. We experience a distant vanishing glacier both intimately and absent-mindedly, tied to it by complex and chaotic cause and effect, where our everyday activities accumulate and exert invisible and abstract forces on a distant land. In this artificial geography, we drift along the dashed routes and contour lines, on an ever-changing map of a data driven landscape. The digitised terrain is presented as an instrument, appearing and vanishing in response to our daily consumptions. When the real places are no longer reachable and the maps fading to blank, the digital ghosts of these remote landscapes exist in the city as a placeholder for the vanishing physical ones, questioning our relationship to a disappearing terrain.

4. Jon Skerritt, Uyuni Super Mine – the landscape of the Bolivian Salar de Uyuni flashes by in the trailer for a Japanese racing game: a future landscape commodified to fuel our electric future and reimagined with the cold efficiency of the world's largest mine, where endless fields of evaporation ponds feed lithium salts into the world market to be monetised in the battery production lines of Asia. This is a mine so large that no single national entity could support it as, like the space industry, lithium mining in Bolivia must be operated by a particular scale of multinational corporation, following the pattern of developed countries forming partnerships with the developing world to extract resources and disperse them across the planet. The Division's Cultural Attaché, Jon allows us to see this landscape only through the cold eyes of the video game and to view one culture through the lens of another. In a new form of place that is caught between cultures, a race plays out in a landscape that has been forever altered in the moment of our green energy revolution. It is a glimpse into the landscapes on the other side of our screens, the landscapes that fuel the games we play for kicks.

5. Patrick Morris, Large Sub-Pixel Array — we understand the world though the images we take of it and our constellation of luminous screens create experiences just as real as any other. In our Department of Instagram Archaeology Patrick has created a landscape within the fabric of the LCD screen itself, a site formed in the canyons of the sub pixel, a territory that can exist nowhere else. The strata of this landscape is an ever-growing mass of 5.4 billion pixels and the 60,000 annual Instagram updates of the Salar de Uyuni in Boliva, one of the most photographed sites on earth. We look out across this hashtag horizon, it stretches 7,680 pixels long and 6,044 pixels wide. We take our first footsteps though the sand of pixels, they shimmer and their RGB hues burn our eyes. Black roots crackle and tangle our feet as we walk, 18 power cords and 15 VGA cables stretch across its surface. The weather is flickering at 60Hz and the cooling fans struggle to keep up. The atmosphere thick with pixel dust and the buzz is incessant. We travel though the screen to this site formed of technology. It is a virgin territory rarely seen, but it is a landscape in which we live most of our lives.

Diploma 7

Evgenia Andersson
Eduardo Andreu Gonzalez
Lorenza Baroncelli,
  Daniela Meyer,
  Swiss Pavilion, Venice
Giulio Bertelli
Stefana Broadbent
Barbara-Ann
  Campbell-Lange
Javier Castañón
  and the TS team
Jane da Mosto, Venice
Kate Davies
Ryan Dillon
Albane Duvillier
Wendy Eagling, Royal
  Corinthean Yacht Club
Alvaro Fernandez
Liza Fior
John Frazer
David Greene
Selim Halulu
Samantha Hardingham
Yijun Huang
Andrew Jin Dar Hum
Sho Ito
Christopher Johnson
Holger Kessler, British
  Geological Society
John Lyall
Tae Hyuk Kim
Yin Lee
Bruce McLean
Lucy Mary Moroney
Sheraz Quiddale Shabbir
Raja O'Sullivan
Jiadong Qiang
Humphry Repton
Mike Russum
Irénée Scalbert
Maddalena Scimemi,
  Venice
Colin Scott,
  ABPmer environmental
consultancy
Toby Shew
Brett Steele
Pier Vittorio Aureli
Gloria Pou Wai
John Walter
Ken Worpole
Yiling Zhang

This year Diploma 7 continued its search for the characteristics of New Nature – possible architectures for a post-print-post-industrial-post-consumer landscape. Our main area of interest, a 50-minute journey northeast of London, was the coastal wetland of Wallasea Island in Essex. Here more than six million tonnes of subsoil – the by-product of London's Crossrail tunnel construction – has been relocated to now function as an aid for managing Britain's retreating coastline. Searching *not-usually-valued knowledge*, students worked in that scratchy layer where subsurface meets ultrasurface, where the very fast meets the very slow. With film-as-sketchbook as the primary means of investigating, accumulating and recording information, moving drawings become the primary mode of representation for proposals based on the tenets of speed, time and interval.

The principal design endeavour was to work out how much or how little architecture is required. Projects were informed by visits to the British Geological Society London, the Royal Corinthean Yacht Club in Burnham-on-Crouch, and workshops in Venice. Theoretical, technical and critical issues were searched through a series of talks and seminars with a diverse group of distinguished artists, architects, environmental scientists, anthropologists, and architectural and landscape historians. Importantly, all the projects developed over the year have contributed to expanding the lexicon of New Nature, and all fall into one of four distinct new chapters:

- Earthly Delight in the New Nature: Intertidal Geospheres
- Politics in the New Nature: Spaces of Collective Attention
- Learning in the New Nature: Digital Bricolage
- New Nature Noospheres

Lucy Moroney, Taking a Bath in the Intertidal Zone
of Wallasea Island – exploiting the temporary
limitations of nature

Top: Sho Ito, Politics in the New Nature, the Westminster Model – a transitory government

Bottom: Albane Duvillier, London's Housing Struggles

Eduardo Andreu Gonzalez, Fragile Monuments – a
system of measurement for a changing coastline

145

London

Top: Christopher Johnson, New Nature Noosphere
Middle: Quiddale O'Sullivan, A Classroom of
Earthly Delights

Bottom: Evgenia Andersson, Bad Weather Park, autumn

London

Diploma 9

Unit Staff
Natasha Sandmeier

Many thanks to
Manolis Stavrakakis for
  his seminars,
  workshops, and cultural
  and geographical
  navigation
Antoine Vaxelaire for
  seminars, tutorials and
  in-house exhibition
Charles Arsène-Henry for
  seminar, superworlds
  and chess
and to our dear friends,
  guests and critics:
Miraj Ahmed
Shumon Basar
Umberto Bellardi Ricci
Doreen Bernath
Valentin Bontjes
  van Beek
Matthew Butcher
Nerea Calvillo
Barbara-Ann
  Campbell-Lange
Javier Castañón
Judith Clark
Marie de Monseignat
Ryan Dillon
Belinda Flaherty
David Greene
Kostas Grigoriadis
Fenna Haakma Wagenaar
Francesca Hughes
Sam Jacob
Lily Jencks
Carlos Jiménez Cenamor
Amandine Kastler
Saskia Lewis
Nacho Marti
Inigo Minns
Carol Patterson
Pablo Ros
Lola Ruiz Garrido
Adiam Sertzu
Takero Shimazaki
Rob Stuart-Smith
Brett Steele
Antoine Vaxelaire
Madelon Vriesendorp
Mike Weinstock
Thanos Zartaloudis
Elia Zenghelis

Factory Made

Since the industrial revolution the factory has confirmed architecture's place in the mass-production of modernism. From James Watts' steam engine, to Henry Ford's assembly line, to Andy Warhol's infamous Factory of pop art, to the invisible ones that yield our digital spaces – for nearly 150 years the factory has housed all kinds of manufactured worlds. At the start of the year unit discussions revolved around factories that make stuff – typewriters, cars, textiles, shoes and drugs – but our conversations led us to an entirely other realm of production. If we were going to use architecture to work on the very issue of architecture culture, then surely where we work and how we work were inevitable questions to ask. Our attention shifted from the assembly of a product towards the assembly of a critical question: What is an architecture factory and what does it make: stuff or identity?

Oliver surreptitiously interviewed architects in the streets of London about pay and gender equality within the profession. His resulting project is a carnival-esque mobile office that shirks identity in favour of pure output, and demands dialogue instead of directives. Arguing that the factory assembles more than it creates Sabrina built a world of 'borrowed' work, grafting her identity from those around her and situating herself at a crucial junction where copyright law and identity theft steadily encroach on the profession. Catarina's factory – a real-life photoshop – exists at the end-stage of production, the realm in which architecture meets its viewer. In her project people and structure are edited away to optimise the audience's experience. This hyperrealism sits in stark contrast to Nara's more ethereal factory of belief. Light is her building material – but she uses it to build uncertainty, transforming terra firma within her spaces into infinite vistas and slipped timescales. Ultimately, the output of Diploma 9's factories is equally a set of cultural conditions and building proposals that address the multifarious world we operate within today.

Students
Anouk Ahlborn
Felix Brinkhege
Nara Ha
Maridia Kafetzopoulou
Sabrina Morreale
Oliver Pershav
Andra Miruna Mazilu
Catarina Sampaio Cruz
Andreani Stephanou
Djordje Stupar
Alexander Zhukov

2

3

1. (previous page) Nara, Factory of Belief — 150 of Manhattan's 500+ churches don't have a dedicated space; instead they occupy drab offices, schools, starkly lit shops, and halls. This project is dedicated to bringing the qualities and experiences of the sublime to the everyday.

2. Sabrina, Copy Machine — Sabrina claims she was never taught to draw and as a result has built a career out of tracing and appropriating. Her mission is to embed a less precious attitude towards authorship into architectural production.
3. Miruna Factory of Islands — a desert landscape impregnated with relics of events and artefacts, forcing questions of what lives longer: the moment or the mass?

4

5

4. Catarina, Selfie Machine – in a world without image-editing, Catarina builds the architectural-edit – a construction system that slims, tints, smoothes and even erases away offending structures. The Kim Kardashian of architecture, it's a super-savvy archi-selfie-machine.

5. Anny, Context Machine – while Jean Prouvé insisted that his site was his factory, Anny argues this leads to unplaceable buildings, and instead she creates a context machine to force architecture into contextual collisions, leading to more robust and versatile buildings.

6

7

8

6. Oliver, Future Office Factory – 'Are you a hedgehog or a fox?' asks Oliver to architects in London. His ideal architectural office addresses gender and pay equality in our profession.

7. Felix, Inversion Machine – infinite houses respond to the contemporary live-work continuum in which no one can quite tell where one begins and the other one ends.
8. Djordje, Preservation Machine – preservation walks a fine line between nostalgia and continuum. Djordje allows for neither as he entombs offending architecture in concrete.

9

10

11

9. Anouk, Format Factory – frame, plinth and format provide the location, ground and bedrock for content – and this is where Anouk builds her factory.
10. Maridia, Threshold Machine – the cinematic experience of zooms and splices is how Maridia wants to experience architecture. Jumping between thresholds we witness a career's worth of buildings.

11. Sasha, Boundary Machine – public space has disappeared from the modern city. What we are left with are spaces magnanimously loaned to us by corporations. Sasha obliterates the harsh border created by Novartis by elevating it to reveal a vast new public realm beneath.

Diploma 10

Unit Master
Carlos Villanueva Brandt

Constructed Situation
Workshop
Jan Willem Petersen

Technical Workshop
Alex Warnock-Smith

Tokyo Workshop
Professor Tom Heneghan
Tamao Hashimoto

Skidmore Owings &
Merrill Collaboration
Daniel Ringelstein
Alida Bata
Gareth Edwards
Martin Grinnell
Stuart Marsh
Dimitri Jajich
Bernhard Rettig

Direct Urbanism: Scan and Insert
In reaction to masterplanned impositions, Diploma 10 has experimented with an alternative form of transformation: insertions as spatial interventions. To create these insertions, we scanned a polemic London territory that included the ideological vision of the Churchill Gardens Estate and the current commodity-led development in Nine Elms. Having revealed the variables that make up the space of the city, isolated the live realm and identified the interactions that exist between structures, situations and the forces of change, we tweaked these to generate new transformative structures, situations and strategies from the scale of the city to that of architecture.

In the Churchill Gardens Estate:
Hunter's insertion of lightweight structures, enveloping a multilevel BID, creates a new form of integrated transformation; Steve opens up Churchill Gardens to the city's users by inserting focal points for political, community and cultural groups; Sorina, questioning the ideal of the modernist estate, inserts city-like junctions to create alternative social interactions; Yonatan combines the mechanisms that control the individual, groups and communities to colonise the estate with a new type of school; and Fearghus starts to fragment the weaponised NHS by inserting a freestanding A&E into Churchill Gardens.

In Nine Elms:
Zeina counteracts the lack of spaces of engagement in the existing development by inserting a series of composite centralities; Frag challenges the masterplan by combining similar development strategies into a new type of block-sized insertion that internalises the street; Pablo, by turning a Nine Elms tower on its side, creates a new barrier that juxtaposes territorial control with an increased social complexity; Ben inserts smart urban systems to create a spatial and digital interface in front of the US Embassy; and Camilla asks: 'London as a social commodity is currently underrated: so why not insert a trajectory of different scaled encounters?'

Students
Zeina Al-Derry
Yonatan Buchhandler
Hunter Devine
Ben Jones
Fragkiskos Konstantatos
Steven Price
Fearghus Raftery
Pablo Sanchez Lopez
Camilla Sand
Sorina Siddall

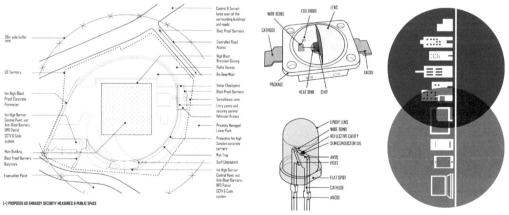

1. Ben Jones — an interactive digital screen
creates a feedback system with the new
US Embassy in Nine Elms.

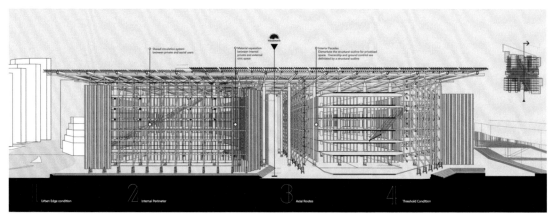

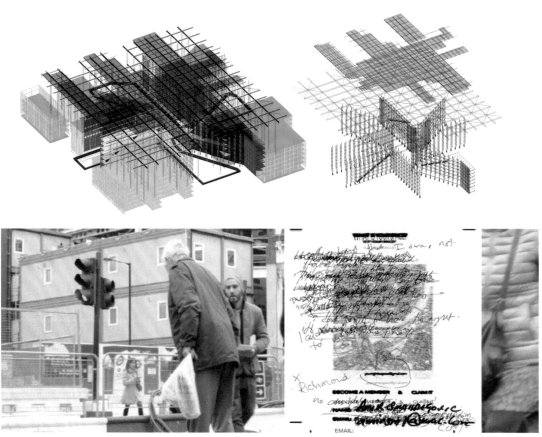

2. Fragkiskos Konstantatos – a new type of block-sized insertion internalises the street to challenge the Nine Elms masterplan.

3. Hunter Devine – in the Churchill Gardens Estate, integrated lightweight structures, enveloping a multilevel BID, create a new form of transformation for London.

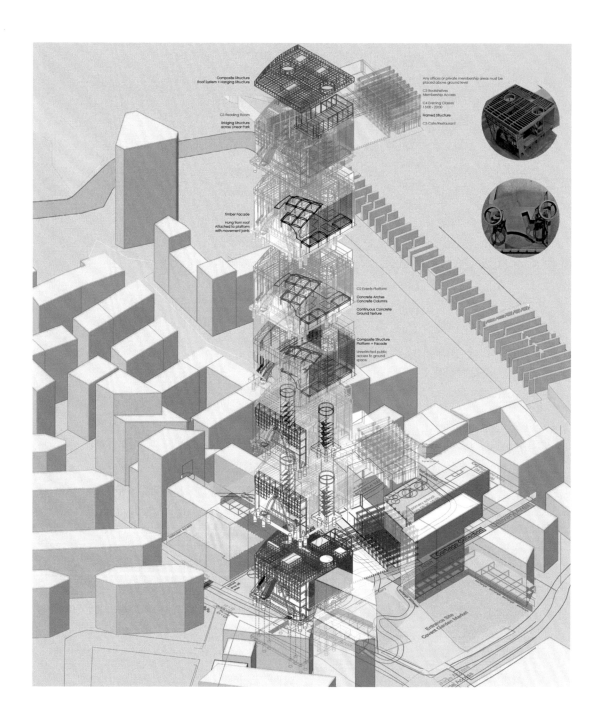

4. Zeina Al-Derry – a composite centrality counteracts the lack of spaces of engagement in the Nine Elms development.

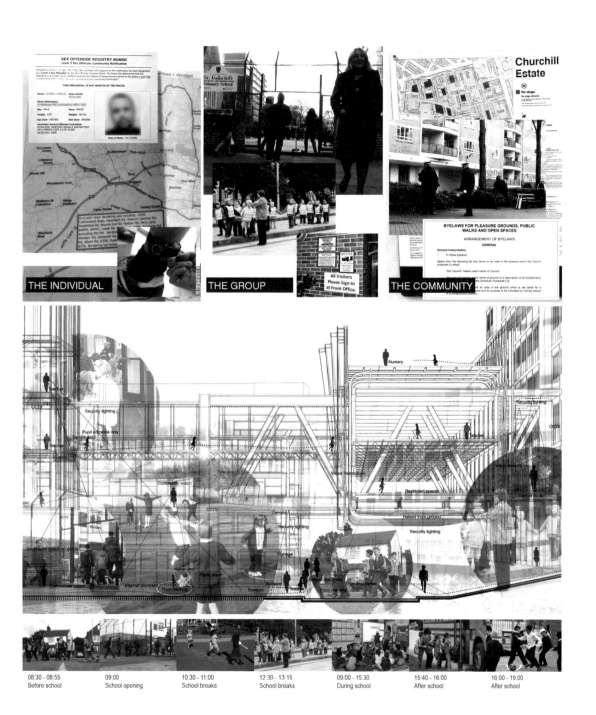

5. Yonatan Buchhandler – the mechanisms that control
the individual, groups and communities are combined
to colonise the Churchill Gardens Estate with a new
type of school.

Diploma 11

Unit Staff
Shin Egashira

Special thanks
London Seminars
and Regular Critiques:
Nicholas Boyarsky
Peter Carl
Kate Darby
David Grahame Shane
David Greene
Elizabeth Hatz
Hugo Hinsley
Peter Thomas

Tokyo Seminars:
Shigeru Aoki
Hidenobu Jinnai
Masao Noguchi
Makoto Uyeda

Tokyo Workshops:
Tamao Hashimoto
Tom Heneghan
Kanto Iwamura
Atsushi Iwata
Taebeom Kim

Hooke Park:
Charlie, Georgie
 and Tia Corry-Wright

Jurors and
Guest Critics:
Chiaki Arai
Pierre d'Avoine
Kate Davies
Ryan Dillon
Raha Farazmand
Summer Islam
Jon Lopez
Inigo Minns
Benjamin Reynolds
Akira Suzuki
Dora Sweijd
Sylvie Taher

This year Diploma 11 sought to re-read the area between London's King's Cross and Farringdon stations through all the things that are marginalised and fragmented by the forces of economic and political change. Triggered by a series of recent developments such as the arrival of Crossrail and planning proposals for Mount Pleasant, we questioned processes of so-called gentrification by looking for cultural expressions of the unplanned city. Much of our work addressed the effects of such processes of transformation and how we could think of them differently.

Our investigations were led not by research in the most banal sense of the word but rather by being playful, naïve and childish. Each discovery was distilled on the drawing board, to reveal hidden mechanisms and complexities within the city. Group sections and axonometric collages quickly translated into each student's individual interests: could diminishing institutional buildings like the Royal Mail Sorting Office and Smithfield Meat Market be reconciled with their adjacent historical and infrastructural layers? Is it possible to conceive of construction sites as inhabitable spaces? Could erased places of production be integrated into the new Crossrail station? Could city water systems and building services provide the basis for informal public spaces? Is there a way to distribute the functionalities of the British Library and Barts Hospital across the city? Where is the place for the youth when land value is so high?

We found the workshop tabletop to be our primary platform to try to answer such questions throughout the year. Materialisation explored the beauty of incompleteness and temporality when combined with permanent details. We learned from the contextual subtleties of London, where programme and spatiality continue to transform while buildings remain defined by rigid configurations. Our challenge has been to give form to place by reusing what it is able to gather and transmit.

Students
Khalid Alsugair
Vasilis Argyropoulos
Roberto Boettger
Theclalin Cheung
Panos Demiris
Lena Emanuelson
Lelia Ku
Erez Levinberg
Joan Lim
Ami Matsumoto
Mark Mcglynn
Mahsa Ramezanpour

1

Through the year we tested our ideas by collaging the existing with the new and our own interventions. (Diploma 11 Model Collage 1) We've dealt with the topics of gentrification in the context of the River Fleet, spanning the distance from King's Cross to Farringdon, focusing on the infrastructure of the area and exploring ideas such as the reconfiguration of the masterplans that make up the Farringdon Crossrail site. Using gaps between the proposed developments, residual spaces are opened up with techniques of retention and excavation. By strategically linking a series of productive activities along this new spine the station is transformed into a hub, not only a circulation space for passengers but one for materials and local

2

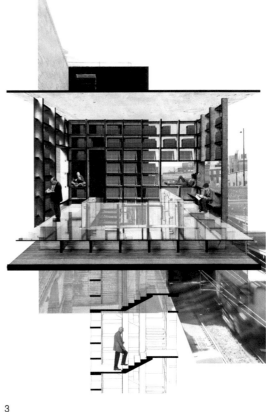

3

4

processes as well (Erez Levinberg 4). We looked at the proposed and possible development sites around the station and explored how to use them for alternative programmes during the construction phase (Mark Mcglynn). Investigations into a series of underused spaces left incomplete by the construction of Metropolitan line inspired the idea of the Street

Academy, which reactivates underused facilities by inviting misfit students to explore and interact with the cityscape (Theclalin Cheung 2). The disused train platform hidden along the River Fleet is reimagined as a 'micro library', salvaging the overloaded British Library collections to curate reading rooms in the city (Joan Lim 3). Seeking an alternative to the commercial

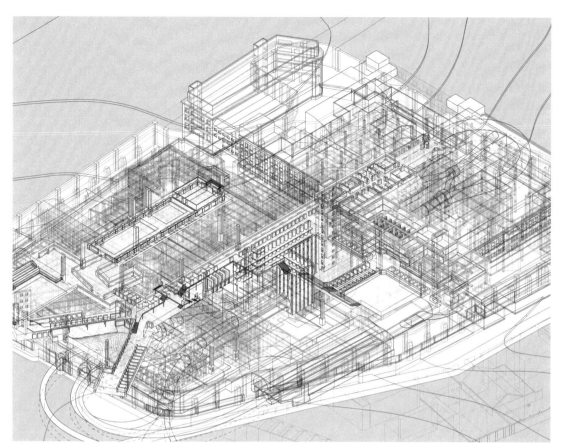

5

development of the Royal Mail Mount Pleasant Mail Centre, interventions of stripping, cutting and inserting new amenities made the site a new hub for the surrounding community (Mahsa Ramezanpour 10). By uncovering the footprints of the cold bath, prison, workhouse and all the pre-existing buildings beneath Mount Pleasant, a network of old fragments emerged as an inverted landscape. Along this cut will be a series of the kind of local facilities neglected by the recently approved development scheme for Mount Pleasant (Lelia Ku 5). The water station is proposed as a habitable local infrastructure whose intention is to slow the rapid gentrification by exposing structures and historical layers preserved under the sorting office

6

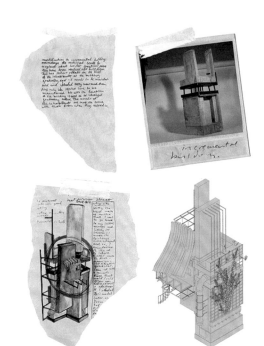

7

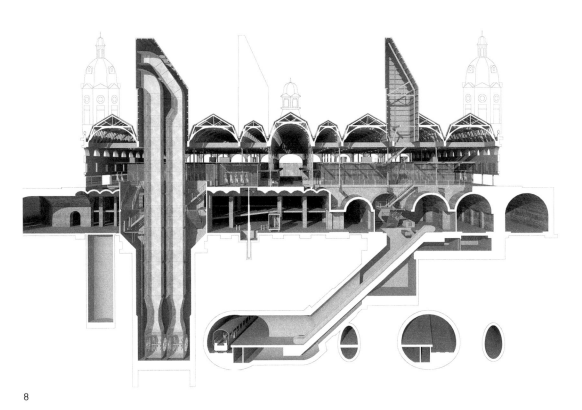

8

(Khalid Alsugair 11). Could the city space become an environment for healing in cases where hospitals no longer provide the spatiality and time essential for recovery after treatment? The proposed insertions of urban furniture aim to turn small patches of wilderness and hidden alleyways and spaces into suitable healing environments for vulnerable people in the city.

(Ami Matsumoto 6). A building has now three stages in its life: planning, construction and, finally, inhabitation. How could the lines between what is ephemeral and permanent be blurred and questioned? How could these three stages become one? (Panos Demiris 7). Smithfield Meat Market is another infrastructure that is slated for redevelopment. It is important to revive

164

9

10

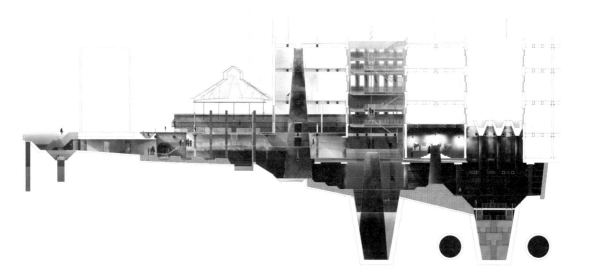

11

this once great place by opening it up to the public and adding to the existing building without infringing on current daily operations (Vasilis Argyropoulos). As the meatpacking industry shrinks in line with declining demand, its obsolete infrastructural elements are revealed through a process of dismantling, cutting away and underpinning. (Roberto Boettger 8). Based on an investigation into the 'Incidental Spaces' of Farringdon, a design methodology was created to integrate a new type of public space – one with no commercial value – into the city. Such spaces will be a valuable addition in areas where existing communities are being pushed out by gentrification (Lena Emanuelsen 9).

Diploma 14

Staff
Pier Vittorio Aureli
Maria Shéhérazade
 Giudici

Thanks to
Fabrizio Ballabio
Monia De Marchi
Elias Guenoun
Adrian Lahoud
Charles Rice
Davide Sacconi
Francisco Sanin
Irénée Scalbert
Thomas Weaver

The street, the block and the room: these are the most common spaces of existence. Everywhere, at any time, we dwell within these places, and for this reason we assume they are innocent backdrops for our lives – stages for the everyday. Yet these spaces represent the *summa* of how human subjectivity has been tamed and moulded within predictable social patterns. Life and work are now one and the same; labour cannot be confined within specific 'workplaces'. For this reason, domestic space – the space of reproduction – becomes the most strategic vantage point for considering how life itself – as *bios*, as *dynamis* – is put to work. Issues such as gentrification and the credit crunch are truly brought to bear when they are seen as part of the enslavement of life as a source of economic value. Here, our common spaces become insidious spheres where dwelling happens in a state of permanent precariousness. This condition clashes with the ideological cliché of the home as a reassuring space of intimacy and family values. Instead, the intimacy of the domestic becomes the locus of a familiar horror.

This year Diploma 14 opened the Pandora's box of our contemporary horror as it emerges in our daily routines. We looked at dwelling on three scales – the street, the block and the room – in order to analyse how economy, politics and form have shaped subjects and habits. This analysis was used as the starting point for a molecular revolution within and against domestic space with special focus on the architecture of the interior as an arena for radical spatial and social invention.

Students
Anastasija Binevic
Michela Bonomo
Alex Butterworth
Lili Carr
Kate Finning
Jesper Henriksson
Jenny Hill
Richard Leung
Luis Ortega
Emmanuelle
 Siedes Sante
Louise Underhill
Andrea Wong
Lara Yegenoglu
Yantian Zhou

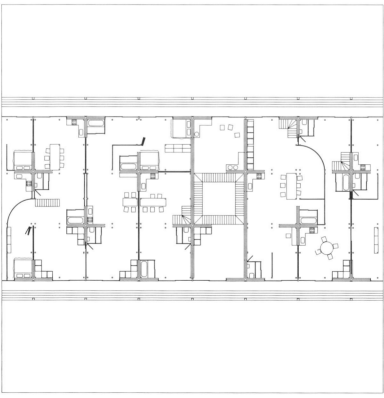

1. Louise Underhill, Frames – the reinvention
of the London terrace house

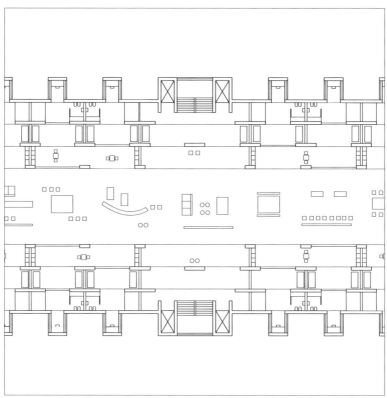

2. Michela Bonomo, Gradient – student housing
in Belgrade

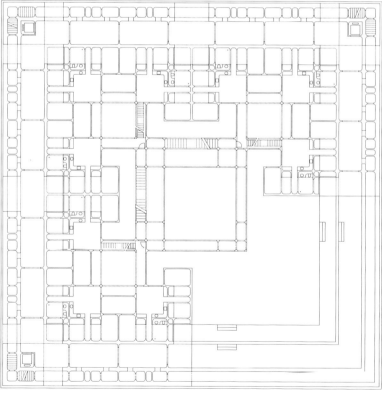

3. Lara Yegenoglu, Mahalle – housing unit
for 800 people in Istanbul

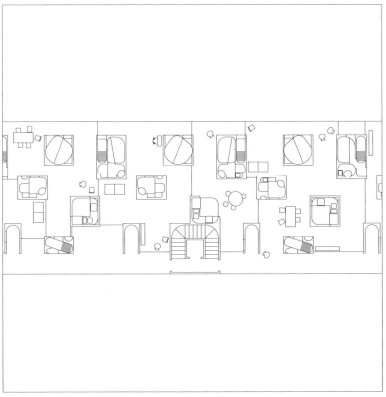

4. Andrea Wong, Cores – social housing
prototype for Singapore

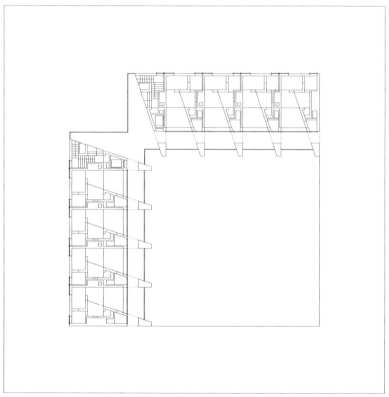

5. Jesper Henriksson, A House for My Self — prototype
for single-occupancy homes in Stockholm

Diploma 16

Unit Masters
Andrew Wai-Tat Yau
Jonas Lundberg

Consultants
Duncan Berntsen
Elian Hirsch
Pedram Seddigazeh
Karin Hedlund

Acknowledgements
Thanks to all the
supporting staff of the
AA School and to our
visting critics:
Jeroen van Ameijde
Jonathan Bell
Duncan Berntsen
Carlos Villanueva Brandt
Young Wei-Yang Chiu
Shin Egashira
Kostas Grigoridis
Ken Hogg
Adam Holloway
Jeremy Kim
Michael Kloihofer
Ashkan Sadeghi
Rebecca Spencer
Dora Sweijd

Diploma 16 continues its exploration of innovative and visionary design responses within of regenerative architecture and urban formation, set in East London and addressing large-scale infrastructure and extreme urbanisation in our rapidly changing environment. Can the design and materialisation of architecture as both infrastructures and cities capacitate a positive ecological footprint exceeding the adverse environmental effects of construction and building operation? Is it possible to do so without compromising design quality and sensibility while instilling a sense of hope and optimism forged by new technology and human endeavour?

METATROPOLIS 2050 searches for design novelty in architecture and cities based on the incidental parameters between urban expansion and large-scale infrastructure where decentralised social organisation and dense urban living is necessitated by our need to sustain the planet. The change in paradigm from sustainability to regenerative design requires new forms of architecture and urbanism. This ECOTOPIA of sorts is associated with lean infrastructure, energy production, resource harvesting and waste management.

Using a variety of material, fabrication and production processes the projects are developed as urban prototypes which are adapted and tested based on specific urban contexts. A central part of the unit's work is the production of large-scale models and super-scale singular composite drawings representing both artefacts, time-based changes and metabolism. Students are encouraged to develop their own design repertoire and communications skills based on generative and associative modelling techniques, environmental simulation and digital fabrication. The critical design relationship between novel material production, fabrication and construction processes, architecture and new urban living is central to the design work. We focus on the formulation of creative responses to architecture in the development of proto-cities that anticipate a new regenerative future. We aim for a final manifestation of an architecture that responds to the promise of regenerative design, a positive environmental impact and the hope for a sustained planet.

Fifth Year Students
Anand Naiknavare
Dimitar Dobrev
Jaewon Lee
Jerry KK Lam
Jin Kyu Moon
Nick Ping-Hsiang Chen
Tom Hatzor
Xiao Von Chua

Fourth Year Students
Federico Turina
Kerry Dickinson
Nurul Atira Binti
  Che Ariffin
Peng Qin
Su Yi Choi
Thomas Veiteberg Holan

2

3

1. (previous page) Jaewon Lee, The Levitating Garden City 2100, eighth wonder of the world?
2. Jaewon Lee, Hanging water-based gardens at 8840m elevation

3. Kerry Dickinson – model for floating inhabitation, articulating the trifoil profile, to promote connections between inside and outside, attraction and repulsion, public and private space

174

4

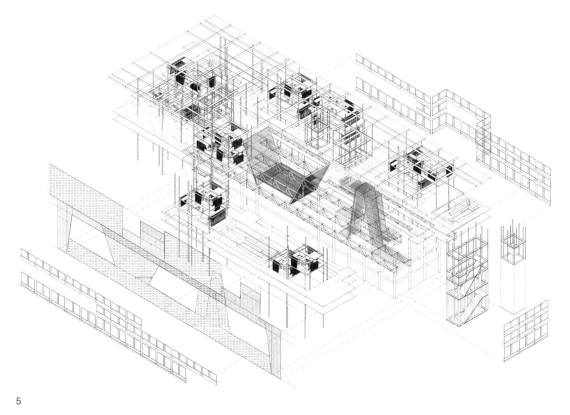

5

4. Jerry KK Lam, Field condition – a new structural type hovering above London's industrial brown field sites, dissolving and transforming the existing urban plan

5. Jerry KK Lam – how do you build with only air and timber? An air labyrinth using air as a new material boundary and housing various thermo-landscapes

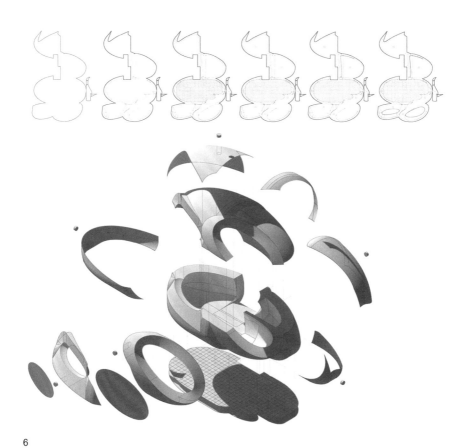

6

7

6. Federico Turina – using tailoring on the fabric formwork to control unit form, internal spaces and thicknesses

7. Federico Turina – 2050 model for single-person inhabitation using new construction techniques to promote temporary dwelling using minimum resources

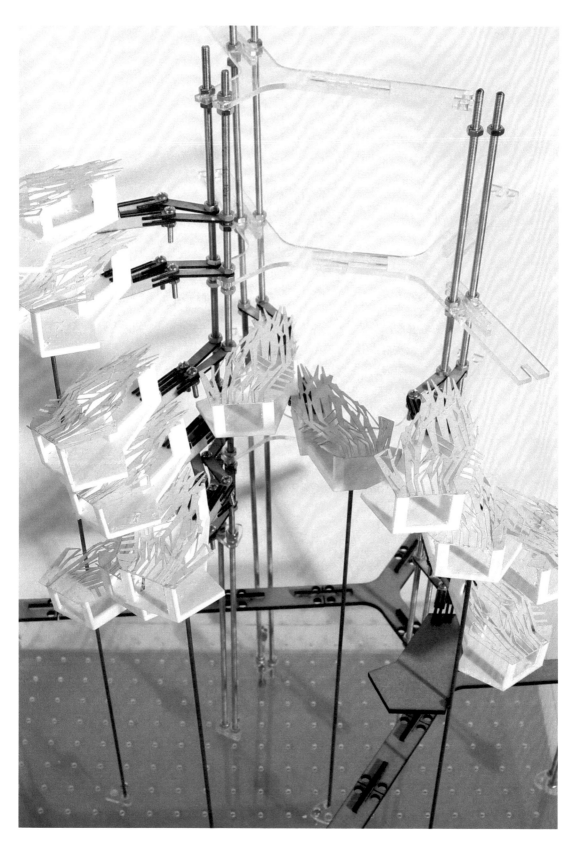

8. Nurul Atira Binti Che Ariffin – a lived-in tree or a forest?

Diploma 17

Staff
Dora Sweijd
Theodore
   Sarantoglou Lalis
Kasper Ax

Acknowledgements
Miraj Ahmed
Win Assakul
Daniel Bosia
Barbara-Ann
   Campbell-Lange
Javier Castañón
Yannick Denayer
Cristina Diaz Moreno
Ryan Dillon
Shin Egashira
Didier Faustino
Felix Fassbinder
Kostas Grigoriadis
Thomas Jensen
Ilina Kroushovski
Tyen Masten
Pablo Ros
Nathalie Seroussi
Theo Spyropoulos
Robert Stuart-Smith
Brett Steele
Manja van de Worp
Carlos Villanueva Brandt
Andrew Yau

<u>Latent Territories: Spaces for Knowledge Exchange</u>
In the past decade, the rapid expansion of transportation and information networks has produced profound territorial transformations as well as radical mutations in the way we exchange knowledge and occupy space. A counter-effect of these technological changes is the contraction and devaluation of the physical public realm and the homogenisation of culture and our built environment. This year's edition of latent territories operated within this critical condition and continued its investigations into the socio-political role of infrastructural and architectural form in defining new modes for coexistence in the contemporary city.

This year we focused our work on rethinking the organisation and experience of spaces for knowledge exchange in the age of digital content beyond institutional and professional frameworks. We observed widespread building obsolescence as well as greater informal use of space in the practices of learning and working.

We started the year by investigating form integration of multiple design objectives through a series of tectonic investigations. We prioritised the performative and behavioural attributes of form for their capacity to materialise relational spaces and reposition the body in society through action and the triggering of senses. We addressed informality through a greater emphasis on ergonomics and material definition. Concurrently we investigated the socio-political role of partition and vision as elements producing social organisation and control. Projects debated the changing notion of public space and the conditions through which architectural form reflects the relationship between the individual and the collective.

Within these conditions, projects questioned the role of programme and site as traditional drivers for architecture in order to develop formal apparatuses that prioritise both social interaction and a redefinition of boundaries to allow greater resilience towards change.

Students
Luca Allievi
Nailu Chen
Daniel Schandl
   Christiansen
Ritika Daswani
Philip Doumler
Neha Gandhi Dhiren
Raz Keltsh
Agata Pilarska
Maria Elena Popovici
Jonathan Wong Chi Ho
Di Zhan
Yu Zheng

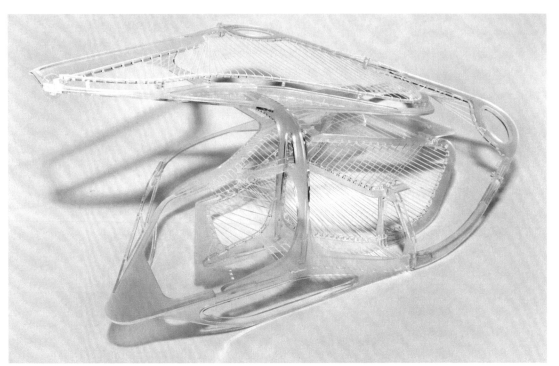

2

3

1. (previous page) Maria Elena Popovici, Complex Learning Grounds: An Institutional Alternative in the Technological Society, modulation of space through the absolute use of columns – harbouring an understanding of spaces dedicated to knowledge exchange through freedom of use and inquisitive variation rather than programmatic partitioning

2. Philip Doumler, After Hours: The City's 24-hour Existence – the project explores the way the city responds to its connection to different time zones within the context of the current era of information. What would be the nature of the urban public space that allows social encounter and knowledge exchange within a 24-hour framework?
3. Di Zhan, Social Cores

4

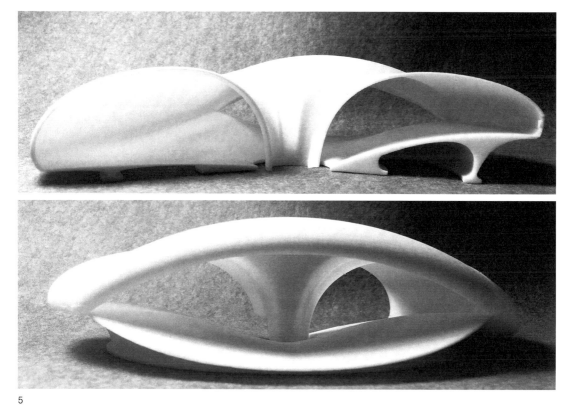

5

4. Nailu Chen – a three-dimensional framework
that establishes visual and physical connections,
facilitating new modes of open-source collaboration
and non-hierarchical organisation of space

5. Yu Zheng – looking into the moments where the
urban educational space collapses into the domestic
sphere to reformalise a new spatial typology through
the ceiling articulations

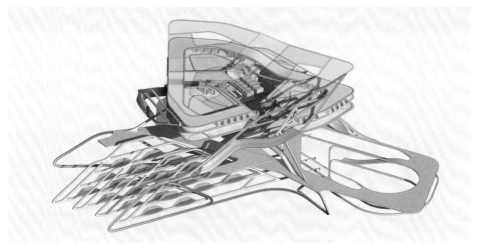

6

7

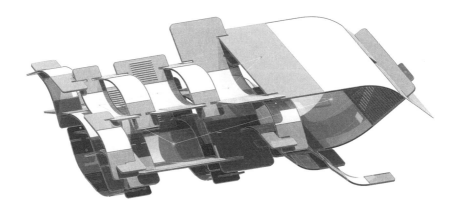

8

6. Philip Doumler, After Hours: The City's 24-hour Existence – the new public typology is addressed through the conditions of 'the edge', a reinterpretation of the beam as an architectural element, and an exploration and hybridisation of its structural, programmatic and social attributes within a continuous, self-supporting framework loop.

7. Ritika Daswani, Reversible Active Spaces – the project investigates variable boundary conditions through the use of the ground in order to create a programmatic cluster of swimming pools, parking and event spaces in Sarcelles, France.
8. Jon Wong

9

10

9. Daniel Schandl Christiansen, Informal Host: Eroding Knowledge Spaces – maker labs, artist studios and an auditorium set below a walkable roof structure infiltrate an urban leftover terrain. Spaces are affected by surface flow patterns and the wearing out of a composite material promoting a less institutional space for knowledge exchange.

10. Raz Keltsh, Curricular Constellations – a pedagogical formation of knowledge clusters pursuing curricular interaction

Diploma 18

Staff
Enric Ruiz Geli
Pablo Ros
Felix Fassbinder

Assistant
Ioana Giurgiu

Thanks
Olga Subirós,
  architect and curator
Samantha Hardingham
Barbara-Ann
  Campbell-Lange
Javier Castañón
Nacho Martí
Theo Sarantoglou Lalis
Julia Tcharfas,
  artist and curator
Hans-Willi Notthoff,
  artist, Museum Island
  Hombroich
Hareth Pochee, physicist
Katrin Wittwer,
  Greenpeace
Henrik Düker,
  Greenpeace
Karen Wiltshire, biologist
Jan Beerman, biologist
Biological Institute
  Helgoland (BAH) of
  the Alfred Wegener
  Institute
Helmholtz Centre for
  Polar and Marine
  Research
Detlev Bruckhoff,
  architect
Magdalena Lodzinska,
  yoga professor
Denis Devaris,
  environmental
architect, Hacienda
  Cristoforo
Dr Marco Koschorreck,
  quantum physicist
Dr Christoph Schäfer,
  CMS Collaboration,
  CERN
Dr Peter Adams,
  physicist, CERN
Marc M. Cohen,
  astrotecture, NASA
Dr Jim Haseloff, biologist,
  University of Cambridge

Atmospheric Architecture of Particles

After four years of investigations into global warming, Diploma 18 spent this year researching the Atmosphere, specifically the 'Architecture of Particles'. We interpreted the environment on the molecular level to design strategies of intervention in both the tectonic/material and the climatic/incorporeal, using computational dynamics to explore nano-scale behavioural patterns. This modelling of ecologies led us to understand relations in macro-scale environments. We visited the lignite mine in Gartzweiler, Germany. On the islands of Heligoland we met environmental activists, and on Tenerife we met people who live in harmony with the environment. We experienced the anthropocene at the origins of pollution but also followed the rhythm of nature. Diploma 18 atmospheric projects proposed solutions from the infrastructural to the molecular scale in order to raise green consciousness and activism in architecture. They include:

- Utopia of weathers: Soft infrastructures, domestic experiments, visceral enquiry, anthropogenic unity
- Spaceship Mind: Quantum entangled migration to exoplanets
- Splintering Architecture: The Inequality of Technological Singularity
- Sensational Landscape of Data-scenarios: Layers of terrain physicality and invisible reality of our senses
- Spring Stations: Nomadic landscape healing the environmental disaster of the Aral Sea
- Ethical gold: retrofitting nature and employment in the Peruvian Amazonia
- Helgoland: [iwussasasdcnsdinobeycyrmeoeyantlilmtntasm tstfrfqfbieilipwtaouusivrflgloerdiuoigicnermmetfssychaxks artfimiapisty isanptiyismanrtoclgoyniaeasenscindbhmcnip yagltieumrrpuaallcetscompchaos]
- Ocular City: decrypting the invisible urban contamination
- Airpocalypse : The Inventory of World Resource – designing a blue sky
- ATLAS of inadvertent invention hybrids
- Terra Violet: A Living Lab for UV Mutation Research
- GMO Civilisation: Journey to bio-eternity with GMO, magnetism and permaculture

Students
Lingxiu Chong
Krists Ernstsons
Dunya Hatem
Donika Llakmani
Salvador Folque
Ruth Gattegno
Naida Iljazovic
Marietta Kakkoura
Bianca Moldoveanu
Ibrahim Muasher
Pavlos Pierides
John Yim

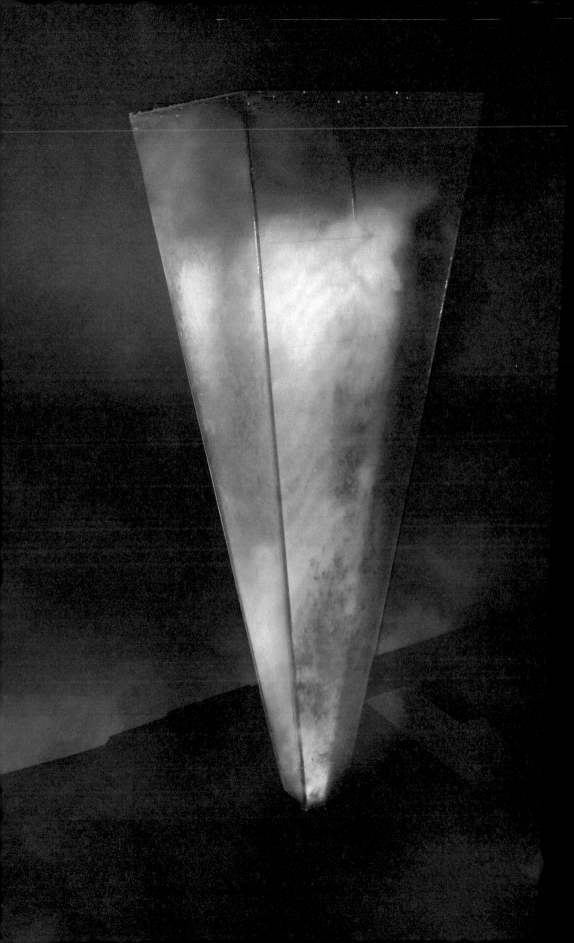

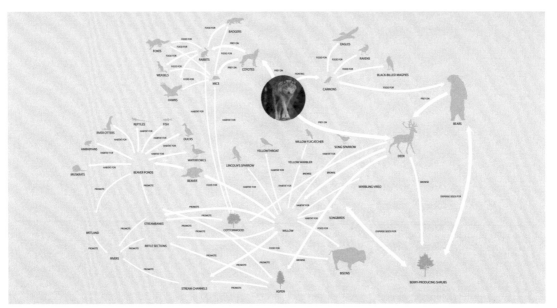

2

3

4

1. (previous page) Bianca Moldoveanu   3. Donika Llakmani
2. Naida Iljazovic   4. Ruth Gattegno

186

5

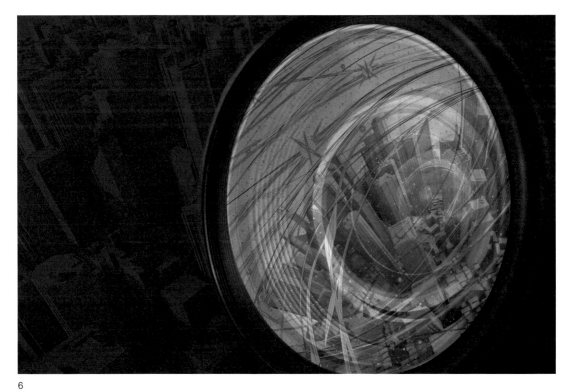

6

5. John Yim
6. Marietta Kakkoura

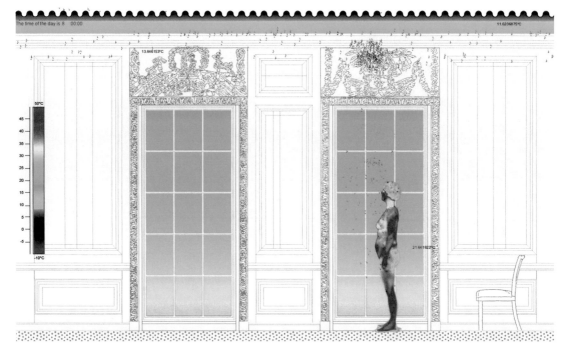

7

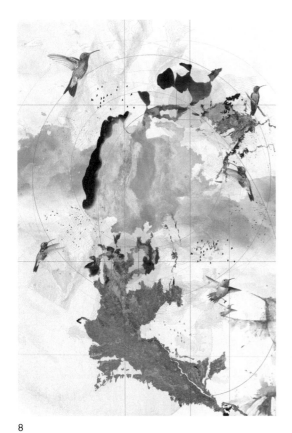

8

9

7. Lingxiu Chong
8. Salvador Folque
9. Pavlos Pierides

188

10

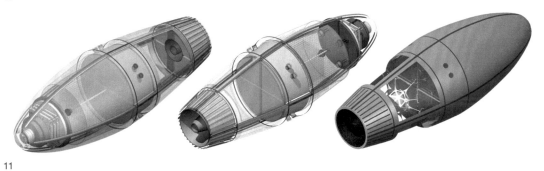

11

12

10. Dunya Hatem
11. Krists Ernstsons
12. Ibrahim Muasher

The programmes in History & Theory, Media Studies and Technical Studies make up an essential part of every year of the Undergraduate School. In term-long courses students obtain knowledge and gain experience related to a range of architectural learning. These courses also provide opportunities for those approaching architecture from the different agendas of the units to come together in shared settings. History & Theory Studies includes courses that develop historical and theoretical knowledge related to architectural discourses, concepts and ways of thinking through the skill of writing. Media Studies helps students develop skills in traditional forms of architectural representation as well as today's most experimental forms of information and communication technology. Technical Studies offers surveys as well as in-depth instruction in material, structural, environmental and other architectural systems. This leads to technical submissions, which build upon the ideas and ambitions of projects related to the work in the units.

Together, the various courses on offer in Complementary Studies allow students the opportunity to establish and develop their own interests and direction in the school.

History & Theory Studies

Director
Mark Cousins

Course Lecturers /
Course Tutors
Pier Vittorio Aureli
Mollie Claypool
Mark Cousins
Ryan Dillon
Christopher Pierce
Brett Steele
Sylvie Taher
Zaynab Dena Ziari

Teaching Assistants
Fabrizio Ballabio
Shumi Bose
Susan Chai
Nerma Cridge
Lionel Eid
Pol Esteve
Winston Hampel
Alison Moffett
Ricardo Ruivo
Emmanouil Stavrakakis

Consultants
Edward Bottoms
Judith Clarke
William Firebrace
Patrick Keiller
Roberta Marcaccio
Christopher Turner
Thanos Zartaloudis

Administrative
Coordinators
Belinda Flaherty
James Hulme

Thank you to our critics
Kate Davies
Costandis Kizis
Natasha Sandmeier
Yasmin Sharif
Manijeh Verghese
Liam Young

In recent years the AA has provided the resources for a more ambitious vision, enabling us to reconsider what the basic objectives of teaching history and theory at the school should be. Strange as it may seem, we believe that the concentration of the programme should be on the parallel issues of writing and drawing. To take writing first, the most serious and decisive way in which a student can engage with the building is not just to look at it, but also to write about it. Description and analysis combine powerfully in the memory, and the gradual acquisition of the skill of architectural writing provides students with an ability to document and analyse what they see, which is vital in contemporary architectural practice for those who want a creative career. We have continued the Dennis Sharp Prize for Excellence in Architectural Writing in the Diploma School and the Writing Prize in each year of the Intermediate School. These provide an initiative for written work as well as an open forum for students to present their essays. Hopefully, we are convincing students that writing is an indispensable pleasure allowing them to express their ideas in a powerful way. It is perhaps more obscure to say that we are concerned with drawing, but for all the dramatic changes brought by the digitalisation of design over three decades there are still many functions embedded in drawing for which the computer is no substitute. Writing and drawing should both be seen as forms of notation with which students can express ideas as well as document things they see and encounter at the school and beyond. It is difficult for us to think of an architect deprived of scribbling.

A future goal of the programme is to assist and train students in ways in which they can present their work. Given the gap between how students design and how they talk about their design work there is a real opportunity for the programme to help with the preparation of presentations. Needless to say this is not only a vital intellectual tool, but one which will be significant in their future work.

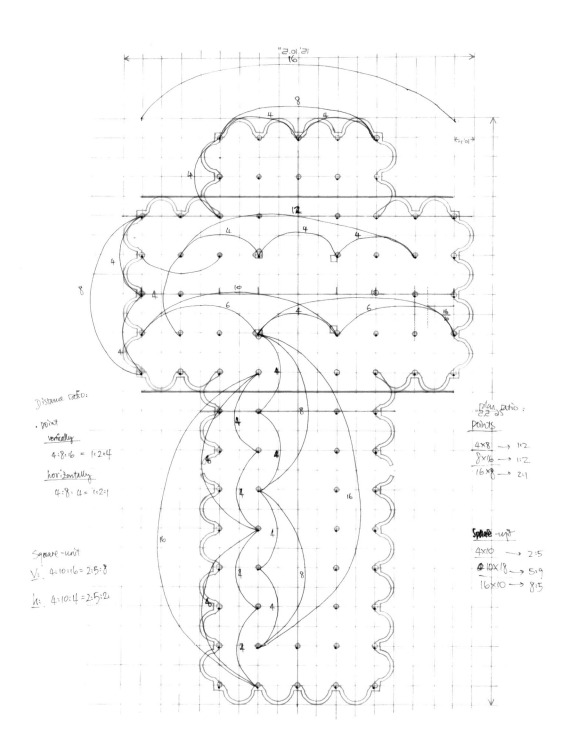

1. Xuecheng Wang, HTS First Year, The Rebirth
of Human Scale – drawing of Santo Spirito
consisting of modules and their multiples

SIMONPIETRO SALINI, *NOVITATEM MEAM CONTEMNUNT EGO ILLORUM IGNAVIAM*: THEY DESPISE MY NOVELTY, I THEIR TIMIDITY
First Year Writing Prize
It almost seems to me as if I was trying to invent a new logic behind those structures. A logic centred on the disintegration of the clarity behind each composition of my etchings, where I was gradually departing from a coherent reading of the spaces that seemed to transform and distort into an unsolvable puzzle. I had created a labyrinth wherein I could not locate the exit.

OLUKOYE AKINKUGBE, THE INESCAPABLE BIAS OF REPRESENTATION
Second Year Writing Prize
The inherent quality of photo documentation to render an air of significance to an otherwise insignificant occurrence exhibits the might and readiness of this form of representation to influence the sentiments of an indifferent audience, not presupposing indifference because such an audience is none the wiser or merely uninterested, but more owing to the fact that the presented documentation is finite in its manifestation of representation.

JANE WONG, THE BURNING HOUSE
Third Year Writing Prize
In shooting the apotheosis Tarkovsky insisted on using only one camera for the scene. The house, which was painstakingly built over the course of five months, was set aflame to the faith of one lens, yet the machine jammed midway through the destruction. An accidental sacrifice, the house burned to the ground without being captured on film. Reshooting came at the agonising cost of reconstructing the house in two weeks. The burning house is thus preserved in the suspension of the second take. We shall not see an end to it.

ZEINA AL DERRY, THE MELANCHOLIC CITY OF MIRAGES
Dennis Sharp Prize 2015
Compared to his contemporary Iraqi architects, Rifa'at Chadirji possessed a rather liberal spirit in abstracting from history, as he did not copy exact formation and was not bound by traditional principles of proportion or composition... Historical forms were reduced to geometrically simple volumes – a hint, an essence that had little or no physical similarities to his designs. The stronger the abstraction of tradition the easier it was for him to merge it with what he described as the universal spirit of the age.

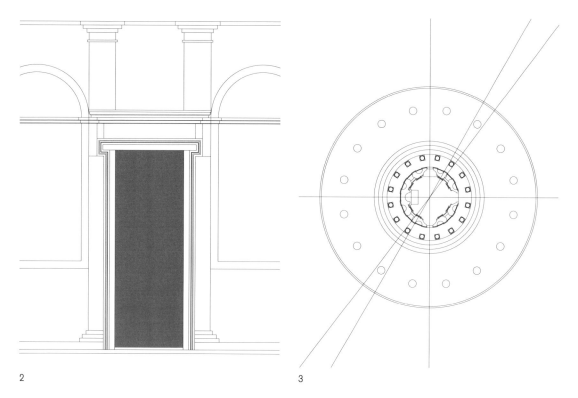

2

3

Equality!

In 1922
I began to walk into a dream
that I never again left
life in the modern city

I had made detailed plans for a
contemporary city of 3,000,000
inhabitants

I had created new dimensions,
I had made room for the basic
pleasures
the sky and the trees
everybody's chosen companions

Sun in the room
a window filled with blue
awakening to a wave of greenery

there, in the city

4

2. Hexuan Yu, HTS First Year – detailed drawing of the main portal of Tempietto, excluding the two columns
3. Hexuan Yu, Plan of Tempietto

4. Moad Musbahi, HTS First Year, Pavillon du Temps Nouveau; Le Corbusier's imaginary form or a rough series of adverts; *a perfume rises and grips the passerby*

Media Studies

Department Head
Kate Davies

Department Staff (Core)
Miraj Ahmed
Charles Arsène-Henry
Kasper Ax
Shany Barath
Sue Barr
Valentin Bontjes
 van Beek
Apostolos Despotidis
Shin Egashira
Gary Freedman
Anderson Inge
Alex Kaiser
Oliviu Lugojan-Ghenciu
Antoni Malinowski
Alison Moffett
Joel Newman
Capucine Perrot
Caroline Rabourdin

Department Staff (Lab)
Ran Ankory
Chris Dunn
Andres Harris
Joshua Newman
Vincent Nowak

The AA Media department is an experimental testing ground for exploring and interrogating the processes and tools involved in making architecture – the tools with which we speculate, manipulate and play; compute, control and test; communicate, seduce and provoke. It operates a diverse multidisciplinary programme where unexpected collisions and obsessive attention to detail expose rich seams of creative potential. By actively testing modes of production through focused acts of doing and making, AA Media presents a range of opportunities for students to develop individual practice and hone dexterity with both established and progressive media.

The department is made up of staff who possess a breadth of expertise encompassing architecture, the arts and technology and this year's courses address a wide range of creative media including drawing, video, photography, animation, narrative, textiles, analogue and digital fabrication, interactive and web-based media, fieldwork, curation and electronics. Alongside a compulsory curriculum for First Year and Intermediate students, the department runs full-day workshops, computer lab courses, talks and demonstrations open to curious minds from across the entire school. As techniques and concepts in fabrication, computation and representation continue to undergo radical changes, AA Media deploys a range of tools – from pencil to point-cloud – aimed at both reinforcing and reinventing the methods in which students approach design and architecture.

1

2

1. Taek Gyun Won – Disobedient Photography
workshop with artist Steven Pippin

2. Rose Mary Florian Rodriguez – Da-Da Digital
with tutor Kasper Ax

197

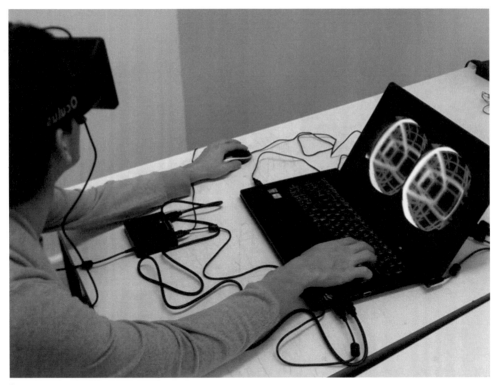

3

4

3. Kyle Jonathan Ingber, The Household Glitch Mounted
Regiment with tutor Oli Lugojan-Ghenciu
4. Yu-Hsiang Wang, Projection and Speculation with
tutor Miraj Ahmed

5. (opposite) Painting Architecture class
with tutor Alex Kaiser

198

Technical Studies

Head of Technical
Studies
Javier Castañón

Diploma Master
Javier Castañón

Intermediate Master
Kenneth Fraser

Administrative
Coordinator
James Hulme

Design Tutors
Giles Bruce
Christina Doumpioti
Wolfgang Frese
Pablo Gugel
Martin Hagemann
David Illingworth
Julia King
Antiopi Koronaki
Nacho Martí
Federico Montella
Yassaman Mousavi
Amin Sadeghy
Nina Tabink
Manja van de Worp

Course Lecturers
Carolina Bartram
Giles Bruce
Phil Cooper
Paola Daro
Chris Davies
Christina Doumpioti
Ian Duncombe
Wolfgang Frese
Evan Greenberg
Ben Godber
Martin Hagemann
David Illingworth
Emanuele Marfisi
Nacho Martí
Thomas Oosterhoff
Nina Tabink
Paul Thomas
Giancarlo Torpiano
Manja van de Worp
Mohsen Zikri
Giancarlo Torpiano

Special Course Lecturers
Evan Greenberg
Elif Erdine
Axel Körner
Antiopi Koronaki
Yassaman Mousavi

Very special thanks to
Belinda Flaherty for the
great work she does
keeping everyone and
everything moving. Very
special thanks also to
Evan Greenberg for his
unconditional support
and a very warm welcome
to James Hulme for being
willing to dive into the
deep end straight away.

Technical Studies can be likened to an iceberg, in that one sees only about a tenth of its mass. In this sense the Projects Review shows a small sample of what Technical Studies (TS) achieves during the year. Our 'solo exhibition' was the High Pass Exhibition, where we saw what the dedication of the TS staff and enthusiastically committed AA students can produce. A token sample of these efforts follows.

Third and Fifth Year students have continued to embark on their own projects of research and experimentation intimately related to their unit design work. The TS design tutors aim to provide every student with the wherewithal to materialise the ambitions, ideas and concepts born in the intimacy of the unit.

All of this is what can be seen above the surface, but most of Technical Studies remains hidden in the silent work put into each day, throughout the year, which enables students to produce such interesting projects. The Technical Studies programme stands as a complete coherent technical education over five years and constructs a creative collaboration with the material demands of individual unit agendas. This goal requires a constant reinventing of all that makes up the programme. This year the First Year has seen one of the biggest changes, but likewise the Special Courses mainly offered to Fourth and Fifth Year students have helped transform the landscape of options on offer.

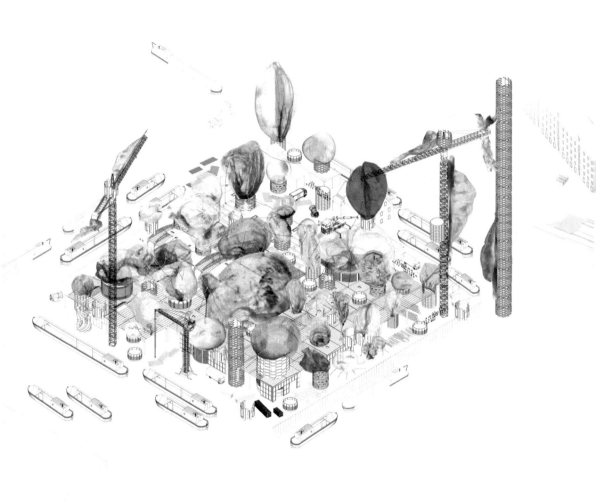

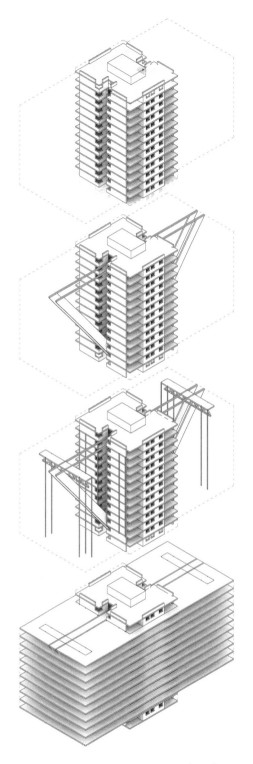

1. (previous page) Dalia Frontini (Inter 9), Fermenting Papirøen – Noma restaurant is moving to Papirøen Island and consuming the existing warehouses. Converting them into kitchens, halls and fermentation laboratories. Papirøen becomes the main forum for cooks and scientists in Copenhagen to inhabit the experimental kitchens and harvest gases.

2. Cliff Tan (Dip 1), ModelMead – the project explores the possibility of building over the existing towers of Thames Mead to create an architecture that allows for meaningful circulation, interaction and an enjoyable space. The extension cantilevers out from the existing concrete building and features a structure consisting of diagonal struts that extend the entire length of the tower, forcing inwards at the base, and pulling outwards in tension at the top, resulting in a closed structure that is held only vertically from the top.

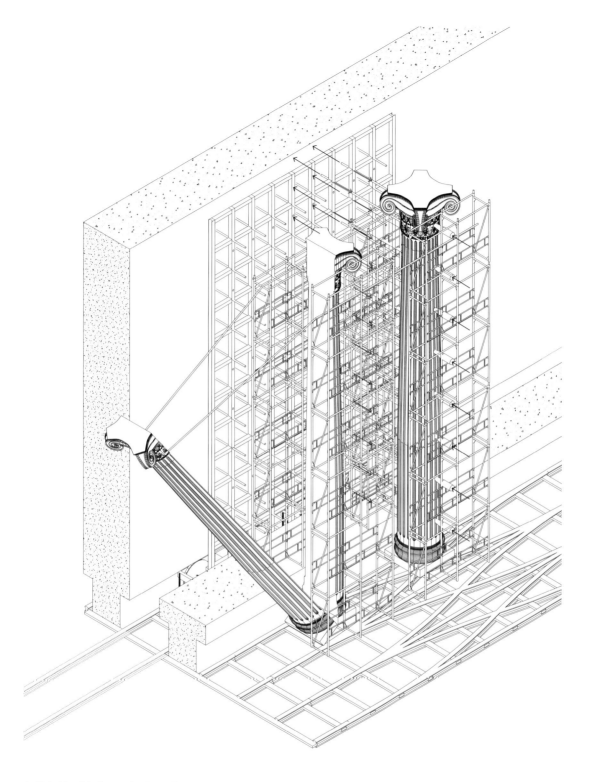

3. Gleb Sheykin (Inter 7), River of Facades, the
Depository of Stolen Images – this vast exchange
accumulates a bank of both historical and
contemporary facades by stealing them from the city.
Beyond simply curating and storing the facades it
renders them as a dynamic element, testing how they
interact with other samples and thus creating a new
drive for architectural experimentation and
construction in Berlin.

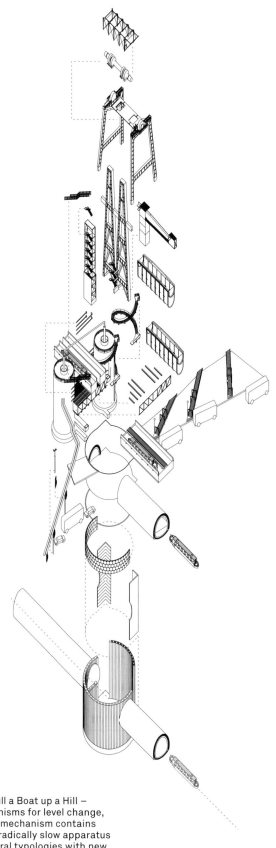

4. Jane Wong (Inter 5), To Pull a Boat up a Hill –
reinterpreting canal mechanisms for level change,
each component within the mechanism contains
a unit of duration to form a radically slow apparatus
that hybridises infrastructural typologies with new
social potentiality.

5

6

5. Louise Underhill (Dip 14), Framing the Home –
the proposal aims to create a new form of terraced
housing by addressing the party wall and what exactly
individualises families within the city. By thinning the
structure and pulling it apart the clear divisions and
hierarchies are removed, reintroducing the potential
for interaction and negotiation between neighbours.

6. Catarina Sampaio Cruz (Dip 9), The Architectural
Edit – this technical work explores the possibility of
a self-editing architecture through different cloaking
mechanisms based on refraction, reflection and lenses.
The result is a building that erases itself, freeing
spaces from columns, beams and other structural
elements in an attempt to criticise the way architecture
is experienced today.

The AA Graduate School includes postgraduate programmes offering advanced studies in one of the world's most dynamic learning environments. Full-time master's programmes include 12-month MA and MSc and 16-month MArch options. The Design Research Lab (AADRL), the AA's innovative team-based course in experimental architecture and urbanism, offers an MArch. Emergent Technologies & Design (MArch/MSc) emphasises forms of architectural design that proceed from innovative technologies. Sustainable Environmental Design (MArch/MSc) introduces new forms of architectural practice and design related to sustainability and the environment. Landscape Urbanism (MA) investigates the processes, techniques and knowledge related to the practices of contemporary urbanism. Housing & Urbanism (MA/MArch) rethinks urbanism as a spatial discipline through a combination of design projects and contemporary theory. History & Critical Thinking (MA) encourages an understanding of contemporary architecture and urban culture grounded in a knowledge of histories and forms of practice. Design & Make (MArch) allows students to pursue workshop-based design while imagining alternative rural architectures. Projective Cities (MPhil) is dedicated to research-and-design-based analysis of the emergent and contemporary city. AAIS researches and applies alternative forms of collaboration through spatial performance and design. The part-time Building Conservation course offers a two-year programme leading to an AA Graduate Diploma. Complementing these, the AA PhD programme fosters advanced scholarship and innovative research in the fields of architecture and urbanism through full-time doctoral studies. A PhD by Design programme provides a setting for advanced research and learning for architects, designers and other qualified professionals.

The AA is an Approved Institution and Affiliated Research Centre of The Open University (OU), UK. All taught graduate courses at the AA are validated by the OU. The OU is the awarding body for research degrees at the AA.

Design Research Laboratory

Director
Theodore Spyropoulos

Founder
Patrik Schumacher

Course Masters
Shajay Bhoosan
Robert Stuart-Smith

Course Tutors
Pierandrea Angius
Doreen Bernath
Mollie Claypool
Ryan Dillon
Apostolos Despotidis
Winston Hampel
Oliviu Lugojan-Ghenciu
Mostafa El-Sayed
Tyson Hosmer

Technical Tutors
Albert Taylor
Edward Moseley
Alessandro Margnelli

Software Tutors
Torsten Broeder
Michail Desyllas
Manos Matsis
Paul Jeffries
Karoly Markos
Jorge X Mendez-Caceres
Ashwin Shah

Programme Coordinator
Ryan Dillon

External Examiners
David Ruy
Chris Williams

Invited Critics
Philippe Block
Mark Cousins
John Frazer
Jason Kelly Johnson
Marta Malé-Alemany
David Pigram
Max Schwitalla
Brett Steele

This year the DRL concluded the second year of its new design research agenda Behavioural Complexity, which builds on the scenario- and material-based research outcomes of its predecessor, Proto-Design. The work investigates architecture as an instrument of interaction in which social scenarios are coupled with material behaviours and life cycles that aim to open up speculative questions about how we live and the role that architecture can actively play.

To achieve this, behavioural, parametric and generative methodologies of computational design are combined with physical computing and analogue experiments to create dynamic and reflexive feedback systems. The result is the development of new forms of spatial organisation containing adaptive characteristics that are not type- or site-dependent but tested within scenarios of evolving ecologies and environments in order to develop novel design proposals concerned with the everyday. The iterative methodologies of the studio focus on investigations of spatial, structural and material organisation, engagement with contemporary discourses on computation and materialisation in the disciplines of architecture and urbanism.

The possibilities of Behavioural Complexity are explored in four parallel research studios. Theodore Spyropoulos' studio, 'Self-Aware – Self-Structured Robotic Ecologies Towards a Behavioural Model for Architecture', investigates autonomous self-aware and assembled systems that explore machine learning, collective building and environmental conditioning. 'Tectonic Articulation: Making Engineering Logics Speak', led by Patrik Schumacher, instrumentalises engineering and fabrication logics for the purpose of articulation: the adaptive differentiation structure, volumes and envelopes according to environmental performance. Robert Stuart-Smith's studio, 'Behavioural Production: Investigations into Swarm Printing', develops adaptive, rapid and on-demand construction enabled by swarm 3D-printing that orchestrates design and production as a singular creative process able to respond to diverse social and economic time-based scenarios. Shajay Bhooshan's studio, 'Metamorphosis: Prototypes as Applied Research in Architecture, Engineering and Manufacturing', attempts to research and speculate on 'when machines will design and build' in terms of architectural design and how can we describe, evaluate and search for the right designs.

Phase 2 Students
Soulaf Aburas
Doguscan Aladag
Dmytro Aranchii
Karthikeyan Arunachalam
Leyla Asrar Haghighi
Agata Banaszek
Mengxian Bao
Paul Clemens Bart
Sai Pratiek Bhasgi
Nik Arief Bin Nik
 Ab Rahman
Delfina Bocca
Duo Chen
Yiqiang Chen
Cosku Cinkilic
Victor Corell
Camilla Maria
 Degli Esposti
Faten El Meri
Alexandra Katerina
 Garcia Lipezker
Maria Luisa Garcia
 Mozota
Flavia Ghirotto Santos
Maha Moustafa
 Habib Abdelraouf
Yuqiu Jiang
Dachuan Jing
Sasila Krishnasreni
Baiye Ma

Evangelia Magnisali
Karim Mohamed
 Anwar Abdel
 Salam Mohamed
Juan Jose Montiel
Giannis Nikas
Georgios Pasisis
Ilya Pereyaslavtsev
Akshil Bharat Rawal
Jose Antonio
 Rodriguez Gonzalez
Maria Alejandra
 Rojas Jaramillo
Carolina Saenz Marrufo
Mattia Santi
Melhem Sfeir
Tahel Shaar
Ahmed Moshen Shokir
Daniel Simaan Franca
Antonios Thodis
Junfeng Tong
Pavlina Vardoulaki
Maria Paula
 Velasquez Garzon
Wan-Shan Wu
Liu Xiao
Houzhe Xu
Wei-Chen Yeh
Yiwen Zhang
Yuchen Zhu

Phase 1 Students
Sara Abou Saleh
Ashwin Balaji
Anandkumar
Maria-Eleni Bali
Vladislav Bek-Bulatov
Marta Bermejo Rosique
Aditya Bhosle
Pierre Bianchi
Aleksandar Bursac
Raissa Carvalho Fonseca
Li Chen
Nai-Yi Chen
Alejandro García Gadea
Suzan Ibrahim Abed
Jitesh Jadhav
YoungAh Kang
Hitesh Katiyar
Assad Khan Jaffer Khan
Yeonsuk Kim
Ramzi Omar Koduvayikkal
Lisa Kuhnhausen
Andreas Kyriakou
Chiara Leonzio
Yuan Liu
Ruxandra Claudia Matei
Dieter Hans Matuschke
Esteban Naranjo
Yooyeon Noh
Kyle Onaga
Necdet Yagiz Ozkan

Andrew Potter
Avneesh Rathor
Rui Qui
Martina Rosati
Rithu Mathew Roy
Patchara Ruentongdee
Irina Safonova
Johnathan Shillingford
Lyudmyla Semenyshyn
Kai-Jui Tsao
Georgia Tsoli
Anju Veerappa Satish
Astrid von Mühlenbrock
Qiao Zhang
Weixin Zhao

1. OwO
Studio: Theodore Spyropoulos
Assistant: Mostafa El Sayed
Team: Agata Banaszek (Poland),
Camilla Degli Esposti (Italy), Ilya Pereyaslavtsev
(Russia), Antonios Thodis (Greece)

2. WIRED
Studio: Shajay Bhooshan
Robotic Consultant: Gregory Epps, RoboFold Ltd
Team: Alexandra K G Lipezker (Italy), Evangelia
Magnisali (Greece), Georgios Pasisis (Greece),
Sai Prateik Bhasgi (India)

3. OwO
Studio: Theodore Spyropoulos
Assistant: Mostafa El Sayed
Team: Agata Banaszek (Poland),
Camilla Degli Esposti (Italy), Ilya Pereyaslavtsev
(Russia), Antonios Thodis (Greece)

4. Infusion
Studio: Shajay Bhooshan
Robotic Consultant: Gregory Epps, RoboFold Ltd
Team: Soulaf Aburas (Syria), Giannis Nikas (Greece),
Mattia Santi (Italy), Maria Paula Velasquez (Colombia)

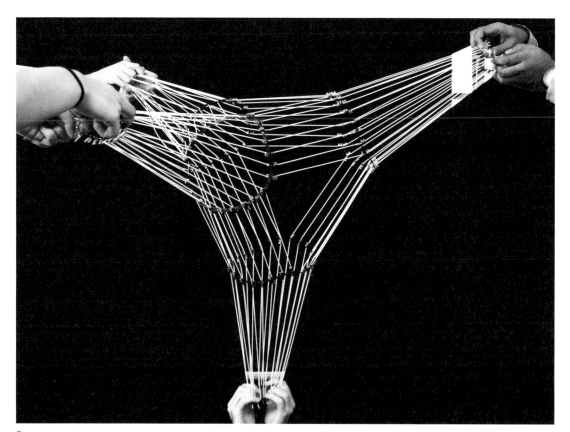

5

6

5. Tensional Integrity
Studio: Patrik Schumacher
Assistant: Pierandrea Angius
Team: Carolina Saenz (Mexico), Delfina Bocca
(Argentina), Faten El Meri (Canada),
Jose Rodriguez (Spain)

6. Aerial Printed Infill
Studio: Robert Stuart-Smith
Assistant: Tyson Hosmer
Team members: Duo Chen (China), Liu Xiao
(China), Sasila Krishnasreni (Thailand),
Yiqiang Chen (China)

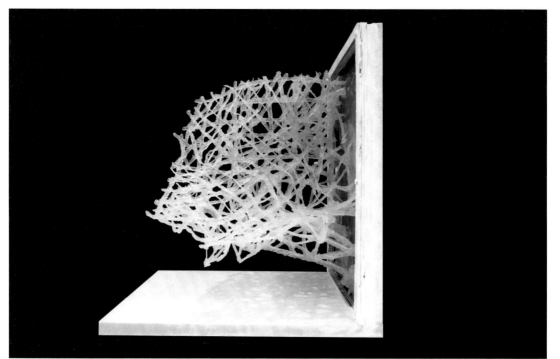

7

8

7. Aerial Printed Infill
Studio: Robert Stuart-Smith
Assistant: Tyson Hosmer
Team: Duo Chen (China), Liu Xiao (China), Sasila
Krishnasreni (Thailand), Yiqiang Chen (China)

8. HyperCell
Studio: Theodore Spyropoulos
Assistant: Mostafa El Sayed
Team: Pavlina Vardoulaki (Greece/Bulgaria),
Houzhe Xu (China), Coşku Çinkılıç (Turkey),
Ahmed Shokir (US/Egypt)

9

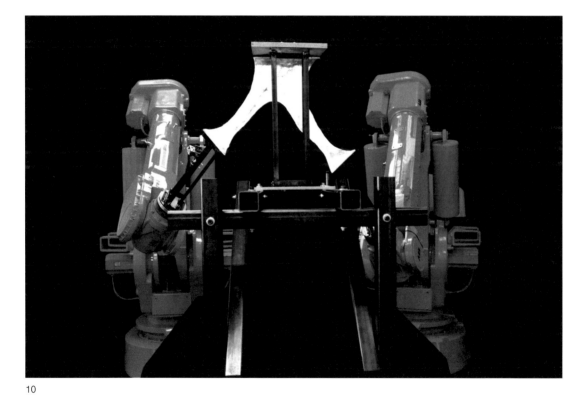

10

9. Tensional Integrity
Studio: Patrik Schumacher
Assistant: Pierandrea Angius
Team: Carolina Saenz (Mexico), Delfina Bocca
(Argentina), Faten El Meri (Canada),
Jose Rodriguez (Spain)

10. Infusion
Studio: Shajay Bhooshan
Robotic Consultant: Gregory Epps, RoboFold Ltd
Team: Soulaf Aburas (Syria), Giannis Nikas (Greece),
Mattia Santi (Italy), Maria Paula Velasquez (Colombia)

11

13

14

11 & 12. Phase 2 Final Jury, January 2015 – Invited
critics: Philippe Block, Mark Cousins, John Frazer,
Jason Kelly Johnson, Marta Malé-Alemany, David
Pigram, Max Schwitalla, Brett Steele

12

13 & 14. DRL Studio drawing and model display during
External Examination, March 2015

Emergent Technologies and Design

Directors
Michael Weinstock
George Jeronimidis

Studio Master
Evan Greenberg

Studio Tutors
Mehran Gharleghi
Manja van de Worp

Visiting Tutors
Suryansh Chandra
Axel Koerner
Antiopi Koronaki

Visiting Lecturers
Francis Aish,
    Foster + Partners
Janet Barlow,
    University of Reading
Alan Dempsey, NEX
Sylvia Felipe, HYBRIDa
Jian Kang, University
    of Sheffield
Jan Knippers, ITKE /
    University of Stuttgart
Wolf Mangelsdorf,
    Buro Happold
Jordi Truco,
    HYBRIDa / ELISAVA

The Emergent Technologies and Design programme is focused on the concepts and convergent interdisciplinary effects of emergence on design and production technologies, and on developing these as creative inputs to new architectural design processes. The programme continues to evolve through the development of our research in studio, seminar coursework and dissertations. We aim to produce new research each year, building from our interests and expertise in material organisation and the design and development of systems in a variety of scales. This continuation of work is focused on the interdisciplinary effects of emergence, biomimetics and evolutionary computation of design and production technologies, as well as on developing these as creative inputs to new architectural and urban design processes. The instruments of analysis and design in Emergent Technologies and Design are computational processes. The seminar courses and core studio are designed to familiarise students with these instruments, their associated conceptual fields and their application to architectural design research. The courses are extensively cross-linked, thematically and instrumentally, with each other and the core studio. In Core Studio 1 the focus is on the exploration of material systems and their development into differentiated surfaces and assemblies. These assemblies demonstrate the potential for integrated structural and environmental performance producing local microclimatic variations that define spatial arrangement. In Core Studio 2 we investigate a larger and more complex piece of the city, examining urban systems and generating new material, social and ecological organisations.

**MSc Students
2013/2014**
Faisal al Barazi
Giorgos Bitsianis
Rebecca Bradley
Stanley Carroll
Maria Fernanda Chaparro
Silvia Daurelio
Alessandro Guidetti
William Haviland
Anja Hein
Amro Kabbara
Antiopi Koronaki
Olga Kravchenko
Francisco Ernesto
    Pastore
Omar Quesada Arias
Camille Saad
Niki Vergini
Min-Kai Yang
Lei Zheng

**MArch Students
2013/2015**
Shahd Abdelmoneim
Radhika Amin
Alessandra Fabbri
Leoncio Jose
    Garcia Gallardo
Samidha Kowli
Amritha Krishnan
Alessandra Lazzoni
Suhash Patel
Abhilasha Porwal
Balamurugan Rajakumar
Rachelle Spiteri
Daniel Zaldivar Alcantara

Phase II Students
Sulaiman Alothman
Arnold Tejasurya
Ashwini Ashokkumar
Natasha Aygunyan
Nicolo Bencini
Parantap Bhatt
Chaitanya Chavan
Thanisorn Devapalin
Spyros Efthymiou
Lorenzo Franceschini
Giulio Gianni
Elif Hazar Karahan
Panit Limpiti
Arpi Maheshwari
Francis McCloskley
Antonia Moscoso
Gabriele Motta
Achraf Mzily
Akshay Narwekar
Carlos Ochando
Kuber Patel
Lorenzo Santelli
Natalie Sham
Yutao Song
Antoniya Stoitsova
Yifei Sun
Patrick Tanhuanco
Di Zhou Arpita Parmar
Felix Tseng

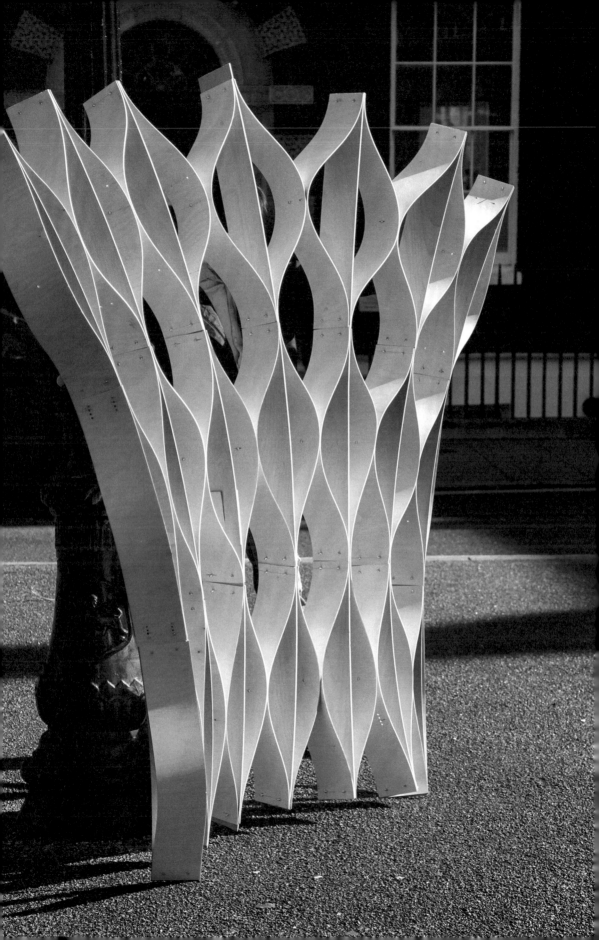

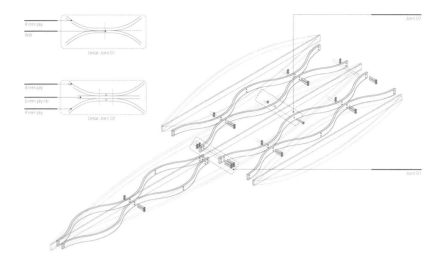

2

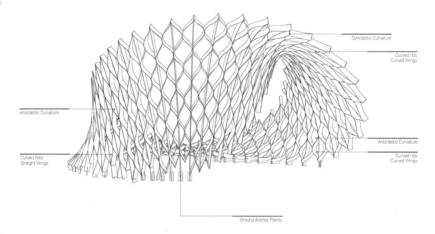

Synclastic Curvature

Curved ribs
Curved Wings

Anticlastic Curvature

Curved Ribs
Straight Wings

Anticlastic Curvature

Curved ribs
Curved Wings

Ground Anchor Points

3

4

1 (previous page), 2–4. Emtech students and staff –
The Twist, Design/Build Project

5

6

5 & 6. Radhika Amin (MArch), Antiopi Koronaki (MSc),
Samidha Kowli (MArch) and Rachelle Spiteri (MArch) –
Responsive Growth Systems

7

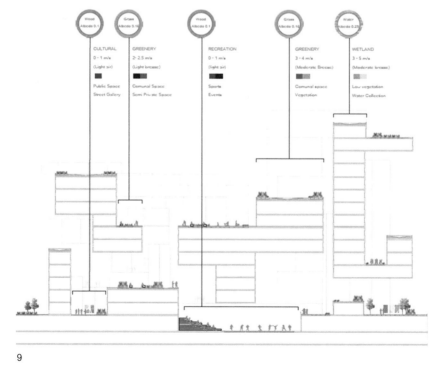

8

9

7–9. Maria Fernanda Chaparro Chaparro (MSc),
Silvia Daurelio (MSc) – Adaptable Morphodynamics

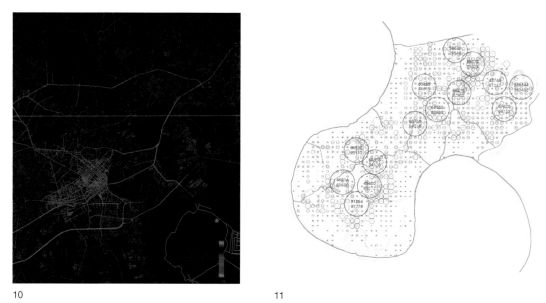

10   11

12

13

10–13. Alessandra Fabbri (MArch), Leoncio Jose Garcia
Gallardo (MArch), Alessandra Lazzoni (MArch), Suhash
Patel (MArch) – Hydrological Urban City

223

MA History and Critical Thinking

Director
Marina Lathouri

Staff
Mark Cousins
John Palmesino
Douglas Spencer

Visiting Tutors
Tim Benton
Fabrizio Gallanti
Siri Nergaard
Manuel Orazi

Visiting Speakers
Pedro Alonso
Mario Carpo
Tina Di Carlo
Alejandra Celedon
Jackie Cooper
David Cunningham
Adrian Lahoud
Louis Moreno
Benjamin Noys
Sophia Psarra
Anthony Vidler
Alexandra Vougia
Thanos Zartaloudis

The 12-month programme in History and Critical Thinking is a unique platform for enquiry into history, theoretical arguments and forms of architectural practice. Its aim is three-fold: to connect contemporary debates and projects with a wider historical, cultural and political context; to produce knowledge that relates to design and public cultures in architecture; to explore writings of history as well as new forms of research, communication and practice. The course is organised around lectures, seminars, debates, writing sessions and workshops which offer students opportunities to expand disciplinary knowledge in a broad cultural arena and within a variety of viewpoints.

Writing as a practice of thinking is central to the course, and different modes such as essays, reviews, short commentaries, publications and interviews allow students to deploy a diverse line of questioning to articulate various aspects of their study. Seminars with distinguished designers, critics, journalists, writers and curators introduce diverse perspectives and skills.

This year, the Term 1 workshop 'Design by Words' focused on books and writing, enabling students to explore the relationship between text, image and design. In Term 2 the one-week workshop 'Architecture in Translation' helped students develop a critical view of architecture's translatability in light of institutional, legal and economic constraints, cultural specificities and political ideologies. As part of the research seminar in Term 3, the unit ventured to Bologna and the Emilia-Romagna Region to develop the final thesis while participating in daily seminars and architectural visits.

Vertical connections in the school were reinforced by collaborations with AA Design Units and participation in juries, joint seminars with PhD students and the HCT Term 2 Debates on Architecture Politics with visiting speakers, creating a venue for debate within the School and a point of interaction with the broader academic and architectural community.

Students
The programme again
drew a wide variety of
students from Australia,
Chile, China, Cyprus,
Kuwait, Mexico, Romania,
India and the US.

Amina Al-Failakawi
Rajeel Arab
Shengze Chen
Melissa Hollis
Elena Palacios
Savia Palate
Stefan Popa
Daniela Puga
Rachel Serfling
Sunaina Shah
Davi Weber

AMINA AL-FAILAKAWI, RE-ESTABLISHING LOCAL VERNACULAR AS A CONTEMPORARY INTERFACE OF THE GULF CITY – Cultivating the local vernacular in architecture in the Arabian Gulf is not a call to resurrect its traditional aesthetic elements, rather it is a pursuit to revive the fundamental components that have endured under harsh climatic conditions, yet have failed to be accommodated in today's structures. To this end, close attention will be given to the living unit and the courtyard house.

RAJEEL ARAB, TERRITORIES OF ANXIETY – The thesis investigates the Muslim ghettos in Indian cities which have grown out of recent religious and political conflicts and constitute urban enclaves of anxiety, fear and insecurity. Considering that contention, resistance and dissent among communities discourage co-existence, the question here concerns the ways in which these pockets negotiate their presence in the city and how these multiple negotiations affect the whole of the city at a socio-economic, political and cultural level.

SHENGZE CHEN, MARKET ECONOMY AND THE DISPOSABLE ARCHITECT – The thesis is an attempt to understand the relationship between market economy and postmodern space production since the 1970s. In particular, it investigates the changing role of state policies on social projects to challenge the seemingly dispensable role of the architect in the market economy.

MELISSA HOLLIS, TEXTURAL CARTOGRAPHIES OF THE CITY AND SELF – The thesis is concerned with the textual cartography of both the 'imaginary' and the 'real' in contemporary 'urban fiction' and the specific forms of spatial organisation that demonstrate contemporary subjectivities that have been produced out of the material conditions of metropolitan experience that are deeply inscribed within the architectural structures of the city.

ELENA PALACIOS, THE INTERIOR IS NOT A ROOM – We normally identify the notion of interior with a room or some sort of enclosure. However what makes us recognise an image or three-dimensional space as an interior is not its potential quality as a room but the iconography of the objects contained within it. The interior is always looking to expand, and the room to contain.

SAVIA PALATE, THE DIY NATION – What is the form of a nation? Historically, in times of crisis, individuals have shown a tendency to build communities from scratch. Nowadays, nationalism's loss of credibility, along with the delusion of proliferating rights at a (digital) global scale, requires architecture to once more redefine its boundaries.

STEFAN POPA, TRACES IN THE SNOW: THE SUSTAINABILITY DILEMMA OF WINTER SPORTS – The thesis interrogates how movement informs the design and implementation of the Winter Olympic Games as an event and as an urban phenomenon, in focusing on the particular concept of 'movement organisation' at the 1994 Winter Olympic Games in Lillehammer, Norway. The thesis comments on concepts of environmental impact, efficiency and effort with the aim of understanding what can be called the 'sustainability dilemma' of winter sports.

DANIELA PUGA, BUILDING BY COLLECTING – The thesis explores the act of collecting as a critical way of engaging with the existing, which mediates between the particular and the universal and has the potential to define or transform boundaries. This is discussed through the creation of the collection of Aby Warburg (1866–1929).

RACHEL SERFLING, THE CONTINUED RISE OF THE ARCHITECTURAL RENDERING: THE SLOW DEATH OF 'ARCHI-SPEAK' – The thesis explores the politics of the aesthetics of photorealistic renderings and their larger effect on the discipline, including how the current deficit of architectural language is a consequence of the ascendancy of this very particular type of visual. Not another cultural critique, this theme will instead be scrutinised through tracing the historical usage of images in architecture contrasted with an analysis of the contemporary image.

SUNAINA SHAH, TECHNOLOGY AS A RHETORIC FOR HUMAN PROGRESS – For a long time, the idea of using new technology has been seen as a sign of progress. This thesis studies the notion through the works of the German-Jewish graphic artist, gynaecologist and writer Fritz Kahn (1888–1968), giving special consideration to Gilbert Simondon's (1924–1989) philosophical discourse on technology and ontology. Both figures bring together the areas of technology and biology or ontology, which is then discussed within the framework of modernist discourse on architecture.

DAVI WEBER, BODY IN SUSPENSE – Rather than measurements and data of physical relations, this study explores cultural and perceptual accounts of space: the content that escapes drawings. It is concerned with spaces between as the architectural material – dense, palpable, charged, ductile and unquantifiable.

MA HCT visit to Aldo Rossi's San Cataldo Cemetery in Modena, Italy, photo Marina Lathouri

Housing & Urbanism

Staff
Jorge Fiori
Hugo Hinsley
Lawrence Barth
Abigail Batchelor
Nicholas Bullock
Florian Dirschedl
Elad Eisenstein
Dominic Papa
Elena Pascolo
Anna Shapiro
Naiara Vegara
Alex Warnock-Smith

Contributors
Luiz Amorim
Jose de Souza Brandao
Alfredo Brillembourg
Ricky Burdett
Kathryn Firth
Ruurd Gietema
Sascha Haselmayer
Sam Jacoby
Jonathan Kendall
Evelyne Labanca
Jo McCafferty
Roberto Muniz
Alessandro Rizzo
Jonathan Rose
Junia Santa Rosa
Antje Saunders
Patrik Schumacher
Simon Smithson
Peter Thomas
Carlos Villanueva Brandt
Juliana Muniz Westcott
John Worthington

The Housing and Urbanism (H&U) Programme engages architecture with the challenges of contemporary urban strategies. Metropolitan regions show great diversity and complexity, with significant recent global shifts in the patterns of urban growth and decline. Architecture has a central role to play in this dynamic context, both in developing spatial strategies as part of urban policies and in generating new urban clusters and types. Housing is explored both as a major critical aspect of urbanism and as a means to reflect upon changing ideas of living space and domesticity, identity and public space.

Offering a 12-month MA and a 16-month MArch, the programme engages with cross-disciplinary research as well as design application work. Combining workshops, lectures and seminars, and a final MA thesis or MArch project, the programme explores the interplay between graphic tools and writing in order to develop ideas and research about the urban condition, and to develop skills for intervening as urbanists through spatial design.

There are three current research themes of H&U work: the role of urbanism in enhancing innovation environments and knowledge-based clusters; the idea of living space and housing, and issues of mix, density and urban intensification in which architecture is viewed dynamically in relation to a process of urbanisation; and the exploration of an appropriate urbanism to address urban irregularity and informality and to engage with the interaction of spatial strategies and urban social policies.

This year's design workshops explored several of London's major redevelopment areas while also undertaking work in Recife, Brazil, in collaboration with the Federal University of Pernambuco. The workshops addressed the processes of urban development related to knowledge-based economies and the potential for synergies between existing and new urban cultures. The programme's work was complemented by a study visit to Sweden. As in previous years, the work of the H&U programme forms the foundation for international collaborations and publications.

Students
MA and MArch Phase 1
Nour Saleh Ahmad
  Abdel Hamid
Elesban Anadón Vargas
Alise Ãrgale
Danya Zoe Bali
Annu Boban
Ashwin Bungarnayak
Pimlada Bunluthangthum
Laura Caicedo Lopez
Gabriel Trinkel Dal Maso
Mariel Chris Drego
Renata Catalina
  Guerra Mena
Fengxu Guo
Yun-Ting Hsieh
Nirmal Sylvester
  John Britto

Charita Kishore Rupa
Olga Konyukova
Magdalena Elzbieta Lach
Yanchen Lin
Tanzela Monsoor
Goutham Nijalingappa
Juan Fernando
  Orozco Ramirez
Amanda Blair Palasik
Sana Aziz Rehman
William Joseph Sergison
Jay Pankaj Shah
Kanishk Sinha
Satyadeep Sonar
Ariel Nicole Westmark
Irene Willy
Bingjun Xu
Xiao Lu Yang

MArch Phase 2
Asli Arda
Mariana Cenovicz Moro
Natalie Clemens
Ivo Barros
Vaishali Enos
Nayeli Galindo Cano
Shaleen Jethi
Gayathri
  Kalyanasundaram
Sharmila Kamalakkannan
Keval Kaushik
Piyush Naresh Makwana
Ioana Ochoa Alvarado
Solachi Ramanathan
Zheyu Shi
Sasiwimol Utaisup
Nikita Uday Vora
Christina Voutsa

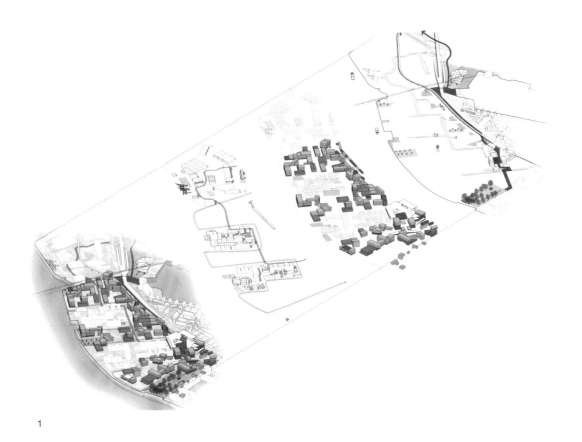

1

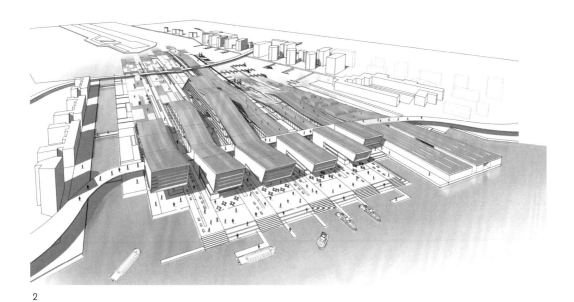

2

1 & 2. Developing new productive areas
of Royal Docks, London

Design Workshops
Design Workshops are a major part of H&U's teaching
and research, engaging with rapidly changing areas
of London and with a large programme of housing
intervention in Recife, Brazil. Each workshop tests
research and proposals, exploring how different urban
conditions can develop a more productive spatial
fabric to support a knowledge-based economy.

3

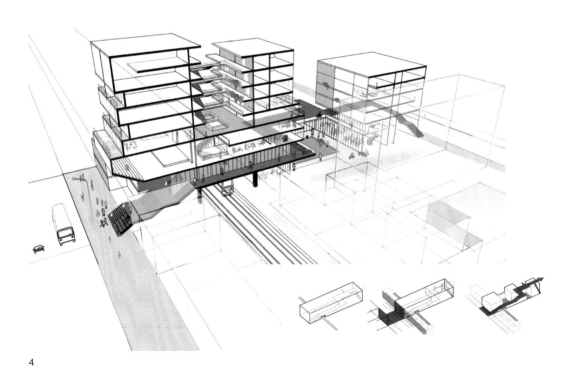

4

3 & 4. London: station area intensification –
proposal for knowledge-economy quarter and dense
residential district around Tottenham Hale station

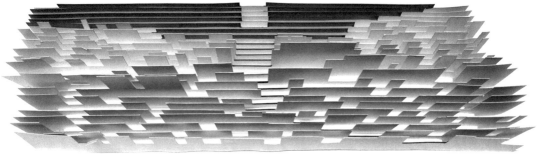

5

6

5. London: Portland Place research –
compressed sectional study

6. London: 'Culture and knowledge quarter' in Olympic
Park – study for shared-knowledge environment

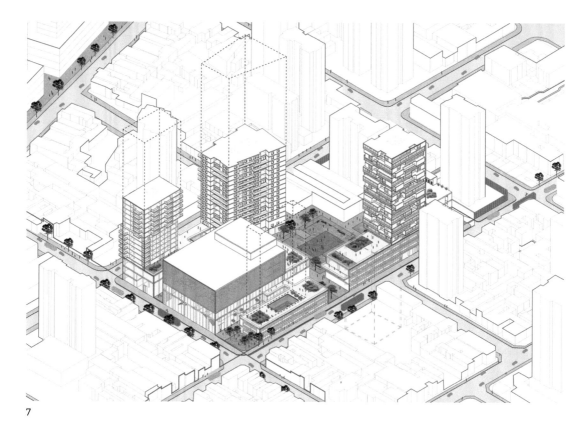

7

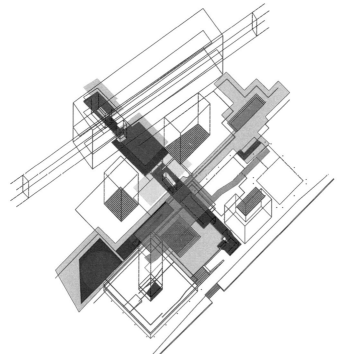

8

MArch Design Theses
Students produced individual design theses, focused on shared research themes of mobility and integration; productive ecologies; resistance and transformation. Above are images from two theses studying potential of intensification at transport interchanges, on the theme of mobility and integration.

7. Mariana Cenovicz Moro, São Paulo, Brazil – station district intensification
8. Vaishali Enos, Bengaluru, India – station district intensification

9

10

11

9. Studio debate
10. Reading the territory
11. Density study on slopes

Housing as Urbanism – Recife, Brazil
This intensive design workshop in Recife addressed
the potential of new housing development linking
existing and new urban cultures related to new
transport infrastructure. This is a continuing research
programme in collaboration with the Federal University
of Pernambuco and the National Housing Secretariat
of the Ministry of Cities.

Landscape Urbanism

Co-Directors
Alfredo Ramírez
Eduardo Rico

Studio Master
Clara Oloriz

Seminar Tutors
Tom Smith
Douglas Spencer

Technical Tutors
Gustavo Romanillos
Giancarlo Torpiano
Vincenzo Reale

Visiting Lecturers
Andrew Goudie
Andrew Fowler
Clon Ulrick
Tom Coulthart
Marti Peran
Teresa Stoppani

Landscape Urbanism explores the emergence of territory, understood as a political technology, as a field of design practice. In understanding practice through territory, the agency of the designer can extend beyond disciplinary divisions – between architecture and planning, between urban design and landscape architecture or engineering – to uncover the physical and social dynamics at stake in the making of the landscape. In the process, geographic knowledge and practices, such as cartography and geomorphology, are reappropriated to address fundamental questions of contemporary territorial conditions.

A Pan-European Atlas of Radical Cartographies

In October 2000 the European Landscape Convention in Florence became the first pan-European project to attempt to define the entire European territory from a cultural perspective. It promised a collective sense of territorial specificity supported by comprehensive studies of charters and tailor-made recommendations. However, the decidedly encyclopaedic spirit of the Florence Convention was trumped by a stubborn reality governed by the practices of property developers and, perhaps more crucially, by labyrinthine policies that never translated into meaningful systems of space production. Within this rift – between the utilitarian and the cultural practices of European policies – Landscape Urbanism has sought to explore how productive and natural formations can generate the basis of a pan-European project for territories that are neither generic nor iconic, conventional nor touristic. The programme is concerned both with the geomorphological formations of relevant landforms and with the actual cultural, political and economic forces that drive their social formations. The primary outcome of this year's work has been the production of a set of cartographies which form an Atlas of radical cartographies documenting the future of European environments. These cartographies are seen as projective machines with a capacity to unveil the glitches between conflicting systems – tectonic landscapes, political governance, land administration – and to propose alternatives for their future in the form of projects and design intentions at territorial scales.

Students
Dimitra Bra
Howe Chan
Ting-Fu Chang
Lida Evangelia Driva
Xiabin Hu
Da Kuang
Keyin Li
Paulina Lizlova González
Tong Kit Lo
Elena Longhin
Liam Robert Mouritz
Silvia Guiomar Ribot Gil
Difeng Sun

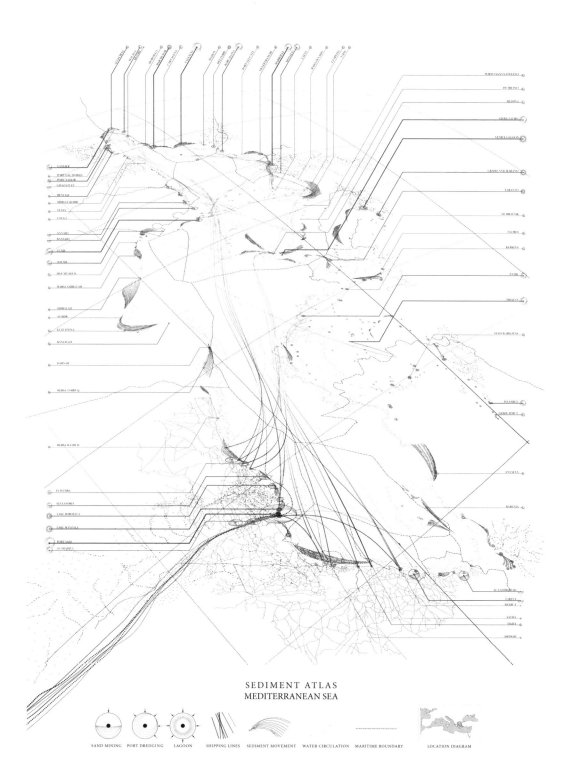

SEDIMENT ATLAS
MEDITERRANEAN SEA

SAND MINING   PORT DREDGING   LAGOON   SHIPPING LINES   SEDIMENT MOVEMENT   WATER CIRCULATION   MARITIME BOUNDARY   LOCATION DIAGRAM

1. Liam Mouritz, Ting Fu Chang and Xıabın Hu,
Sediment Atlas of the Mediterranean Sea – at any
given moment in time, sediment is in motion in the
Mediterranean. The Sediment Atlas is an attempt
at articulating this process, with the intention of
highlighting the territories in which an intervention
may be warranted.

SOCIAL FORMATION
LAKE MANZALA

INPUT
FISH FEED
FISH FRY

OUTPUT
FARMED FISH

INTENSIVE
FISH FARM

SEMI INTENSIVE
FISH FARM

EXTENSIVE
FISH FARM

ILLEGAL
HOSHA FISH FARM

LOCATION DIAGRAM

0   2   4   6   10
                    Km

2. Liam Mouritz, Ting Fu Chang and Xiabin Hu, Social Formations, Lake Manzala, Egypt – humans have depended on Lake Manzala for thousands of years, both for their livelihood and their food. In the last 30 years this level of consumption has shifted from traditional subsistence fishing towards the mass-production of fish, a pattern that has developed from the intensive to the extensive and from the legal to the illegal, with several categories in between.

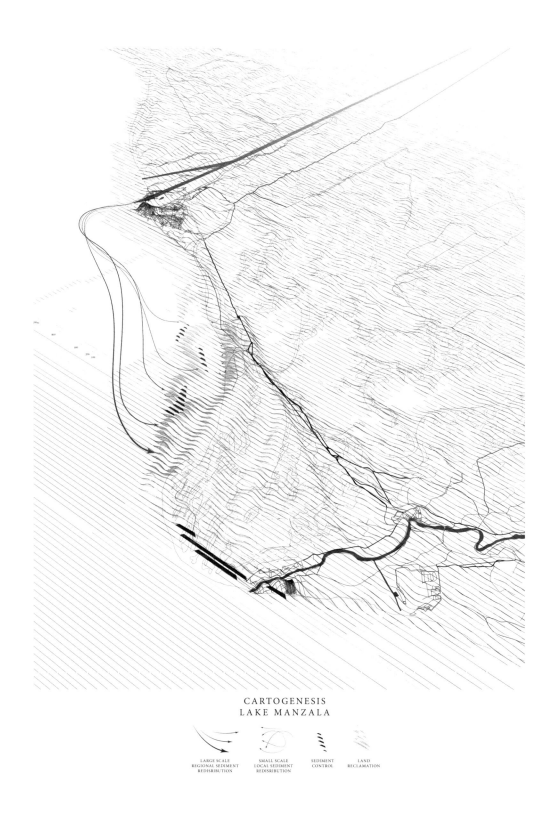

CARTOGENESIS
LAKE MANZALA

LARGE SCALE
REGIONAL SEDIMENT
REDISRIBUTION

SMALL SCALE
LOCAL SEDIMENT
REDISRIBUTION

SEDIMENT
CONTROL

LAND
RECLAMATION

3. Liam Mouritz, Ting Fu Chang and Xiabin Hu, Cartogenesis, Lake Manzala, Egypt – this map explores how the knowledge acquired from the geomorphology and social formation can be intersected to envision new territories. Here, we speculate on human deposition of sediment along the coastline, intensifying the existing formation of coastal spits, from which this new land can support a variety of integrated saltwater fish-farming practices.

Simulation results

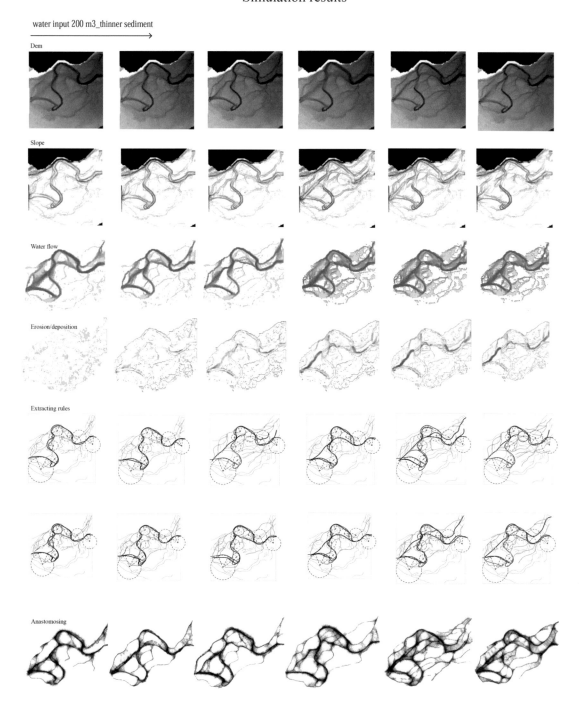

4. Silvia Ribot, Lida Driva, Dimitra Bra, Anastomosing
Rivers, digital simulations —experimentation with
CAESAR software simulations testing the possibility of
fluvial avulsions through time, following the theoretical
model by Bart Makaske for the anastomoses of rivers

Social formations

5. Silvia Ribot, Lida Driva, Dimitra Bra, social formation patterns in the Spanish region of Navarre – indexing shows forms of labour around different seasons within the industrial and agricultural fields surrounding the Arga and Aragon rivers. Settlement and labour patterns are constantly redefined by the use of lands to suggest new ways of organising this territory.

Sustainable Environmental Design

Directors
Simos Yannas
Paula Cadima

Course Masters
Nick Baker
Klaus Bode
Gustavo Brunelli
Jorge Rodriguez Alvarez

Studio Tutors
Herman Calleja
Mariam Kapsali
Byron Mardas

Contributors
Kanika Agarwal
  Mahadevwala
Carole Aspeslagh
Meital Ben Dayan
Magali Bodart
Angeliki Chatzidimitriou
Jason Cornish
Peter Chlapowski
Larissa De Rosso
Christian Dimbleby
Arnaud Evrard
Brian Ford
Joana Gonçalves
Alan Harries
Catherine Harrington
Richard Hawkes
Dean Hawkes
Andreas Matzarakis
Joy-Anne Mowbray
Fergus Nicol
Mileni Pamfili
Rajan Rawal
Harald Røstvik
Jean-François
  Roger France
Amedeo Scofone
Helge Simon
Becci Taylor
Leonidas Tsichritzis

External Examiners
Bill Gething
Alan Short

Sustainable Environmental Design engages with real-life problems affecting buildings and cities throughout the world. Providing alternatives to the global architecture and brute force engineering that are still the norm in most large cities requires new knowledge about what makes a sustainable environment and how architecture can contribute to this. Design research for the SED masters programme is driven by strict performance criteria following a process of *adaptive architecturing* that proceeds from inside to outside, attuning the built form and its constituents to natural rhythms and inhabitant activities. Key objectives of all SED projects are to improve environmental conditions and quality of life in cities, achieve independence from non-renewable energy sources and develop an environmentally sustainable architecture able to adapt and respond to changing urban environments.

Refurbishing the City, the SED research agenda, continued this year with team projects in Terms 1 and 2 (Phase 1) and individual dissertation projects in Terms 3 and 4 (Phase 2). London was the laboratory for the team projects, providing real sites and buildings for hands-on fieldwork and environmental measurements. Following these investigations were computational simulations in the studio to explore performance improvements and responses to social trends, climate change and technical developments. Some 40 recent residential buildings studied in previous years were revisited, providing a good sample for comparative environmental assessments. The results of these studies were starting points for Term 2 design research briefs on sites in the Royal Docks area of East London.

Fifty dissertation projects, situated in as many cities and more than 30 different countries, were started or completed this academic year, encompassing widely different climates, building types, architectural features and operational conditions. Projects in India, an exhibition of 12 recent dissertation projects by SED students from India, was put on display at the PLEA 2014 international conference in Ahmedabad.

MSc & MArch Phase 1 Students
Antonio Costa Almeida
Irech Castrejon
Juanito Alipio De La Rosa
Maria Francisca
  Echeverri
Sandheep Ellangovan
Sheila Esteve
Oindrila Ghosh
Irene Giglio
Lu Jing
Aarushi Juneja
Michelle Kuei
Jennifer Liao
Aly Mahmoud
Nimmiya Mariam
Daniel Chad McKee
Mariana Moniz

Mattis Mussault
Wasinee Prasongsumrit
Luis Arturo Reyes
Maria Teresa Sanchez
Cindrella Semaan
Victoria Soto Magán
Avgousta Stanitsa
Monica Toledo
Julia Torrubia
Olga Tsagkalidou
Tolga Uzunhasanoglu
Ameer Varzgani
April Wang
Jiaji Yang
Daniel Zepeda

MArch Phase 2 Students
Han Chen
Adriana Comi

Camilla Diane El-Dash
Mahmoud Ezzeldin
Francisco Godoy
Anahí González
  San Martín
Madhulika Kumar
Ayelet Lanel
Rhiannon Taylor Laurie
Gabriela Nuñez-Melgar
Artem Polomannyy
Ganesh Pulavarnattham
  Sivakumar
Hyosik Pyo
Jorge Ramirez
Andrea Rossi
Praew Sirichanchuen
Svilen Todorov
Pierluigi Turco
Mariyam Zakiah

1

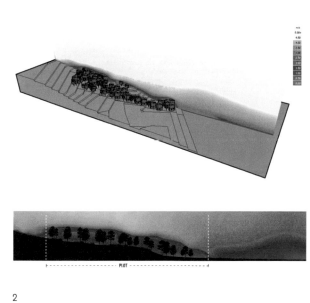

2

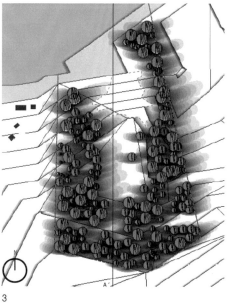

3

1–3. Francisco Godoy, Eco-Tourism in Chile, Hotel on
Chiloé Island, Patagonia 42°46'S 73°46'W

241

4

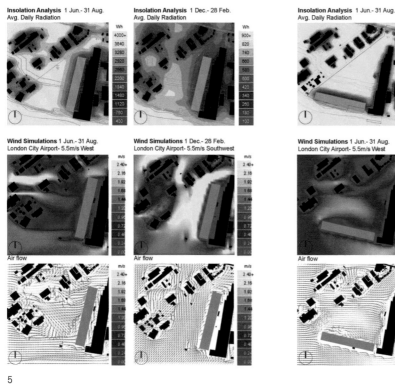

Insolation Analysis 1 Jun.- 31 Aug.
Avg. Daily Radiation

Insolation Analysis 1 Dec.- 28 Feb.
Avg. Daily Radiation

Wind Simulations 1 Jun.- 31 Aug.
London City Airport- 5.5m/s West

Wind Simulations 1 Dec.- 28 Feb.
London City Airport- 5.5m/s Southwest

Air flow

5

4–5. Sandheep Ellangovan, Lu Jing, Daniel Chad
McKee, Jiaji Yang, Proposals for riverfront
development, Royal Docks, East London 51°30'N
0°01'E

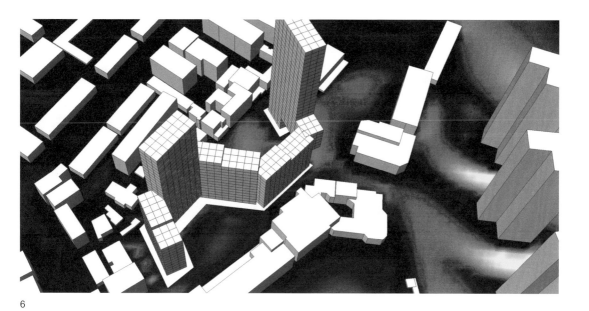

6

7

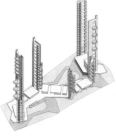

Landscape and access route

Pilotis and amenity space

Circulation

Roof garden and shading

8

6–8. Han Chen, High-Density Residential Community,
Wuhan, China 30°35'N 114°18'E

9

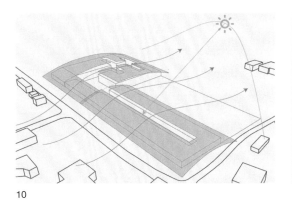

10

11

12

9. Madhulika Kumar, School of Dance and Music on the
River Kaveri, Trichy, India 10°48'N 78o41'E

10–12. Andrea Rossi, Pierluigi Turco, Migrant Centre
and Primary School, Lampedusa, Italy 35°30'N 13o36'E

244

13

14

15

Option 1

Option 3

Option 5

13–15. Ganesh Pulavarnattham Sivakumar, Affordable
Housing in Thanjavur, India 10° 46'N 79°07'E

Conservation of Historic Buildings

Staff
Andrew Shepherd
David Hills
Martin Cook

It has been an unusual year for Building Conservation, with only a single cohort rather than the usual two years of students. This academic year it was decided that an 18-module teaching pattern should be developed relating to the original core contents/aspects of the ICOMOS syllabus on which the course is based. These modules include Conservation Philosophy, Recovery and Surveying Historic Buildings, Building Diagnostics, Conservation and Regeneration, Heritage Law and Planning, Archaeology and Conservation Practice, Various Materials and their Conservation, as well as an expected historical development of building types and materials. The students graduating this year have benefitted from this model, enjoying a study weekend in Dublin (eighteenth-century architecture), among other events.

Highlights were a visit by Charles Brooking, who brought part of his Venice Biennale display (272 items only!) to the lecture rooms of the AA, as well as a sustainability workshop for Bedford Square and environs carried out with other students and young professionals.

Thanks are offered to our course co-ordinator, Danielle Hewitt, who has taken up other responsibilities at the AA and elsewhere, to the students and to my colleagues David Hills and Martin Cook. And we always still try to have fun on Fridays!

Students and Theses
Timothy Brooks, *Paternalistic authoritarianism or social responsibility? The Development of Purpose-Built Housing for the Elderly in England 1945–79*

Faye Davies, *Does the name Eugenius Birch mean anything to you? The Life and Selected Works of Eugenius Birch (1818–1864)*

Michael Garber, *A Prospect of Ruins: discovery, exploration and contemplation*

Joana Guedes de Carvalho, *Is Ornament Crime? Westminster Cathedral – a proposition*

Waleed Hassan, *The Mosque in Britain: British Heritage?*

Joao Lopes, *Landfill of Nuggets: Reclaimed, Salvaged and Recycled Materials in Today's Building Conservation*

James Moore, *Poverty to Progress: An Introduction to the Evolution of Kilkenny Farm Buildings, 1700 – Present*

Camilla Prizeman, *John Prizeman, Architect (1930–1992)*

Lisa Shell, *Saving Dalston Lane: What went wrong?*

1. Eighteenth-century decorative plasterwork, Dublin
2. Practical instruction in mixing lime plaster
3. Lecture with Charles Brooking on architectural
components ©BB22

Design & Make

Programme Director
Martin Self

Studio Masters
Charley Brentnall
Toby Burgess
Kate Darby

Visiting Tutors
Mark Campbell
Kostas Grigoriadis
Jos Smith

Visiting Critics
and Speakers
Francis Archer
Keith Brownlie
Sophie Le Bourva
Richard Burton
Barbara-Ann
  Campbell-Lange
Shin Egashira
Evan Greenberg
Anderson Inge
Niall Jacobson
Steven Johnson
Arthur Mamou-Mani
Ricardo de Ostos
Carol Patterson
Christopher Pierce
Bob Sheil
Theodore Spyropoulos
Brett Steele
Peter Thomas
Jeroen van Ameijde
Emmanuel Vercruysse
Thomas Weaver

Site and Workshop
Supervision
Oscar Emmanuel
Jack Hawker
James Stubbs

Engineering Support
Arup (Francis Archer,
  Charlotte Briggs,
  Coco van Egeraat,
  Naotaka Nimami)

Students of the MArch Design & Make programme design and construct buildings at Hooke Park, the AA's woodland campus in Dorset. The 16-month course is structured around a series of design-build projects that develop and test architectural responses to material, site and processes of construction. These projects lead to the design and construction of permanent buildings as part of the growing Hooke Park campus as well as the production of an individual thesis by each student.

This year's agenda has been to use emerging scanning and fabrication technologies to test new applications of locally grown timber. Phase 2 students Yingzi Wang and Sattaveesa Sahu completed their Biomass Boiler House in January. This building contains the boiler, chip-store and buffer tank for the district heating system that now provides heat energy to all of the Hooke Park campus. It consists of stacked, naturally curved tree trunks, all of which were 3D-scanned to form a database of geometries from which a smoothly flowing and sinuous curved wall was composed. These curvatures form part of an architectural landscape strategy and also contribute to the structural stability of the wall.

The 2014–15 students are continuing this research in the form of a Woodchip Barn to store the long-term supply of woodchip for the biomass boiler, enabling the Hooke Park estate to process and use its own timber for renewable heat production. A core ambition in the project is to use tree fork junctions within a structure so that the natural strength of the fork joints is exploited. Again, 3D-scanning techniques are being developed that will capture the geometry of each component. This information will then be used to help place each component within the structure and to define tool-paths for fabrication using Hooke Park's robot arm.

Phase 1 Students
Mohaimeen Islam
Zachary Mollica
Swetha Raju
Sahil Shah
Yang Yung-Chen

Phase 2 Students
Sattaveesa Sahu
Yingzi Wang

2

3

2. Sattaveesa Sahu and Yingzi Wang,
The Biomass Boiler House – built into a slope in the
centre of the campus with an accessible roof deck,
photo Valerie Bennett
3. Bespoke tooling was developed for the Boiler House
fabrication to allow naturally curved timber to be
used in the structure. This rolling chainsaw produces
a rain-shedding chamfer cut on each element.

1. (previous page) Vivian Yang Yung-Chen and Zachary
Mollica, 'Inhabitable Tetrahedron' – term 1 Core Studio
project aimed to act in contrast to the form of the
mound it is suspended above and to provide a minimal
inhabitable enclosure, photo Valerie Bennett

4

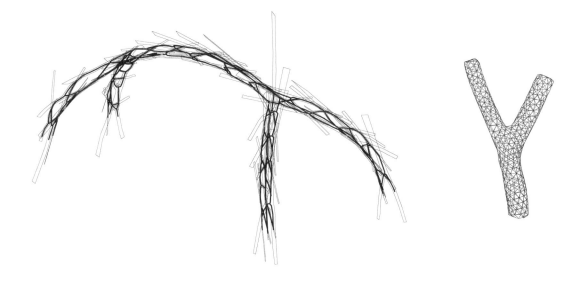

5

4. Mohaimeen Islam, Swetha Raju and Sahil Shah The 'Big Fish' Term 1 project – consists of a series of kerfed timber ribs on which around 400 strips of larch and ash were laid. The final form emerged over five days in an ad-hoc process devised to maximise the inhabitants' experience of the terrain, trees, sunsets and views. Photo Valerie Bennett

5. Strategies for the 2015 Design & Make Wood Chip Barn project currently in development include methods for incorporating the 3D-scanned geometries of tree forks within a truss structure

Projective Cities

Programme Staff
Sam Jacoby
Adrian Lahoud
Maria Shéhérazade
  Giudici
Mark Campbell

Consultants
Philip Clemens
Samaneh Moafi
Mehran Gharleghi

Visiting Lecturers
Andrew Higgott
Alex Lehnerer
Senan Abdelqader

We thank all of our jurors

The MPhil in Architecture and Urban Design pursues original enquiries into the city within diverse political, economic, social, historical and cultural contexts. The ambition of Projective Cities is twofold: first to define the status and methods of design research. This is understood both as an intellectual problem, exploring the relationship between theory and design for knowledge production, and as a practical problem, looking at how design research can affect practice. Design and writing practices are complementary forms of reasoning that provide different forms of knowledge and evidence fundamental to any comprehensive design research. Second, the programme aims to develop the means of architectural urbanism as an alternative to design doctrines defined by a conventional separation of architecture, urban design and planning. The city and its design are not understood as singular problems but as interrelated questions with specific articulations at different scales. These ambitions are framed by a number of propositions: that architectural and urban plans are intelligible as formal and theoretical products of disciplinary activity as well as the collective outcome of socio-political forces; that design and research are inseparable; that knowledge production and formal production are methodologically linked; that architecture and urbanism are symbiotic modes of enquiry driven by relevance and agency within a field. This field is defined in terms of distinct diagrams that are always *social* and *spatial*.

Projective Cities is divided into a Taught Year 1 and a Research Year 2. During the first year each term is organised around design studies, theory lectures and writing and skills workshops that introduce the programme's theoretical and practical foundations and methods. In the third term of Year 1, students complete their dissertation proposal. This is developed in the following Research Year 2 into a comprehensive designed and written dissertation.

Students and Research Projects

Francesca Romana Forlini, *The Critical Mass of French Housing and Culture*

Guillem-Jaume Pons, *Private Brussels*

Ji Yoon Gu, *Housing for Bureaucrats by Bureaucrats*

Leonhard Clemens, *Hotel as Political Institution*

Naina Gupta, *Palaces without a People: Creating a Transnational Constituency*

Runze Zhang, *Rituals, Protocols, Domesticity and Higher Education in Cambridge*

Simon Goddard, *Lille Immaterial: the Knowledge Economy, Welfare State and Post-Industrial City*

Tianyi Shu, *The Superblock in Xi'an*

Valerio Massaro, *Urban Loneliness: Housing for the Old*

Yana Petrova, *Domesticity and Social Production*

Yating Song, *Tertiary Shenzhen: Labour Mobility and Urban Transformation*

Yu-Hsiang Hung, *Beyond the Neighbourhood: The Shi-Jie in Kaohsiung City*

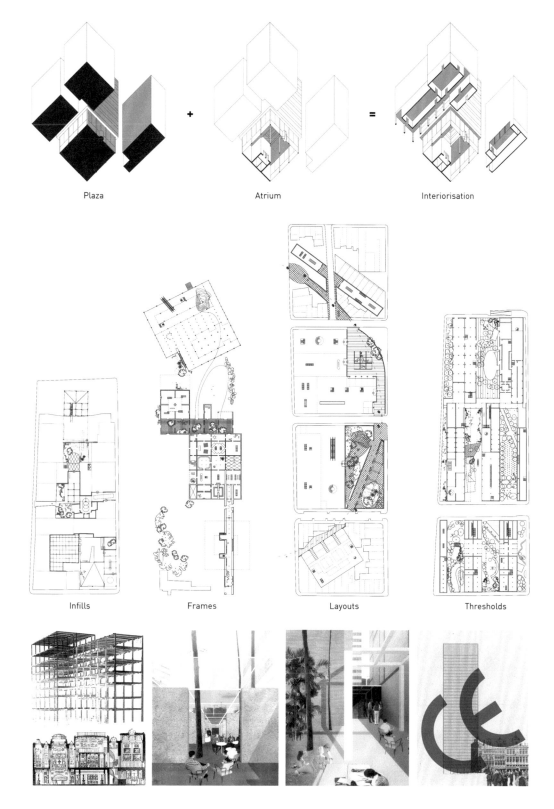

Plaza + Atrium = Interiorisation

Infills   Frames   Layouts   Thresholds

1. Guillem-Jaume Pons, Private Brussels: Interiorisation as a new provision of the public realm – a subversive practice challenging traditional categories of urban space (from plaza and atrium to interiorisation). Four proposals using an interior strategy of infill, frame, layout and threshold.

Images: Generic vs specific. An enfilade of semi-exterior rooms forms differentiated entrances to offices; interiorisation of an infill between a new office and existing buildings; European manifesto – the new administrative institutional building of the EU.

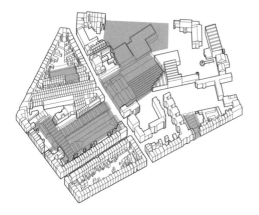

Post-industrial urban block

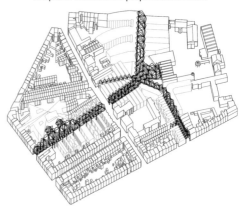

Proposed arcade to re-purpose urban block

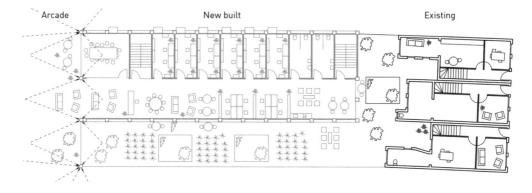

Arcade   New built   Existing

2. Simon Goddard, Lille Immaterial: In an ironic twist, the knowledge economy is not urban but post-urban. This is evident in Lille where once factories were an integral part of a Haussmannian urban fabric. The project transforms the post-industrial block through the insertion of an arcade as a device of improved business clustering that repurposes the block's interior for contemporary productive use while generating amenities for neighbourhood residents.

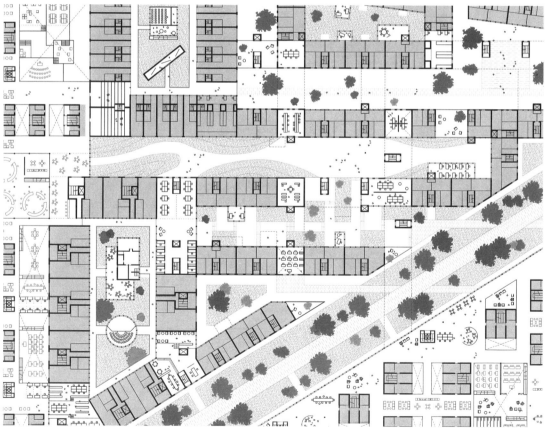

3. Yana Petrova, Domesticity and Social Production:
Proposal for housing and social spaces in the new
Science City in Copenhagen – perspective and
fragment of ground floor plan

PhD

PhD Directors of Studies
Pier Vittorio Aureli
Lawrence Barth
Mark Cousins
Jorge Fiori
Hugo Hinsley
George Jeronimidis
Marina Lathouri
Brett Steele
Michael Weinstock
Simos Yannas (PhD
   Programme Director)

Second Supervisors
& Advisors
Doreen Bernath
Vida Norouz Borazjani
Paula Cadima
Mark Campbell
David Cunningham
Socratis Georgiadis
Sam Jacoby
Adrian Lahoud
Spyros Papapetros
Nina Power
Patrik Schumacher
Eduardo Rico
Douglas Spencer
Thomas Weaver
Thanos Zartaloudis

Doctoral studies at the AA combine advanced research with a broader educational agenda, preparing graduates for practice in global academic and professional environments. Current PhD topics encompass architectural theory and history, architectural urbanism, advanced architectural design, the city, emergent technologies and sustainable environmental design. Under each of these strands, doctoral candidates may either follow the traditional route of a text-based thesis or a studio-based option of a PhD in architectural design.

This year's PhD Programme events included research seminars by Mark Cousins and Pier Vittorio Aureli in Term 1 and by Marina Lathouri in Term 2. A lecture series on research issues organised in Term 1 by Gabriela García de Cortázar featured invited speakers Ross Adams, Jane Alison, Amy Concannon, Kevin Donovan, Valeria Guzman Verri, Enrique Walker and Thanos Zartaloudis. A conference on Algorithms and Actualisation organised by Elif Erdine and Ali Farzaneh in December included presentations by PhD in Architectural Design students and keynote speakers Mark Burry, Xavier de Kestelier and John Frazer. Three symposia, held in Terms 2 and 3, provided opportunity for critical exchange across the programme's diverse research areas, encompassing some 25 presentations that included projects started this year, research continuing from previous years and projects completed during the year. Over all three terms the programme's PhD candidates contributed to conferences, teaching and publications within and outside the AA. External events included the Building II, a symposium organised by AA PhD students with colleagues from Princeton, Harvard and Columbia as a follow-up to the Building event held at the AA last year; paper presentations at eCAADe 2014, Northumbria University; PLEA 2014 at CEPT University, Ahmedabad, India; SAAL at the University of Coimbra, Portugal; Data Across Scales at the Harvard Graduate School of Design.

Students
Nihal Al Sabbagh
Eleni Axioti
Alvaro Arancibia Tagle
Francisca Aroso Pinto de
   Oliveira
Arthur Aw
Merate Barakat
Alejandra Celedon
Jingru Cyan Cheng
Elif Erdine
Ali Farzaneh
Gabriel Felmer Plominsky
Gabriela García de
   Cortázar
Kensuke Hotta
Serena Jarvis
Niloofar Kakhi
Costandis Kizis
Mohammed Makki
Olivia Marra
Patricia Martin del Guayo
Samaneh Moafi
Arturo Revilla Perez
Ricardo Ruivo Pereira
Davide Sacconi
Ivonne Santoyo Orozco
William Hutchins Orr
Thiago de Soveral
Emmanouil Stavrakakis
Aldo Urbinati
Alexandra Vougia
Jingming Wu

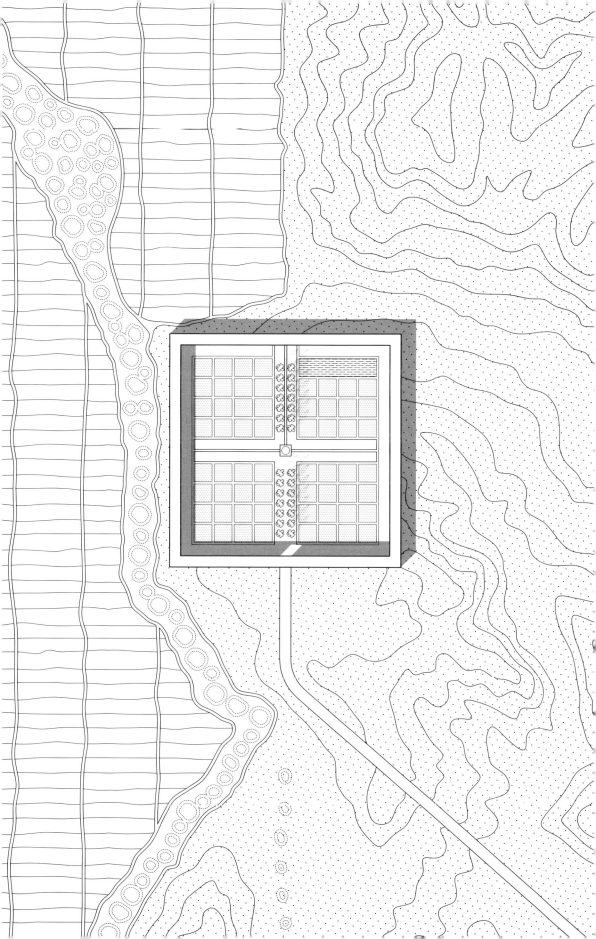

PhD Projects

NIHAL AL SABBAGH, URBAN DESIGN AND OUTDOOR
THERMAL COMFORT
Supervisors: Simos Yannas, Paula Cadima
In Dubai, environmental conditions have been impaired by a
built environment that creates uncomfortable and unappealing
outdoor spaces. The current study aims to improve pedestrian
thermal comfort to prolong the distances that can be travelled
by walking at different times of the year. The influence of
different design strategies are being investigated in the two
urban communities of Greens and Jumeirah Lakes Towers.

ALVARO ARANCIBIA TAGLE, THE HOUSING DESIGN GUIDE
AND THE RE-SIGNIFICATION OF SOCIAL HOUSING:
POLICYMAKING AND STANDARDS IN SANTIAGO DE CHILE
Supervisors: Marina Lathouri, Sam Jacoby
By challenging current social housing policy and its extreme
dependence on the private market the project investigates a new
regulatory scenario with the housing design guide conceived as
an instrument for urban transformation. The research unfolds and
defines a set of fundamental architectural principles, questioning
and expanding the disciplinary agencies of the housing design
guide and the problem of contemporary design itself.

FRANCISCA AROSO PINTO DE OLIVEIRA, FABRICATION-BASED
DESIGN OF RESPONSIVE TRANSITIONAL SPACES
Supervisors: George Jeronimidis, Michael Weinstock
The design research focused on transitional spaces between
buildings' internal and external environments. New design
paradigms were abstracted from biological models. Digital design
and fabrication techniques were combined to test material
properties and enhance the performative capacity of the new
system. Using a subtractive and formative machining process
the properties of wood were manipulated to meet the desired
performance criteria. PhD completed in 2015.

ELENI A AXIOTI, ARCHITECTURE AS AN APPARATUS
OF GOVERNANCE
Supervisors: Marina Lathouri, Thanos Zartaloudis
Architecture can structure the possibilities of our actions and
ultimately affect the conditions in which power can be exercised.
The thesis addresses this issue by examining how architecture,
functioning through spatial technologies, manages our activities
to become an agent of polity. Covering the historical period from
the appearance of the first welfare state in the mid-1960s until
the beginning of its disintegration with the introduction of a state
of workfare in the West and the dissolution of the Soviet Union in
the mid-1980s, the thesis follows the transition from the concept
of a social subject to the idea of a self-actualising individual.

MERATE BARAKAT, SONIC CITY NETWORKS:
URBAN DESIGN THROUGH ACOUSTIC SENSORY MANIPULATION
Supervisors: George Jeronimidis, Michael Weinstock
This research investigates the potential for using sound as
a primary driver of urban design. Every urban space has a
unique aural signature. The project explores the use of
computational approaches for the development and calibration
of an agent-based engine to simulate aural spatial perceptual
patterns in an urban space. Field measurements were used to
test the veracity of the generated patterns and to validate the
use of these spatial patterns for urban design.

ALEJANDRA CELEDON, RHETORICS OF THE PLAN
Supervisors: Marina Lathouri, Pier Vittorio Aureli
Why did the *plan* dominate architectural discourse and practice
for the last two centuries, and how did this affect the discipline?
The meaning of the word *plan* has changed over time,
registering and triggering disciplinary changes – the relation
between drawings and words, between objects and discourse.
Such changes correlate with a shift in the definition and scope
of the discipline – from the building, to the drawing (*disegno*)
of buildings as objects, to the building as a device for organising
and managing the city – that sees the building as an urban piece.
PhD completed 2014.

JINGRU CYAN CHENG, HUKOU REFORM AS URBAN REFORM
Supervisors: Pier Vittorio Aureli, Sam Jacoby
This thesis aims to put forward a systematic project for the
twenty-first century Chinese city at both an architectural and
territorial level. In the next two decades, Chinese cities will be
confronted by a reform of the *hukou* (household registration)
system and consequently the new challenges of urban growth
and densification. The forthcoming reform aims to abolish this
fundamental rural-urban dichotomy. The current predominant
planning model, the mega-plot, is an outcome of a fundamental
contradiction between state-driven planning and market forces.
The *hukou* reform will exacerbate its collapse but also present
an opportunity for radical urban reform in China.

ELIF ERDINE, GENERATIVE PROCESSES IN TOWER DESIGN:
ALGORITHMS FOR THE INTEGRATION OF TOWER SUBSYSTEMS
Supervisors: George Jeronimidis, Michael Weinstock,
Patrik Schumacher
The focus of the thesis is on developing a generative system of
design that offers simultaneous integration and differentiation
throughout the subsystems of a concept for a tall building
during the conceptual design phase. The overall performance
of the tower system is measured via progressive Finite Element
Analysis (FEA) procedures in order to calculate the changes
in the structural behaviour as each subsystem is introduced to
the overall tower system. PhD project completed in 2015.

GABRIELA GARCÍA DE CORTÁZAR, GETTING THERE
Supervisors: Mark Cousins, Pier Vittorio Aureli
The thesis proposes a history of orientation in the nineteenth and twentieth centuries by looking at London and the parallel development of transport and the popularisation of orientation devices (maps, guides, signs and systems). It proposes that the instalment of the view from above is intimately related to the control of movement, achieved through one and the same action: its arrest. Detention of movement is the central aspect of modern city control, and is therefore at the core of both power and knowledge. The thesis will explore the relationship between rest (the designed state of the street – the urban territory as established by its plans), unrest (the unwanted potential state) and arrest (the tool through which the second is turned into the desired first).

ALI FARZANEH, COMPUTATIONAL MORPHOGENESIS
OF CITY TISSUES
Supervisors: George Jeronimidis, Michael Weinstock
The research focuses on computational morphogenesis, a process by which digital objects come into existence and develop their form. Embedded digital information in the model controls the phenotype of the digital objects, similar to how a genome in living systems is responsible for the phenotype of the organism. It includes, but is not limited to, properties that define its physical proportions – area, height and orientation, which, as the object develops, become more and more complex by added features.

GABRIEL FELMER PLOMINSKY,
ADAPTIVE URBAN SOCIAL HOUSING
Supervisors: Simos Yannas, Paula Cadima
The central problem addressed by this project is the fuel poverty and the poor environmental conditions experienced by low-income groups in social housing around Santiago. The research investigates the parameters influencing the environmental performance of social housing schemes. The outcome of the project is a replicable housing prototype for different urban areas and climate regions of Chile.

KENSUKE HOTTA, PROGRAMMABLE ARCHITECTURE
Supervisors: George Jeronimidis, Michael Weinstock
This project introduces a new strategy for robotic architecture as an intelligent system. Information flow between Genetic Algorithms (GA) and user input prompt this hybrid system to output the consequent, ever-changing physical form. The hardware is an accumulation of self-sufficient machines dedicated to the actions of sensing, calculating and actuating. As a case study a machine organised using tensegrity-based components of variable forms was proposed. A physical model of this machine was built and tested via the wirelessly connected microcomputer chip Arduino. PhD completed 2014.

SERENA LEHUA JARVIS, ECOLOGICAL INFRASTRUCTURE:
EXAMINING SPATIAL STRATEGIES FOR INTEGRATED
URBAN WATER SYSTEMS
Supervisors: Jorge Fiori, Michael Weinstock,
Douglas Spencer, Eduardo Rico
This PhD project demonstrates that integrated urban
water systems would significantly benefit urban ecology.
The research repositions existing ecological systems such as
wetlands and forests as integral components of the water
cycle, and establishes how infrastructure can be redesigned
as a fluid integration of both built and natural systems. The
project uses the case of London to examine the interdependence
between water and energy systems, focusing specifically on
the Lea River Valley.

NILOOFAR KAKHI, IDENTITY DISINTERRED:
THE USES AND ABUSES OF A PAST IN ARCHITECTURAL
REPRESENTATION OF A PRESENT
Supervisors: Marina Lathouri, Vida Norouz Borazjani
This thesis focuses on the development of the historicist
understanding of collective identity in the architecture of Iran
since the country's modernisation in the 1920s, an architectural
approach that is seen as a consequence of broader socio-
political conditions and nationalist movements ultimately leading
to the revolution of 1979. The thesis examines the politics of
production of architectural knowledge and historiography
while constructing a conceptual platform for assessing such
representations of identity in contemporary architecture. PhD
completed in 2015.

COSTANDIS KIZIS, POSTWAR MODERNISM AND THE
QUESTION OF 'GREEKNESS'
Supervisors: Marina Lathouri, Sokratis Georgiadis
The thesis examines the architectural discussion on modernity
and national identity in postwar Greece via four cases that
attempt to reconcile national stereotypes with modern ideas
while reflecting the problematic process of absorbing modernity.
The thesis will contribute to the dissolution of myths and
constructs in architectural historiography in Greece and add to
recent scholarship on issues of national identity and modernity.

MOHAMMED MAKKI, URBAN ADAPTATION THROUGH
EVOLUTIONARY DEVELOPMENT
Supervisors: Michael Weinstock, George Jeronimidis
The research tackles the urbanisation of harsh climatic regions
in the arctic tundra, within a computational platform to establish
a correlation between the governing factors of the evolutionary
development of natural systems, to the factors that regulate
city development and growth.

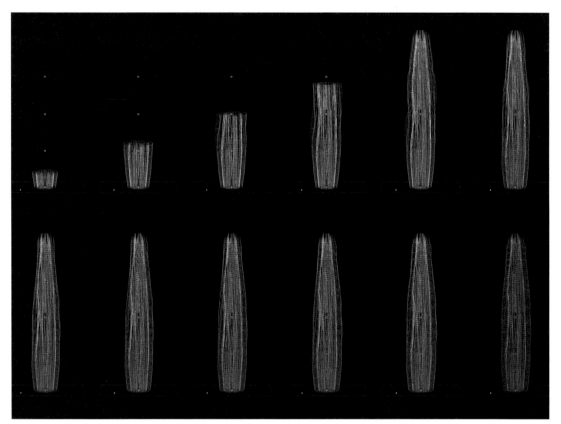

2

3

1. (page 257) Olivia Marra, Garden As Political Form
– reconstruction of a typical Chahar Bagh garden
found around Fars, Iran (drawing based on a 1976
photograph by Georg Gester)

2. Elif Erdine, Generative Processes in Tower
Design Tissues
3. Patricia Martin del Guayo, Environmental Perception
– climate in urban public spaces

OLIVIA MARRA, GARDEN AS POLITICAL FORM –
FROM ARCHETYPE TO PROJECT
Supervisors: Pier Vittorio Aureli, Mark Campbell
The thesis reassesses present and past examples of the garden,
moving towards a genealogy of the spatial and power relations
enacted by emblematic transformations of this archetype.
Focusing on cases in four cities the research aims to trace the
history of the garden from exemplary type of radical enclosure, to
composition of ungraspable limits, to formal tool for urbanisation.

PATRICIA MARTIN DEL GUAYO, ENVIRONMENTAL PERCEPTION:
CLIMATE IN URBAN PUBLIC SPACES
Supervisors: Simos Yannas, Paula Cadima
This dissertation reveals that climatic conditions influence the
way people use public spaces. Fieldwork in London and several
Spanish cities looked at the climatic and social environments in
selected public spaces, focusing on perceptions and reactions to
microclimatic environments and climate-responsive structures.
Through an integrative approach to the design of urban public
spaces the dissertation proposes specific public space on the
outskirts of Madrid. PhD completed in 2015.

SAMANEH MOAFI, HOUSING THE MASSES: DOMESTIC
ARCHITECTURE, GOVERNANCE AND CONFLICT IN IRAN
Supervisors: Pier Vittorio Aureli, Adrian Lahoud
This research begins with an investigation: a radical state-
initiated housing project named Mehr (2007–13) in the Islamic
Republic of Iran. Based on the Mehr scheme, Iran was to
invest in an urgent building programme of four million housing
units spread across the country. The thesis will examine the
instrumentality of Mehr in establishing homogeneity in the
segregated working class as well as the economic processes
that enabled the advent of the project in the first place.

WILLIAM HUTCHINS ORR, PRESCRIPTIVE PRACTICE:
HISTORIES AND THEORY OF ARCHITECTURE
Supervisors: Marina Lathouri, Nina Power
This thesis develops an architectural practice based on Alain
Badiou's theory of subjectivity, drawing on subjective thought's
ability to decide and prescribe the politically actual rather than
possible. In architectural discourse, this 'practice' becomes
the critique of the 'project', the dominant theoretical category
for understanding the field's radical modes – and crucial for
producing a theory of practice that can overcome the stasis of a
structuralist conception of architectural history and production.

ARTURO REVILLA, PROCESSCITY:
ARCHITECTURE AND THE BORDER CONDITION
Supervisors: Marina Lathouri, Brett Steele
This project investigates the border as a conceptual and spatial
condition from which architectural design can reframe its relation

to the city as an object of study. Design is used not as a way
to conclude a consecutive line of arguments, but as a tool
to investigate new relations. With a participatory perspective
in mind, design experiments and small-scale interventions
are used to develop ideas and build a research narrative.

RICARDO RUIVO PEREIRA,
MYSTIQUES OF SOCIALIST ARCHITECTURE
Supervisors: Mark Cousins, Pier Vittorio Aureli
The western historiography of Soviet architecture focuses on
the short period of its first two decades. This PhD project aims to
address these questions at a historiographical level. While paying
attention to historical data regarding the architectural production
of the Soviet Union and its satellite states, the purpose of this
work is to critically reframe the wealth of historiographical
material available today on the subject, focusing on the disparity
between the accounts that deal with the early avant-garde and
those that deal with the currents that superseded it.

DAVIDE SACCONI, ARCHETYPES A PROJECT
FOR THE BRAZILIAN CITY
Supervisors: Pier Vittorio Aureli, Mark Campbell
Tracing within the history of Brazil the occurrence of specific
archetypes – the Jesuit Redução and the Fazenda in the colonial
period, the Avenida and the Predio in mature modernity, and
the Campus in the contemporary city – the thesis constructs
a conceptual framework for the design of archetypes of public
space in Rio de Janeiro, São Paulo and Belo Horizonte. Archetypes
are architectures liberated by programme, where the normative
definition of performances and behaviour is substituted by an
exposed rule, a principle governing conduct and action where
form and activity tend to intimately coincide.

IVONNE SANTOYO OROZCO,
THE ARCHITECTURAL CONSTRUCTION OF CONDUCT
Supervisors: Mark Cousins, Pier Vittorio Aureli
This thesis reconsiders the ways in which architecture has served
the needs of various regimes of power. The task is to understand
not only how spatial experiences have been conceptualised
throughout history but, more importantly, to show how such
categories have motivated specific forms of spatial orderings and
architectural tropes, influencing and even prescribing a specific
type of conduct whose political and economic underpinnings
reveal architecture's role in forms of subjectification.

EMMANOUIL STAVRAKAKIS, THE ARCHITECTURE OF LINEAR B
Supervisors: Mark Cousins, Spyros Papapetros
It is widely acknowledged that Michael Ventris' decipherment
of Linear B was remarkable because he was not a professional
scholar. At the time of his death some obituaries suggested that
perhaps it was something to do with his training as an architect.

This thesis argues that while Ventris lacked others' experience in the field, his advantage came not only from his 'brilliance'; it was also indebted to the forms of analysis he acquired as part of his architectural training. PhD completed in 2014.

THIAGO TAVARES ABRANCHES DE SOVERAL,
SECURITY AND ARCHITECTURE:
VIOLENCE AND THE URBAN DESIGN IN RIO DE JANEIRO
Supervisors: Jorge Fiori, Sam Jacob
In Rio de Janeiro, architecture, topography, legislation and social conflicts have shaped an urban model where fear and security are visible. This thesis investigates the consequences of violence on the morphologies and typologies in Rio, identifying and analysing the shifts in definition and perception of security and violence that have transformed the idea and form of the city over time.

ALDO URBINATI, ARCHITECTURAL EFFECTS
Supervisor: Mark Cousins, Thomas Weaver
The Eiffel Tower has long been regarded as an achievement of engineering and not as an architectural object. Yet, at the same time, it has also come to signify a de facto architectural symbol of the modern era. This thesis aims to clarify this debate while unpicking its associated allegiances by locating the idea of architecture within a much larger cultural field.

ALEXANA VOUGIA, ESTRANGEMENT AND THE METROPOLIS:
AN ENQUIRY INTO THE DISCURSIVENESS OF MODERN FORM
Supervisors: Marina Lathouri, David Cunningham
Alienation, as a concept of philosophy and political theory, emerged as a catalyst for an orchestrated denunciation by the avant-garde movements of the early twentieth century, which opposed the social and cultural predominance of bourgeoisie. In line with the strategy of the negation of a negation, 'estrangement' became a device for distorting artistic form, in pursuance of the de-alienation of the corrupted (alienated) consciousness of the modern subject. The thesis examines how this particular device of 'making strange' was used in architectural practice, especially since the latter can potentially provide the actual stage for social struggle.

JINGMING WU, THE INVENTED CHINESE CLASSICAL GARDEN
Supervisors: Mark Cousins, Doreen Bernath
The Chinese classical garden has been a popular topic in Chinese architecture and urban design for almost 80 years, encouraging the birth of a contemporary architecture that satisfied both Chinese and western audiences. This study investigates the this phenomenon within architectural history and theory writings of the twentieth century. It further considers the ambitions of government and of the architects who invented the term 'Chinese classical garden' as a traditional architecture during the revolution period of the 1950s.

AAIS

Studio Director
Theo Lorenz

Studio Master
Tanja Siems

Studio Tutors and Experts
Andy Dean, music and production
Albert Lang, theatrical direction and spatial composition
David McAlmont, music and history of the arts
Heiko Kalmbach, film direction and dramaturgy
Joe Walkling, choreography, New Movement Collective
Joel Newman, film and sound
Renaud Wiser. choreography, New Movement Collective
Steve Webb, engineering

Thanks to
Stefano Raboli Panserna
Max Babbé
Leanne Chilton
Anne Laubner
Anne Lewald
Daniel Brew
Daniel Daoudi
Alex Tod
Alice Purton
Alex Whitley
Robin Gladwin
Miraj Ahmend
Eduardo Rico
Richard Wentworth
TU Berlin
Mangiabarche Gallery
Ibiza Rocks

EXPATs 'Moving Stone'

Mobility and migration are omnipresent themes in today's globalised world. Affordable air travel, high standards of living and the constant search for creative networks and opportunities all encourage a dispersed lifestyle in which the individual constantly shapes his or her own environment and with it new modes of production. Today's creatives occupy locations of their choosing, making work that is not fixed to a single location or structure, and which undulates around multiple hubs of creativity.

The studio utilised its networks for a series of productions in relation to three 'expat' locations – the islands of Sardinia, Ibiza and Guernsey – and drew on the unique qualities of each to develop an extravaganza of music, dance and spatial performance. We researched how we can become expatriates in spite of 'global citizenship' or virtual networks, and 'unplug' from these in order to feedback with inspired work. Architect Sumaya Islam from Bangladesh, interior designer Mariana Vargas from Costa Rica and designer Dongsoo Koo from South Korea created events that offered fields of interaction with the local environments, materials and scenery while engaging both inhabitants and visitors in immersive performances, workshops and talks.

Collaborating with Mangiabarche Gallery on Calasetta, Sardinia, Ibiza Rocks at Pikes, Creative Guernsey and the New Movement Collective, the studio developed full-scale productions starting with a basecamp on Sardinia which produced the framework for a broader event and cultural festival on Ibiza and finished with a performance and forum of discussion on Guernsey.

Students
Dongsoo Koo
Mariana Vargas
Sumaya Islam

2

3

4

1. (previous page) 'Ex Patria' performance at Ibiza Rocks House with Renaud Wiser, Joe Walking, Alex Whitley and Robin Gladwin of New Movement Collective, David McAlmont and Andy Dean

2. David McAlmont Performing as part of 'Ex Patria' with New Movement Collective, photo Dongsoo Koo
3. Dials at the legendary Pikes/ Ibiza Rocks House
4. Flash performance in Ibiza with New Movement Collective and David McAlmont

5

6

7

6. Joe Walking performing on the cliffs of
Sardinia during the solar eclipse
7. Night shoot of Dial on the cliffs of Sardinia,
photo Dongsoo Koo

5. Film shoot with Heiko Kalmbach and David McAlmont
for the music video of Moving Stone

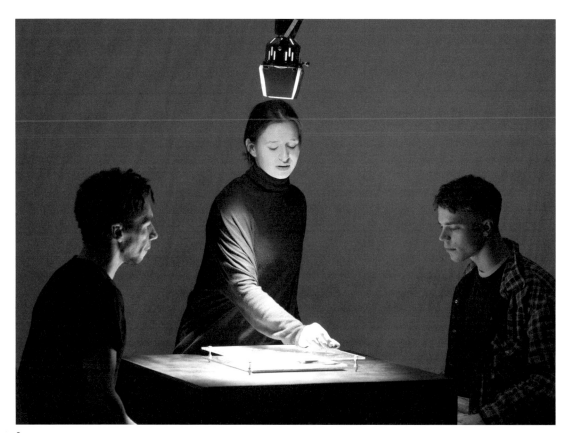

9

10

11

8. (opposite) Moving Stone Performance at the
Mangiabarche Gallery on Sardinia with David McAlmont
and Joe Walking
9. Mariana Vargas directing the 'control table'
at the moving stone performance at the AA,
photo Dongsoo Koo

10. Daniel Brew during recording Session at
'The Square'
11. Sumaya Islam during recording Session
at 'The Square' producing her composition

Launched in Dubai in early 2008, the AA Visiting School (AAVS) has grown into a network of more than 50 annual courses scattered across the globe, from Buenos Aires to London, New York to Hong Kong, onto the Amazon Rainforest and Atacama Desert. Encompassing five continents and countless cultures, AAVS courses take participants on unimaginable journeys to engage with many of the world's most pressing architectural, technological, cultural, urban and social issues.

AAVS is concerned with architectural education in its widest possible conception and offers four kinds of courses: a Semester Programme for visiting students to study alongside AA students in the Undergraduate School; the Summer School, Night School and other short courses organised at the AA in Bedford Square and in Hooke Park; Little Architect, which introduces an awareness of architecture and cities to schoolchildren across London; and an array of Global Schools abroad. Courses are modelled on the AA's famed unit system with individual agendas relating to the particular geographic and cultural conditions of each setting.

AAVS programmes offer participants the rare opportunity to engage with local forms of expertise, and they provide the unique kind of globalised learning experience relevant to architectural education in the twenty-first century. Welcome to a world of continuous architectural investigation, proposal-making and communication – a world where not only architecture, but also architectural learning, is everywhere.

1

2

1. AAVS Tehran
2. AAVS Bilbao
3. AAVS Dubai

274

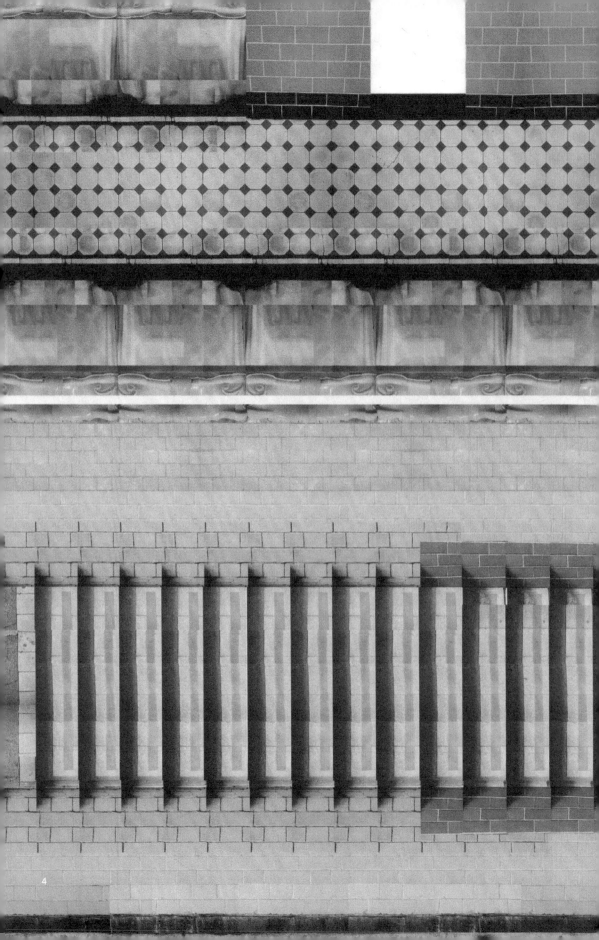

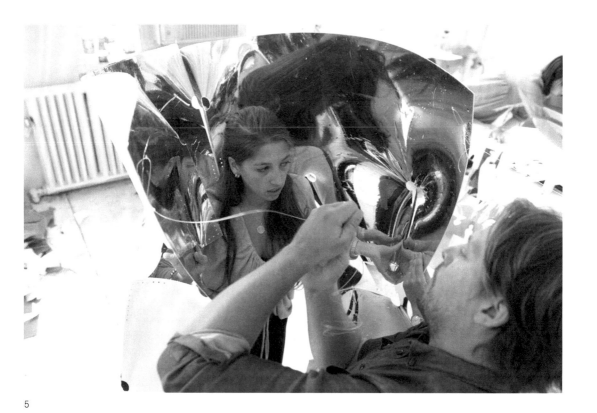

5

6

4. AAVS t-sa forum
5. AAVS New York
6. AAVS Slovenia

7

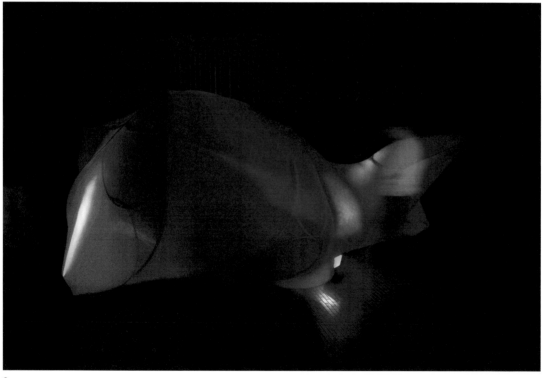

8

7. AAVS San Juan
8. AAVS Madrid

9

10

9. AAVS Las Pozas
10. AAVS Barcelona

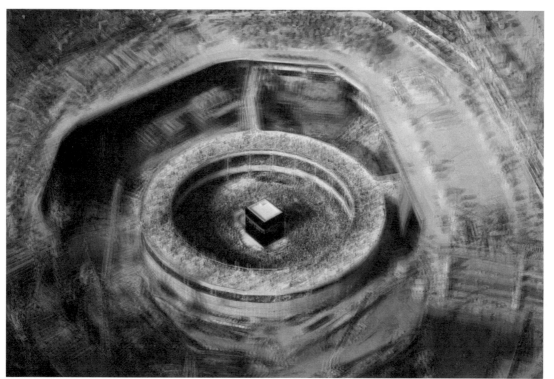

11

12

11. AAVS Makkah
12. AAVS Frankfurt
13. AAVS San Francisco

13

15

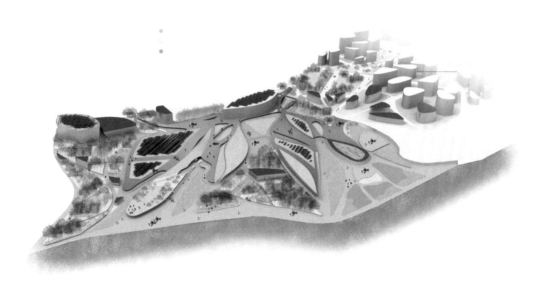

16

14. AAVS SummerMake
15. AAVS Chennai
16. AAVS São Paulo

18

19

17. AAVS Santiago
18. AAVS Jordan
19. AAVS Little Architect

20

21

20. AAVS Unknown Fields Division
21. AAVS Patras

22. AAVS Unknown Fields Division

In addition to units and programmes, the AA extends its academic breadth through numerous courses, initiatives and media. With access to wood, metal and modelling workshops and the digital prototyping lab, students and staff have first-rate equipment to realise projects. Hooke Park, the AA's woodland campus in Dorset, is a 350-acre working forest in an area of outstanding natural beauty. Its facilities, centred on a woodworking workshop, are available to visiting groups of AA tutors and students for teaching activities in the workshop or forest. The AA's Research Clusters also provide opportunities for students, staff and the wider community to investigate specific areas of research, thus expanding and deepening the body of work undertaken at the school. And with a host of live-stream and recorded lectures, programming and microsites, AA Digital Platforms extends the school's presence to the international online community.

HOOKE PARK

RESEARCH CLUSTERS

WORKSHOPS

Hooke Park

Director
Martin Self

Manager
Jez Ralph

Administrator
Merry Hinsley

Workshop manager
Charlie Corry Wright

Workshop supervisor
Edward Coe

Forester
Chris Sadd

Robotics Developer
Pradeep Devadass

Cooks
Georgie &
  Tia Corry Wright

Hooke Park, the AA's woodland campus in Dorset, has continued to host London-based units, visiting schools and the Design & Make masters programme during 2014–15. This year the campus has significantly evolved, with the installation of a new robotic fabrication cell and the completion of the biomass-fuelled district heating system, which is now heating all buildings on campus. In conjunction with this, major upgrades have been made to networking and services throughout the site.

Hooke Park's forest was hit by a storm in 2014. This spring was an opportunity to clear away the damaged and fallen trees, which will not only be used to fuel the new biomass boiler, but also sawn to construct the next group of buildings on campus. Areas where trees were lost have been replanted with a mixture of species that will increase the resilience of the woodland to the impacts of a changing climate and disease. We have also started a community programme for visiting schoolchildren to learn more about the forest. At the same time local users, AA staff and students continue to become more involved with our woodland site.

Activities at Hooke Park this year have included constructions by the MakeLab, Summer DLAB and SummerMake programmes and the second phase of the Maeda Workshop's new gateway project to redevelop the entrance to the estate.

It was with great sadness that the Hooke Park team heard the news of the death in March of Frei Otto, the co-designer of two of the buildings at Hooke Park and an immense and continuing inspiration for staff and students. The further news that he has been named as the 2015 Pritzker Prize laureate adds to the sense that we are privileged to be able to study, work, make, cook and eat in his only UK buildings.

1

2

3

1. SummerBuild programme participants work along MArch Design & Make students to construct the Boiler House

2. Working in the Hooke Park studio space
3. Members of the Maeda Workshop team who are developing proposals for a new entrance to Hooke Park

4

5

6

4 & 5 The MakeLab Visiting School focused on performative envelopes in Easter 2015, designing and testing the characteristics of lightweight and site-specific inhabitable structures.

6. In July 2014 Hooke Park hosted the first of a series of 'Sonic Coast' concerts in the Big Shed.

Workshops

Head of Workshops
William Fausset

Wood & Metal Workshop
Technician
Robert Busher

Model Workshop Master
Trystrem Smith

Wood & Metal Workshop
Student Assistants
Richard Leung
Albane Duvillier
Chris Johnson
Ben Jones
Konstantina Koulouri

Head of Digital
Prototyping
Angel Lara Moreira

Digital Prototyping
Technician
Henry Cleaver

Digital Prototyping
Student Assistants
Ashwini Ashokkumar
Natalie Markantonatou
Norine Chu
Chaitanya Chavan
Ao Tan
Avneesh Rathore
Jane Horcajo
Catarina Sampaio
Iris Gramegna
Alejandro Garcia
Emily Hayden
Lena Emanuelsen
Patrick Morris
Maria Olmos
Mikhaila Fam
Roberto Boettger

Digital Prototyping
Student Assistants
at DRL
Martina Rosati
Sara Abou Saleh

The AA operates four independent workshops located at its home in Bedford Square and at the Hooke Park facility in Dorset. Students are encouraged to use and combine technologies from the different facilities to experiment with a range of tools and materials and to learn about fabrication aspects of the design process. The technologies offered in the different workshops are partially overlapping and range from traditional hand tools for wood and metal work to CNC prototyping machines.

The Wood and Metal Workshop is well equipped with standing machines, hand and power tools for wood, metal and some plastics. Facilities are available for welding, cutting and shaping steel and some other nonferrous metals. The Workshop's machinery supports precise work on hardwoods, softwoods and other panel products. Staff assist the students in determining design and fabrication solutions as well as understanding the properties and processing of materials. Ching's Yard is used for large-scale fabricating projects.

The Model Workshop provides indoor and outdoor working space for a variety of activities, including mould-making and casting, kiln work in ceramics and glass and vacuum-forming. Projects are realised using numerous materials and techniques and range in scale from traditional model-making work to 1:1 concrete castings.

The Digital Prototyping Lab offers a number of digital fabrication technologies including five laser-cutting machines available to students, four CNC-milling machines, two powder-based 3D printers and three FFF 3D printers, operated by two full-time members of staff and a team of 18 student assistants. The lab offers tutorials on digital fabrication techniques and file preparation for groups and individual students and organises independent workshops across the school.

1

2

1. Digital Prototyping Lab   2. Wood and Metal Workshop, photos Valerie Bennett

Research Clusters – Paradise Lost

Cluster Curator
Mark Campbell

Oil was first discovered in the United States in the east-Texas town of Beaumont on 10 January 1901. The area was so pregnant with oil that bubbling gas was frequently seen rising to the surface and the Spindletop rig, which made the strike, unearthed a geyser so powerful it yielded 100,000 barrels of crude oil per day. Beaumont became a boomtown. Naturally, this power and wealth was also manifested architecturally, spawning a commercial district rich with early twentieth-century and Art Deco buildings. In the early-1960s the First Security National Bank, which had profited from the industry, expanded its operation into the modernist First City Building, designed by local architect Llewellyn W Pitts. The signature cast concrete panels that form the facade were designed to shield the sun and provide ventilation. As Beaumont passed into decline (in terms of occupation, if not underlying finances), however, these white panels formed a sharp contrast with the boarded-up buildings throughout downtown. The First City Building has been available to lease since 2008.

The Paradise Lost research cluster is fascinated with the architectural remnants of such economic readjustments. The past four years have been spent exploring such lost paradises in the context of the United States. While the US was the world's greatest economic, scientific and cultural force during the twentieth century, it now faces a kind of unplanned obsolescence; changing patterns of consumption and demand have resulted in a kind of architectural redundancy in which architecture often exists solely as a form of by-product or residue, leaving behind such artefacts as the abandoned Catskills resorts of upstate New York, or the unwanted mass suburbs of California's Salton Sea.

When everything is redundant, what remains? Our means for considering the architectural consequences of these paradises lost are simple. If the symbolic history of the US rests on the heroic potential of production, then we examine the opposite: that which isn't work. More appropriately: that which constitutes non-work when there is no productivity left to define it. The Paradise Lost research cluster is currently working on a publication and accompanying exhibition scheduled for autumn 2015.

First City Building, Beaumont, Texas

Top: Mark Fisher and his 'brother' relax in front of his drawings at the Five Young Architects exhibition, Art Net, 1974. Thanks to James Fairorth and Tait Towers for their initiation of the Mark Fisher Scholarship, established in memory the AA graduate and tutor.

Bottom: Christina Smith at the opening of 'Via Christina'. In 2012 Christina generously donated a gift making possible 'Via Christina' – a new, third-floor corridor uniting all 14 units in the Diploma School.

Development, Partnerships and Sponsorship

Since its founding in 1847, the Architectural Association has been independent and self-supporting. A pioneering UK higher education charity, the AA receives no statutory funding for its School of Architecture, its internationally renowned teaching activities or for its public programme, which is offered free of charge to AA Members and the public.

The Architectural Association and students in the AA School of Architecture are kindly supported each year by generous donations from individuals, institutions, trusts, foundations and corporate sponsors. Such support can take the form of direct financial contributions, or in-kind support for the AA's wide range of yearly activities and initiatives.

Long-term and Capital Support

An independent charitable trust, the Architectural Association Foundation ensures the prudent handling of funds raised in support of scholarships and bursaries for AA students as well as the 2020 Plan – the building improvement and masterplan programme for the AA's Bedford Square campus.

On a yearly basis, the AA Foundation makes available approximately £200,000 and the AA Inc contributes annually another £300,000 towards scholarships and bursaries for AA students.

In recent years the AA has embarked upon a series of improvements to its studios and facilities in Bedford Square. Further plans are underway to implement the changes and improvements to the AA masterplan, the planning permission of which was achieved in December 2012.

Recent projects on Bedford Square have included expansion and improvement of the AA's student workshops, Computing Lab, Modelmaking workshop and the interconnection of all third-floor Diploma unit spaces. Planned additional works will interconnect the properties on the lower floors and create an expanded Library, new Lecture Hall, Prototyping Lab, Exhibition Gallery, entrance and social spaces, and allow full disabled access to the AA's London facilities.

The AA is also continuing to develop its rural campus in Hooke Park, Dorset, where students and staff have designed and built six new buildings during the past five years. Relationships with the local community in Dorset are of great importance to the AA. To cultivate these relationships and to ensure the safekeeping and prudent application of funds raised to develop new facilities and buildings, and to manage and care for the surrounding forest, a separate charitable trust – the Hooke Park Educational Trust – was established in December 2012.

Building projects at Hooke Park have included the Big Shed and the Caretaker's House (2012) and a series of student lodges (2013). These projects have been made possible through the generous support of the Custerson Estate, and the Norah Garlick family through the Horace and Ellen Hannah Wakeford bequest. The direct advice and involvement of Christine and David Price, Tim Wakeford and the members of the Hooke Park Advisory Group have been invaluable to the development of the Hooke Park campus.

Sponsorship & Support for Special Projects

The AA actively seeks to develop outside partnerships for the benefit of school and student activities. The school extends its thanks to the dozens of sponsors and partners who support special projects, study visits and events each year.

Visiting School

This year's growth in the Visiting School and similar initiatives to develop opportunities for interdisciplinary research, exchange and collaboration would not have been possible without the generous support of friends in the academic and professional communities. The AA Visiting School thanks its countless partners, sponsors and friends who have allowed the programme to develop and grow.

Individual thanks for support of research projects, study visits and other events can be found in the introductions to the units and programmes in this book.

How to Give

The AA actively seeks to engage its members and other friends to assist with the organisation's long-term initiatives and with the next series of yearly projects, for which planning is currently underway.

Prospective donors are encouraged to contact the Director's Office to discuss their potential involvement and ideas:

Brett Steele, AA Director
director@aaschool.ac.uk
+44 (0)207 887 4026

Supporters for 2014–15

The Architectural Association gives its sincerest thanks to
the following individuals and organisations who have supported
AA students and key initiatives this year.

1:One
ABC Imaging
Actiu
Adams Kara Taylor
Airlab
Anonymous donors
Arch Daily
Area China
Arkitera
Arquiane
Arup
Les Arts Decoratifs
Atec Consulting
Engineers
AU arquitetura e urbanismo
Autodesk
Baylight Foundation
David Bernstein
Bilbao Ekintza
Blueprint magazine
Robert & Elizabeth Boas
Embassy of Brazil in London
British Arts Council
British Embassy Haiti
Alison Brooks
Buro Happold
Caixa d'Enginyers
Canadian Centre for Architecture
Capital and Counties (CAPCO)
Casa abierta al tiempo
Cassochrome
Catholic University
CCW
Cement and Concrete Institute
Margaret Chow
Cobra CNC
Richard Coleman
Codorniu
Consell Regulator DO Terra Alta
DuPont Corian
Cujae
The Custerson Estate
Daiwa Anglo-Japanese
Foundation
Michael Davies
Design to Production
DS4
DSG
Euro Channel
Nick Evans
James Fairorth & TAIT Towers
FILE
Fletcher Priest Trust
Fondazione Prada SCIN Gallery
Foster + Partners
FRAME China
Frener and Riefer
The Norah Garlick Family
Gensler
German University of Technology
   in Oman (GUtech)
Graham Foundation
The Great Britain Sasakawa
   Foundation
Sir Nicholas Grimshaw
GSA

Guggenheim Bilbao
Hewlett-Packard
HfMT (Music
Academy Cologne)
Hoehler + Partner
Holcim Foundation
IBERO
Istanbul Technical University
Elise Jaffe & Jeffrey Brown
Jotun Paint
Just Swiss
KamKav Construction Company
Bijan Kamvari
Kamvari Architects
The Kaplický Centre
Marian Keyes
Kohn Pedersen Fox
KPF
KunstSalon Foundation
Laing O'Rourke
Gerald Levin
Lisbon Architecture Triennale
Matadero Madrid
MAEDA
MARQ
McNeel Rhino &
   McNeel Grasshopper
Melting Mints
Metro Imaging
Mike Davies, Rogers Stirk
   Harbour + Partners
Music Technology Ltd
Neue Holzbau
New Movement Collective
NUTA
Oaks Prague Czech Centre London
Oikos
Oficina del Historiador
Cuidad de la Habana
PG Bison
Pase Usted
Phillips
Pimpolhos da Grande Rio
Plot
Claire Pollock, Allford Hall
   Monaghan
Liz & Anthony Pozner
Pro Helvetia
Regione Autonoma della Sardegna
Rhino Nest
ROCA
Samoo Architects & Engineers
Shenkar College of Engineering
   & Design
Singapore Polytechnic
Christina Smith
Sociedad Colombiana de
   Arquitectos Bogotá D C y
   Cundinamarca
Storefront for Art and Architecture
Strabag Oman LLC
Studio Gang Architects
The Andrew Szmidla Estate
Tecnalia
TDM Solutions
Theobald and Gardiner

Think City
Tier Time
tomo
Travesia
Tsinghua ADI Colour
UDK
UIC School of Architecture
Universidad Anahuac
Universidad Iberoamericana
Universitaet der Kunste Berlin
Universidad Nacional Autónoma
   de México
University of Chile
University of Hong Kong,
   Shanghai Study Centre
University of Houston
University of Liechtenstein
University of Nicosia
UPV
Urban Space Design
UTS
V-Fund
Villa Arson Nice
Volume
WIX
World Architecture News
Yonsei University
ZHU Long
Zahner Metals
Zeit Stiftung

Staff List

Director's Office
Director
Brett Steele
Personal Assistant
Roberta Jenkins
Academic Coordinator
Barbara-Ann Campbell-Lange
Administrator
Keira Callaghan

Registrar's Office
School Registrar
Belinda Flaherty
Compliance Officer
Krishna Songera
Student Aid & Qualifications Officer
Sabrina Blakstad
Quality Assurance Coordinator
Emma Newbury
Undergraduate School Coordinator
Sanaa Vohra
*Complementary Studies
Coordinator*
James Hulme (temporary)
*Graduate School Coordinator /
OU Administrator*
Clement Chung
Graduate School Coordinator
Danielle Hewitt
(to March 2015)
Professional Studies Coordinator
Rob Sparrow
Filing Assistant
Linda Keiff

Admissions Office
Head
Kirstie Little
*Undergraduate Admissions
Coordinator*
Kristelle Jacobs
Graduate Admissions Coordinators
Imogen Evans
Saira Soarez
Timothy Clarke
Andrew Kershaw (temporary)

ACADEMIC

UNDERGRADUATE

Foundation
Course Director
Saskia Lewis
Studio Staff
Umberto Bellardi Ricci
Taneli Mansikkamki

First Year
Head of First Year
Monia De Marchi
Studio Staff
Shany Barath
Fabrizio Ballabio
Maria Shéhérazade Giudici
Ryan Neiheiser
John Ng

Intermediate School
Unit 1
Mark Campbell
Stewart Dodd
Unit 2
Takero Shimazaki
Ana Araujo
Unit 3
Nanette Jackowski
Ricardo de Ostos
Unit 4
Nathalie Rozencwajg
Michel da Costa Gonçalves
Unit 5
Ryan Dillon
Unit 6
Jeroen van Ameijde
Brendon Carlin
Unit 7
Maria Fedorchenko
Unit 8
Francisco González de Canales
Nuria Alvarez Lombardero
Unit 9
Christopher Pierce
Christopher Matthews
Charlotte Moe
Unit 10
Valentin Bontjes van Beek
Unit 11
Manuel Collado
Nacho Martín
Manijeh Verghese
Unit 12
Tyen Masten
Inigo Minns
Unit 13
Lily Jencks (Maternity Leave)
Jessica Reynolds
Tatiana Von Preussen
(maternity cover)

Diploma School
Unit 1
Miraj Ahmed
Martin Jameson
Unit 2
Didier Fiuza Faustino
Kostas Grigoriadis
Unit 3
Daniel Bosia
Marco Vanucci
Adiam Sertzu
Unit 4
John Palmesino
Ann-Sofi Rönnskog
Unit 5
Cristina Díaz Moreno
Efrén Ga Grinda
Benjamin Reynolds
Unit 6
Liam Young
Kate Davies
Unit 7
David Greene
Samantha Hardingham
Unit 9
Natasha Sandmeier
Unit 10
Carlos Villanueva Brandt
Unit 11
Shin Egashira
Unit 14
Pier Vittorio Aureli
Maria Shéhérazade Giudici
Unit 16
Jonas Lundberg
Andrew Yau
Unit 17
Theo Sarantoglou Lalis
Dora Sweijd
Unit 18
Enric Ruiz-Geli
Pablo Rós
Felix Fassbinder

Complementary Studies
History and Theory Studies
Head
Mark Cousins
Course Lecturers/Course Tutors
Pier Vittorio Aureli
Fabrizio Ballabio
Shumi Bose
Edward Bottoms
Mark Campbell
Susan Chai
Judith Clark
Mollie Claypool
Nerma Cridge
Ryan Dillon
Lionel Eid
Pol Esteve
William Firebrace
Winston Hampel
Patrick Keiller
Roberta Marcaccio
Alison Moffett
Ricardo Ruivo
Emmanouil Stavrakakis
Brett Steele
Sylvie Taher
Chris Turner
Thanos Zartaloudis
Zaynab Dena Ziari

Media Studies
Head
Kate Davies
Department Staff
Miraj Ahmed
Kasper Ax
Charles Arsène-Henry
Shany Barath
Sue Barr
Valentin Bontjes van Beek
Apostolos Despotidis
Shin Egashira
Oliviu Lugojan-Ghenciu
Anderson Inge
Alex Kaiser
Antoni Malinowski
Alison Moffett
Joel Newman
Capucine Perrot
Caroline Rabourdin

Technical Studies
Head / Diploma Master
Javier Castañón
Intermediate Master
Kenneth Fraser
Department Staff
Carolina Bartram
Giles Bruce
Philip Cooper
Chris Davies
Christina Doumpioti
Ian Duncombe
Wolfgang Frese
Ben Godber
Evan Greenberg
Pablo Gugel
Martin Hagemann
David Illingworth
Julia King
Antiopi Koronaki
Emanuele Marfisi
Nacho Martí
Yassaman Mousvi
Federico Montella
Thomas Oosterhoff
Amin Sadeghy
Nina Tabink
Paul Thomas
Giancarlo Torpiano
Manja van de Worp
Mohsen Zikri

Professional Studies
Head
Kathy Gal
Part 1
Javier Castañón
Part 2
Kathy Gal
*Professional Studies
Advisor/Part 3*
Alastair Robertson

GRADUATE

DRL
Director
Theodore Spyropoulos
Founder Director
Patrik Schumacher
Studio Masters
Robert Stuart-Smith
Shajay Bhooshan

Course Tutors
Pierandrea Angius
Mollie Claypool
Apostolos Despotidis
Ryan Dillon
Mostafa El-Sayed
Winston Hampel
Oliviu Lugojan-Ghenciu
Technical Tutor
Albert Taylor

Emergent Technologies
Directors
Michael Weinstock
George Jeronimidis
Studio Master
Evan Greenberg
Studio Tutors
Mehran Gharleghi
Manja van de Worp

History and Critical Thinking
Director
Marina Lathouri
Programme Staff
Mark Cousins
John Palmesino
Douglas Spencer

Housing & Urbanism
Directors
Jorge Fiori
Hugo Hinsley
Programme Staff
Lawrence Barth
Abigail Batchelor
Nicholas Bullock
Florian Dirschedl
Elad Eisenstein
Diego Grinberg
Dominic Papa
Elena Pascolo
Juliana Ribeiro Muniz
Anna Shapiro
Alex Warnock-Smith
Naiara Vergara

Landscape Urbanism
Directors
Alfredo Ramirez
Eduardo Rico
Programme Staff
Ignacio Lopez Buson
Clara Oloriz Sanjuan
Gustavo Romanillos Arroyo
Douglas Spencer
Tom Smith
Giancarlo Torpiano

Sustainable
Environmental Design
Director
Simos Yannas
Programme Staff
Paula Cadima
Jorge Rodriguez Álvarez
Klaus Bode
Gustavo Brunelli
Herman Calleja
Mariam Kapsali
Byron Mardas

Conservation of Historic Buildings
Director
Andrew Shepherd
Year Master
David Hills
Thesis Tutor
Martin Cook

Design & Make
Director
Martin Self
Studio Master
Kate Darby
Construction Tutor
Charley Brentnall
Thesis Tutor
Mark Campbell

Projective Cities
Programme Director
Sam Jacoby
Programme Staff
Mark Campbell
Maria Shéhérazade Giudici
External Thesis Supervisor
Adrian Lahoud

PhD Programme
*PhD Directors of Studies
& First Supervisors*
Pier Vittorio Aureli
Lawrence Barth
Mark Cousins
Jorge Fiori
Hugo Hinsley
George Jeronimidis
Marina Lathouri
Brett Steele
Michael Weinstock
Simos Yannas
Second Supervisors
Doreen Bernath
Paula Cadima
Mark Campbell
David Cunningham
Socrates Georgiadis
Sam Jacoby
Patrik Schumacher
Douglas Spencer
Thomas Weaver

AA Interprofessional Studio
Director
Theo Lorenz
Studio Master
Tanja Siems

RESEARCH CLUSTERS
Curator
Mark Campbell

VISITING SCHOOL
Director
Christopher Pierce
Coordinator
Andrea Ghaddar
Night School Director
Sam Jacob
Night School Coordinator
Danielle Hewitt
Assistant (temping)
Amy Morrison-Porter

ADMINISTRATIVE

Audiovisual Lab
Head
Joel Newman
Audiovisual and Media Technician
Sepehr Malek

Computing
Head
Julia Frazer
Assistant Head of Computing
Mathew Bielecki
Support Staff
David Hopkins
George Christoforou
Paul Fairman
Wesley Faure
Alexander Medrano
Toby Jakeman
(to May 2015)

Print Centre
Manager
Photios Demetriou

Digital Photo Studio
Head
Sue Barr
Ben Deakin (maternity cover)

Workshops
Head of Wood and Metal Workshops
William Fausset
Workshop Technician
Robert Busher
Model Making Technician
Trystrem Smith
Head of Digital Prototyping
Angel Lara Moreira
DPL Technician
Henry Cleaver

Hooke Park
Head
Martin Self
Caretakers
Charles Corry-Wright
Chris Sadd
Administrative Coordinator
Merry Hinsley
Estate and Development Manager
Jeremy Ralph
Assistant Workshop Technician
Edward Coe

Association
Secretary
Kathleen Formosa
Secretary's Office Assistant
Cristian Sanchez Gonzalez
Head of Membership
Alex Lorente
Membership Manager
Jenny Keiff
Events Coordinator
Joanne McCluskey
*Membership Communications
Co-ordinator*
Bobby Jewell

AA Foundation
P/T Administrator
Amanda Claremont

AACP
Head
Shumon Basar
Exhibition Coordination
Pier Vittorio Aureli
Public Programme Curator
Manijeh Verghese
Research
David Greene
Think Tank
John Palmesino
Ann-Sofi Rönnskog

Exhibitions
Head
Vanessa Norwood
Exhibitions Project Manager
Lee Regan
Exhibitions Coordinator
Sebastian Craig

Library
Librarian
Eleanor Gawne
Deputy Librarian
Aileen Smith
Archivist
Edward Bottoms
Cataloguer
Beatriz Flora
Serials/Library
Web Developer &
Data Protection Officer
Simine Marine

Digital Platforms
Head
Frank Owen
Web Designer/Developer
Zeynep Görgülü (Maternity Leave)
Rico Borza

Print Studio
Manager/Editor AA Files
Thomas Weaver
Publications Editor
Pamela Johnston
Editorial Assistants
Clare Barrett
Sarah Handelman
Art Director
Zak Kyes
Graphic Designers
Wayne Daly
Claire Lyon
Rosa Nussbaum
(to March 2015)

AA Publications
Marketing & Distribution
Kirsten Morphet

Bedford Press
Directors
Zak Kyes
Wayne Daly

AA Bookshop
Manager
Charlotte Newman
Assistant Manager
Andrew Whittaker
Senior Bookshop Associates
Isabel Hardingham
Sonia Makkar
Bookshop Assistant
Raluca Grada Amandi

Photo Library
Librarian
Valerie Bennett
Photo Library Assistant (temping)
Byron Blakeley

Accounts Office
Head of Finance
Geoff Parrett
Finance Manager
Lisa Simmonds
Accounts Staff
George Brown
Angie Denney
Margaret Hayde
Aneta Krygier
Sandra Simmonds

Facilities
Head of Facilities
Anita Pfauntsch
Assistant Manager
Peter Keiff
Security Supervisor
Bogdan Swidzinski
Maintenance & Security
Lea Ketsawang
Ebere Nwosu
Colin Prendergast
Leslaw Skrzypiec
Mariusz Stawiarski
Marcin Falfus
Arkadiusz Osman
Sam Dargan
Healthy and Safety Officer
Jillian Berry

Front of House
Head Receptionist
Philippa Burton
Receptionists
Mary Lee
Hiroe Shin Shigemitsu

Catering/Bar
Head of Catering
Pascal Babeau
Deputy Manager/Barman
Darko Calina
Catering Assistants
Aya Ghislaine Djan
Samy Hedin
Miodrag Ristic
Daniel Swidzinski
Isabelle Kacou
(to March 2015)

Human Resources
Head
Tehmina Mahmood
P/T Adminstrator
Rosanna Innocenti

THOUGHT SHELF

MAKING

CHANGING

SHARED

SPACES

Each year the AA's public programme brings together thousands of members, visitors, critics and provocateurs for the purpose of sharing, discussing and debating architectural ideas, knowledge and agendas. The following section reshuffles how we typically label life at the AA – lectures, exhibitions and symposia – using the idea of space as our framework to offer a glimpse into the events, publications and spontaneous happenings that drive AA life in London, Europe and beyond.

During the past year AA events have been held far and wide – from the front steps of the Venice Architecture Biennale, where we constructed a 1:1 copy of the Maison Dom-ino, to a new concert series at Hooke Park, installations on Bedford Square; to juries in Shanghai, design workshops in Tokyo and more presentations in our Lecture Hall than could fit inside a book (one way we make up for that is with aaschool. ac.uk, a boundless resource for microsites, lecture videos, archival material and more). What we hope you discover is not just a school but an open platform for architectural invention, experimentation and communication.

Brett Steele

2014–15 Events

June

30 June – 11 July
Visiting School
Aditnálta

Visiting School
San Juan

July

7
Member Event
Weekend trip to Venice
Architecture Biennale
and Giorgio Cini
Foundation

7–18
Visiting School
London
SummerMAKE

7–25
Visiting School
London
Summer School

8
Format
Tamara Barnett-Herrin
and Shumon Basar
Kurt Cobain Format *

10
Format
Noemi Blager and
Madelon Vriesendorp
Lina Bo Bardi Format *

14–23
Visiting School
San Francisco

16
Format
Brett Steele and
Shumon Basar
A.R.Chitect Format *

18
Format
Omar Kholcif and
Travis Jeppesen
Chelsea Manning
Format *

18–26
Visiting School
Shanghai

21–30
Visiting School
New York

21 July – 8 August
Visiting School
Dorset

Visiting School
Nicosia

22–31
Visiting School
Sao Paulo

22 July – 8 August
Visiting School
Unknown Fields Division

23 July - 7 August
Visiting School
Bilbao

28 July – 5 August
Visiting School
Taipei

August

1–9
Visiting School
Berlin

11–21
Visiting School
Seoul

13–22
Visiting School
Cologne

22 August –
12 September
Visiting School
Koshirakura/Tokyo

23 August – 9 September
Visiting School
Tehran

26
Hooke Park Event
Stephen Upshaw and
Callie Hough
Concert: Sonic Coast

September

8 September –
19 December
Visiting School
London
Autumn Semester
Programme

22–26
Intro Week

30
Night School Book Club
Owen Hatherley
Across the Plaza: The
Public Voids of the Post
Soviet Society

October

1
AA Film Club
Dark City

3
Exhibition Openings
AA Gallery
Ordinary Takeover
Front Members' Room
Honours 2014
AA Bar
Prizes 2014
Graduate Gallery
Director's Selection
Photo Library Corridor
AA Camera Club 2014

4
Saturday Gallery Talk
Alex Kaiser and
Magnus Larsson
Ordinary Takeover

8
AA Film Club
Gattaca

10
AA 167th Birthday Party
Tales from the Woods
A Theatre of Birthday
Party

13
Night School Run Club
Nash Ramblas to the
Reinvention
of Marylebone

What's Next
Lecture Series
Julia King and Asif Khan
in conversation *

15
Night School
Alex Kaiser and
Magnus Larsson
An Ordinary Evening:
Smashing and Putting
Back Together. Almost.

16
Evening Lecture
Sam Jacob
A Clockwork Jerusalem:
Planning and the
British Psyche *

Member Screening
Between the Folds

17
Memorial Event
Remembering
Kathryn Findlay

20
Evening Lecture
Giles Price
Mega Projects – People
and the Place *

21
Joint Evening Lecture
Mark Pimlott
Propositions for things
and places
Tony Fretton
Buildings and their
Territories *

22
Night Photography
Workshop
Sue Barr

AA Film Club
THX-1138

23
Book Launch
Richard Martin
The Architecture of
David Lynch

27
What's Next
Lecture Series
Alex Kaiser and
Magnus Larsson
An Ordinary Evening *

28
Evening Lecture
Alexander Eisenschmidt
Chicagoism and the
Export of Metropolitan
Architecture *

29
Invitation-Only
Member Event
Class of 1964 Reunion

AA Film Club
Akira

31
Friday Lectures
Mark Cousins
The Gest[ure] *

Night School
Ivor Williams
Open Plan Dying

November

3
AA Council
Ordinary General Meeting

AA XX 100
Interview Transcription
Workshop

Night School Run Club
Taming the Southbank:
Bear Pits, Skateboarders
and Property Developers

3–7
Open Week

3–10
Open Workshop
Elia Zenghelis
The Public Interior

4
Scavengers and Other
Creatures Lecture Series
Lebbeus Woods:
Projecting Realities
Didier Faustino, Theo
Spyropoulos and Liam
Young. Organised by
Nannette Jackowski and
Ricardo De Ostos *

5
Emergent Technologies
Open Lecture
Sylvia Felipe and
Jordi Truco
Time-based Spatial
Formations through
Material Intelligence *

Night Photography
Workshop
Sue Barr

6
Book Launch
Adam Caruso &
Helen Thomas
The Stones of Fernand
Pouillon

7
Architects' Mass 2014

10
Evening Lecture
Elia Zenghelis
On the Road of the
Condenser: 45 years
of Architectural
Conjecture *

11
Evening Lecture
& Book Launch
CJ Lim
Food City

12
AA Film Club
Underground

13
Evening Lecture
Vicente Guallart
Barcelona 5.0: The
Self-Sufficient City *

14
State of the Association
Director's Address

Open PhD Seminar
Ross Adams
The Present Interior: The
Pathology of Space-Time
in the Urban

Friday Lectures
Mark Cousins
The Gest[ure] *

Exhibition Openings
AA Gallery
All Purpose
(À Toutes Fins Utiles)
Front Members' Room
Foreign Correspondence

15
Saturday Gallery Talk
Cédric Libert, Alice
Grégoire, Paul Cournet
and Max Kahlen
All Purpose

17
Evening Lecture
UniversalAssemblyUnit
A Space Animation
Studio *

18
What's Next
Lecture Series
Giulia Foscari
Elements of Venice *

19
AA Film Club
Rear Window

AA Members' Event
Member Visit
Constructing Worlds
Exhibition at the
Barbican

20
Evening Lecture
Deborah Saunt & Tom
Greenall (DSDHA)
Why Architecture Must
Never Stand Still *

21
Friday Lectures
Mark Cousins
The Gest[ure] *

Night School
Crude Hints: AA Night
School at the Soane with
Madelon Vriesendorp

24
What's Next
Lecture Series
AIRBNB Collective
Home 2014 *

25
Evening Lecture
Reinier de Graaf
The Risk of Realism *

26
PhD Seminar
Amy Concannon
Building and Time:
Curating 'Ruin Lust'

AA Collections Talk
FR Yerbury: Representing
Modern Architecture

AA Film Club
Exterminating Angel

27
Evening Lecture
Mi5, Manuel Collado
& Nacho Martín
Improve Your Life! *

December

1
What's Next
Lecture Series
Flavie Audi
Sensual Clarity *

1–10
Visiting School
Chennai
Hyper-threads

2
Evening Lecture
Matthias Kohler
The Robotic Touch:
How Robots Change
Architecture

3
Evening Lecture
Studio Weave
Longest, Loudest,
Spiciest, Scariest: Studio
Weave present their
somethingest projects

4
Evening Lecture
Jacquie Burgess
Co-hosted with
Landscape Research
Group *

Night School Book Club
Keller Easterling
The Action is the Form:
Victor Hugo's Ted Talk

5
Friday Lectures
Mark Cousins
The Gest[ure] *

6
The Architecture
Exchange Series
Mouffe in conversation
with Aureli, Martin,
Weizman and Whiting
How is Architecture
Political? *

8
PhD Open Seminar Series
Jane Alison
Building and Interior:
The Surreal House

Evening Lecture
Vittorio Lampugnani
The Craft of Urban
Design, Reinvented *

Night School Run Club
Soho Nights

9
What's Next
Lecture Series
Max Kahlen & Chris Dyvik
A kitchen table, a small
house, a foyer, a
twin-house, a warehouse
and artist's studio *

Night School Book Club
Strelka Press Series:
Eyal and Ines Weizman
Reading Before and
After: Documenting the
Architecture of Disaster

10
AA Film Club
After Hours

11
Evening Lecture
and Book Launch
Sylvia Lavin
Flash in the Pan

AA Members' Screening
Chasing Ice

12
AA PhD Symposium
Algorithms &
Actualisation
With Keynote Speakers
Mark Burry, John Frazer
and Xavier de Kestelier *

15–19
End of Term Juries

January

3–13
Visiting School
Haiti

7–16
Visiting School
Colchane and Santiago

10–18
Visiting School
Rio de Janeiro

12 January – 24 April
Visiting School
London
Spring Semester
Programme

15
Evening Lecture
Francesca Hughes
The Architecture of Error:
Matter, Measure and the
Misadventures of
Precision *

16
Friday Lectures
Mark Cousins
The Gest[ure]: Gesture &
Rhetoric *

Evening Lecture
Edi Rama, Prime Minister
of Albania
Potential Monuments of
Unrealised Futures

Exhibition Openings
AA Gallery
Potential Monuments
of Unrealised Futures
Front Members' Room
Drawing on Holl
Steven Holl Architects
AA Bar
Salones de Eventos
Freddy Mamani Silvestre

19
Housing & Urbanism
Keynote Lecture
Ruurd Gietema
Pulling Strings Only When
Things Go Wrong *

20
SED Final Jury Event
Brian Ford
The Empirical Tradition
and Innovation in
Architecture *

21
Emtech Keynote Lecture
Jan Knippers
Biological Design and
Integrative Structures *

AA Film Club
Being John Malkovich

22
DRL Keynote Lecture 1
John Frazer
An Evolutionary
Architecture
Reassessed *

23
DRL Keynote Lecture 2
Jason Kelly Johnson *

26
PhD Symposium
AA PhD Candidates *

AA Council
Annual General Meeting

Night School
Crude Hints: AA Night
School at the Soane with
David Chipperfield

27
Book Launch
Nikos Katsikis,
Douglas Spencer and
Jeannette Sordi
New Geographies 6:
Grounding Metabolism

28
MA HCT/PhD Seminar
Alejandra Celedon
Cabinet of Curiosities

Evening Lecture
Mike Davies, Ian Ritchie,
Cristina Garcia,
Piers Gough, Don Gray,
Andrew Holmes
The Culture of
Performance *

AA Film Club
Holy Motors

29
Evening Lecture
Andrea Bagnato, Joseph
Grima, Sam Jacob, Justin
McGuirk, Cat Rossi,
Maria S Giudici,
Marina Otero Verzier
The Quantified Home *

30
Lunchtime Lecture Series
Brett Steele
The Afterlife of Dom-ino

MA HCT Debates
Alexandra Vougia
Prescribing Collective
Experience: The Hellerhof
Housing Estate *

Friday Lectures
Mark Cousins
The Gest[ure]: The
Expression of Emotion *

February

2
What's Next
Lecture Series
Katerina Scoufaridou
SoMe+hing On The Side *

2–12
Visiting School
Jeddah

2–13
Visiting School
Sydney

3
Embedded Intelligence
Lecture Series
David Benjamin
Biological Intelligence *

Evening Lecture
Adam Magyar
Between the Lines *

4
Housing London
Lecture Series
Ben Denton, Martyn
Evans, Pete Jefferys,
Eleanor Dodman
Public vs Private: Who
will provide the housing
London needs? *

AA Film Club
Enemy

6
Friday Lectures
Mark Cousins
The Gest[ure]: Does
Stone Suffer? *

9
Open Week Workshop
Madelon Vriesendorp
Making with Madelon

9–14
Open Week

10
Scavengers and other
Creatures Lecture Series
Assembling Realities
Organised by
Ricardo de Ostos &
Nannette Jackowski *

11
Housing London
Lecture Series
Quantity vs Quality: Can
we deliver and make
great places? *

AA Film Club
The Double Life of
Véronique

12
AA Members' Screening
Archiculture

14
Saturday Gallery Talk
Chris McVoy
Drawing on Holl by
Steven Holl Architects

16
MA History & Critical
Thinking
Jackie Cooper
Publishing Architecture.
Building Discourse. The
editors' story

What's Next
Lecture Series
Jan Nauta
Trial and Error *

17
AActions
Ben Vickers
INFRA_LIFE

AAXX 100 Lecture Series
Alice Rawsthorn
& Sophie Hicks
in conversation *

18
AActions
Marlie Mul
I never felt such emoji

AA Film Club
Eternal Sunshine of
the Spotless Mind

Housing London
Lecture Series
Urban vs Suburban:
Where will we build? *

19
Evening Lecture
Nikolaus Hirsch
Architecture Expanded:
Designing, Building,
Curating, Editing,
Teaching and more

20
Symposium
Future Matters:
The Imminent Reality
of Multi-materiality *

Members' Trip
Tour of Victoria & Albert
Museum's Eileen Gray
Collection

23
What's Next
Lecture Series
OMMX: Jon Lopez &
Hikaru Nissanke
Settings *

24
AAXX 100 Lecture Series
Hilde Heynen & Martha
Thorne in conversation,
chaired by Doina
Petrescu
Feminist Theory and
Starchitecture *

25
*Housing London
Lecture Series*
Housing Young London:
Are we Facing an
Exodus? *

Night School
Oliver Wainwright
Writing About the Unbuilt
City Writing Criticism
Workshop

AA Film Club
Spione

27
Friday Lectures
Mark Cousins
Angelic Despair *

*Exhibition Openings
Front Members' Room*
Jan Kaplický Drawings
AA Bar
Richard Brine: Defensive
Structures in the British
Landscape

28
Saturday Gallery Talk
Amanda Levete
Jan Kaplický Drawings

2
*What's Next
Lecture Series*
Carlos H Matos &
Umberto Bellardi Ricci
Beton Machine *

3
AAActions
Sabel Gavaldon
M/Other Tongue

AAXX 100 Lecture Series
Simon Erridge, Peter
Wilson and Gillian Darley
in conversation, chaired
by Denise Bennetts
Hidden from History:
Royal Shakespeare
Theatre *

4
Evening Lecture
Bjarke Ingels
Hot to Cold *

AA Film Club
Army of Shadows

5
Evening Lecture
Ricardo Bofill
Taller de Arquitectura *

6
HCT Debates
Dis-Locutions –
Architecture and the
Political
Thanos Zartaloudis

*Housing London
Lecture Series*
Housing London Open
Jury

9
AA Council
Annual General Meeting

Evening Lecture
Rem Koolhaas
Elements of Architecture

10
AAXX 100 Lecture Series
Zaida Muxi Martinez &
Liza Fior in conversation,
chaired by Anne Thorne
Urban design from a
gendered perspective *

11
Evening Lecture
Zoe Laughlin
The Performativity of
Matter: Greatest Hits and
New Findings *

AA Film Club
Our Man in Havana

12
Evening Lecture
Alex Lehnerer
Architecture's Present
Perfect *

13
Lunchtime Lecture
Shumon Basar, Emily
King, Jim Stoddart &
Thomas Weaver
Paperback OS: The Book
as Resilient Technology *

16
*Night School Portfolio
Workshop*
Part 1: Preparing a
Portfolio and Applying for
Work

18
*Embedded Intelligence
Lecture Series*
Michael Weinstock
Fabrication Intelligence *

Evening Lecture
Minimaforms: Stephen
Spyropoulos + Theodore
Spyropoulos
All is Architecture *
AA Film Club
The Spy Who Came In
From The Cold

19
Evening Lecture
Spielraum – the
Making of
Barkow Leibinger in
conversation with Brett
Steele, Zak Kyes and
Carson Chan *

20
AA Think Tank
Plan the Planet –
Jaqueline Tyrwhitt
and the Formation of
International and
Global Architecture
Ellen Shoshkes, Keller
Easterling, Kodwo Eshun,
Gediminas & Nomeda
Urbonas, Irit Rogoff,
John Palmesino, Ann-Sofi
Rönnskog *

23
*Night School Drawing
Workshop*
Reinventing the Ruler
with Ordinary Ltd

24
Night School Book Club
Wouter Vanstiphout
Are We the World?

25
AA Film Club
The Ipcress File

9–20
Visiting School
Broken Hill

28
*AA XX 100 / AA
Collections Series*
Iain Jackson
From Croydon to
Chandigarh: Jane Drew
and the Creation of
Tropical Modernism *

30
*Evening Lecture
& Book Launch*
Ingrid Schröder, Manuel
Herz, Rachel Stella
Jenkins & Alex Warnock-
Smith
*African Modernism:
Architecture of
Independence *

1
*Exhibition Openings
Front Members' Room*
Ludwig Leo – Ausschnitt:
Five Projects From 1960s
West Berlin
Graduate Gallery
AA Visiting School

2
Saturday Gallery Talk
Ludwig Leo – Ausschnitt
With Jack Burnett-Stuart
& Gregor Harbusch

5
*Embedded Intelligence
Lecture Series*
Skylar Tibbits
Material Intelligence *

6
Evening Lecture
Robert Horton
What Time Is It There?
Time as a Character in
Contemporary Films

AA Film Club
Mystery Train

7
Evening Lecture
Ilias Papageorgiou, SO–IL
Ambiguous Boundaries

Member Screening
Watermark

8
Exhibition Opening
A Clockwork Jerusalem
AA Gallery

12
*AA XX 100 / AA
Collections Series*
Katie Lloyd Thomas
The New Synthesist:
Proprietary Specification,
Ripolin and Elizabeth
Benjamin's East Wall
(1936) *

14
*Evening Lecture
& Book Launch*
Nathalie Du Pasquier &
Omar Sosa
*Don't Take These
Drawings Seriously
(1981–87)* *

13
AA Film Club
Barton Fink

15
Evening Lecture
Jane Rendell, Sally Shaw,
Miraj Ahmed & Kelly
Chorpening
Site Specifics *

16
Saturday Gallery Talk
Miraj Ahmed
Between Thought
and Space

16–27
Visiting School
Los Angeles

18
Book Launch
Erik Swyngedouw
Liquid Power

19
*AA XX 100 / AA
Collections Series*
Patrick Zamarian
Moth-Eaten Old Students
and Noisy Little
Schoolboys – The AA in
the Postwar Era *

Night School Book Club
Dan Hill
Dark Matter and Trojan
Horses: A Strategic
Design Vocabulary

20
Book Launch
Matthew Beaumont
Nightwalking

AA Film Club
The Shining

21
AA Members' Screening
Sand Wars

23–30
Visiting School
Lyon, France

26
*Exhibition Opening
Photo Library Corridor*
AA Camera Club 2015

27
AA Film Club
2046

June

2
*AA Night School X
Archiboo*
Paul Raftery
Drones, Time-Lapse and
Social Media: How
Technology is Helping to
Tell a Deeper Story About
Buildings

Book Launch
Jacob van der Beugel
& Joanna Bird
The North Sketch
Sequence

3
AA Film Club
Badlands

4
*AA Night School X
Archiboo*
Paul Raftery
Shooting and Sharing
Architecture

5
Book Launch
Takero Shimazaki
t-sa FORUM Vol 5:
Refurbishment

6
Saturday Gallery Talk
Sam Jacob & Wouter
Vanstiphout
A Clockwork Jerusalem

8
AA Council
Ordinary General Meeting

10
AA Film Club
Wild at Heart

13
*AA Night School X
Archiboo*
Liam Young
Telling Stories with
Drones

16
Members' Trip
Peter Rees
Sky Garden @ 20
Fenchurch Street

17
AA Film Club
Zabriskie Point

18
AA Members' Screening
Oscar Niemeyer:
Life is a Breath of Air

24
AA Film Club
Vanishing Point

26
Projects Review 2015

29
Members' Evening
Projects Review 2015

* Available to watch online at www.aaschool.ac.uk

Night School at the Soane Museum with David Chipperfield

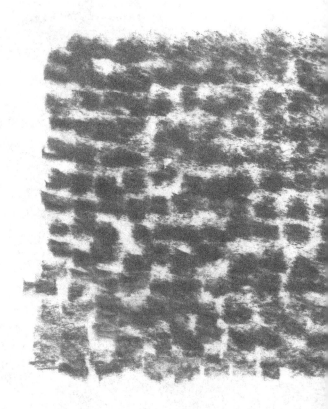

Tiffany & Co, Tokyo, 2008

1:1 spread from *Small Architecture/Natural Architecture* by Kengo Kuma, AA Publications 2015

SHELF SPACE

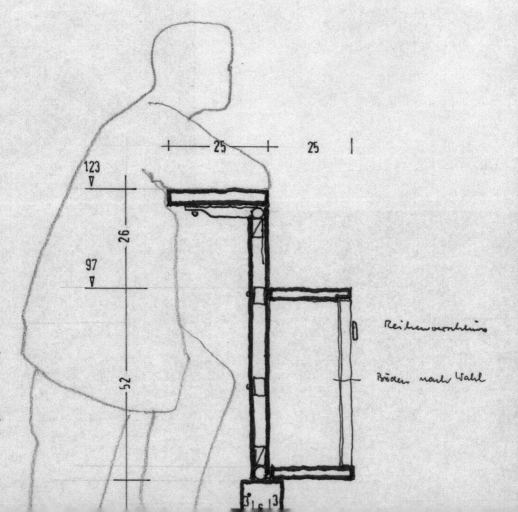

1:1 page from *Architecture Without Content*, Bedford Press 2015

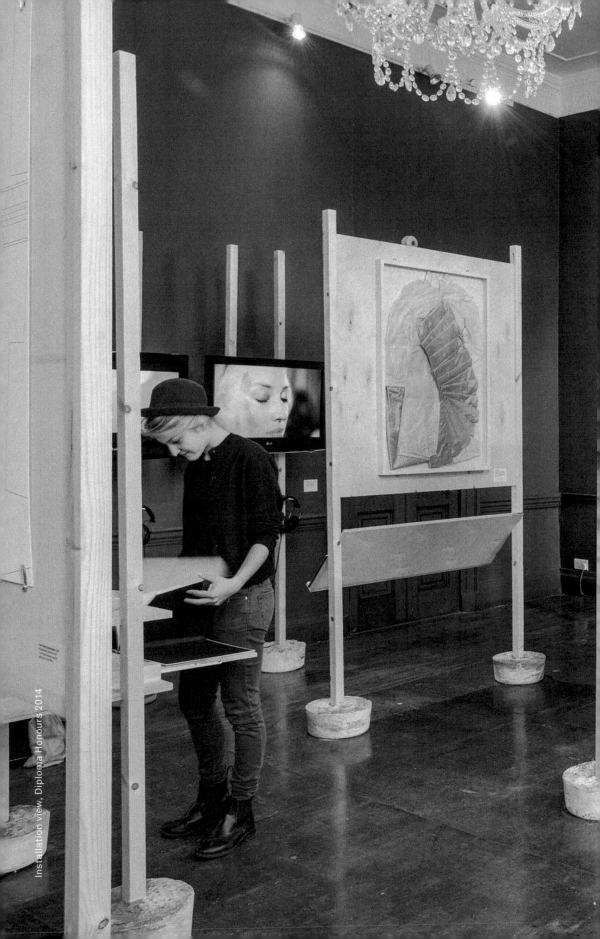

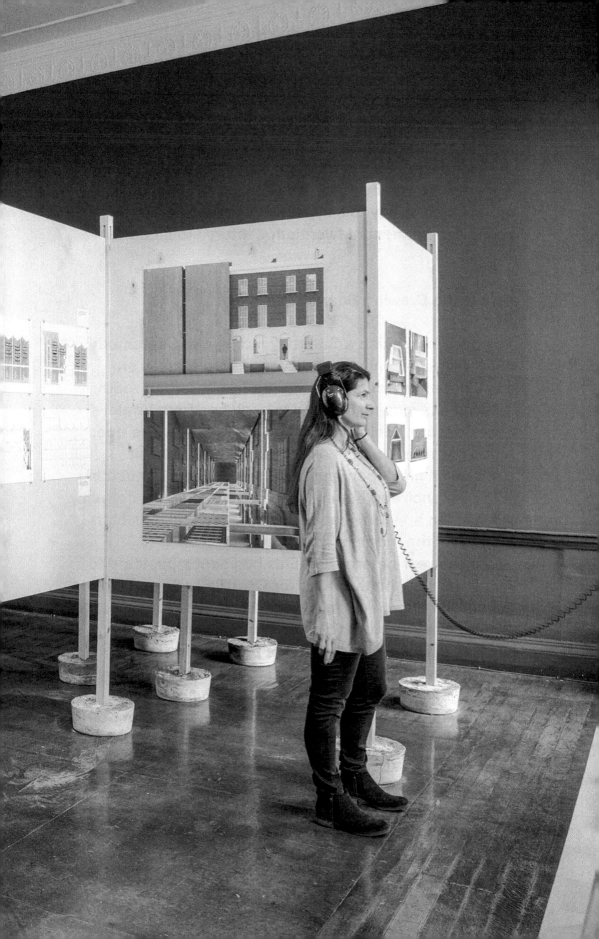

his partnership with Denise Scott Brown later drew him. On the other hand, Alan was also understanding about Peter Eisenman's extreme formalism.

I think both he and I recognised that we were very much on the same wavelength. We both wanted to continue developing the foundational rationale of modernism, we shared many admirations – for the work of Aldo van Eyck, for instance – and, without any specific loyalty to a style, we also held fast to the social commitment of twentieth-century architecture.

Across the Drawing Board   John Miller

You have to imagine a Saturday morning in September 1957. I have recently joined Lyons Israel Ellis as an assistant architect, and am in the front drafting room, drawing and singing inaccurate snatches from Vivaldi's Four Seasons. I think I am alone in the office. The door to the partners' room is directly behind where I sit. Suddenly it flies open and there stands Alan, conducting with his pencil and humming the Vivaldi themes, correctly. His sudden appearance and my surprise make us both laugh. It is the moment we become friends.

The year before, Tom Ellis had sent a postcard to Alan, who was then working for Candilis Josic and Woods in Paris, inviting him to join Lyons Israel Ellis. Alan accepted the offer, replacing Jim Stirling as an associate. When Jim heard about it he sent him a postcard saying, 'On no account must you go to Lyons Israel Ellis. I forbid it.' Alan later commented, 'Pure dog in the manger.'

Before Paris, Alan had been part of a London County Council team that included Sandy Wilson and Peter Carter.

1:1 pages from *Colquhounery*, edited by Irina Davidovici (this page) and *Flash in the Pan*, by Sylvia Lavin (opposite) AA Publications 2014–15

in a state in which architecture performs as a palpably manifest substance instead of a detached and abstract system, while building moves in the opposite direction and fades into liminality.

In 1963 Andy Warhol began looking for a new workspace. In January 1964 he moved into a derelict building

on East 47th Street where Billy Linich, better known as Billy Name, soon covered the space in tinfoil and aluminium industrial paint, a combination he had first used in his downtown apartment.[5] It is said that the periodic repainting of the Mid-Hudson Bridge near his family home in Poughkeepsie inspired Billy's décor. But of course there were many examples of silverised architecture, from Richard Neutra, who had used

Billy Name, Andy Warhol at The Factory, c1964

paint on wood framing in most of his well-known mid-century houses in Los Angeles to Isamu Noguchi, whose own downtown studio was painted with aluminium paint at the suggestion of Buckminster Fuller.[6] But while an architect responding to such precedents would no doubt have understood that the aluminium in the paint had been intended to grant the painted surface the status of metal construction, Warhol and his peers read the aluminium paint and the tinfoil indiscriminately as silver.[7]

In other words, Warhol did not think of silver as a material, as an architect would understand the concept: none of the things he associated with the colour of the Factory – astronaut suits, the silver screen and mirrors – were actually made of silver in 1963. Instead, silver was an effect that, particularly when exaggerated by stage lights, animated the Factory's interior and made the ambience of the space itself a machine for producing endless, shifting images. As if to emphasise the nature of this apparitional environment, a disco ball – the quintessential proliferator and environmental diffuser of quasi-serial images – occupied a prominent position on the Factory floor.

127

Body Building

Sam Jacob

I get a pump when the blood is running into my muscles. They become really tight with blood. Like the skin is going to explode any minute. It's like someone putting air in my muscles. It blows up. It feels fantastic.

This is Arnold Schwarzenegger – bodybuilder, the Austrian Oak, five times Mr Universe, seven times Mr Olympia and star of blockbuster movies – describing the sensation he gets when he works out. He's talking about the way it feels to continually tear his muscle fibres, to pump blood though his veins, to feel the body physically transforming, shapeshifting into his trademark exaggerated form.

Here he is again, now talking about the way he thinks about his body:

You don't really see a muscle as a part of you, in a way. You see it as a thing. You look at it as a thing and you say, well, this thing has to be built a little longer, the bicep has to be longer, or the tricep has to be thicker here in the elbow area. And you look at it and it doesn't even seem to belong to you. Like a sculpture.

ie is not the only one who thinks like this. What he's really articulating is an idea about the body as something other than a natural evolutionary inheritance. He, like all of us, recognises that human biology is a site of cultural imagination, a place where a vast range of societal forces, ideals, dreams, ambitions and also fears reside – where our sense of self and identity, our humanity, is constructed. Bodies, in other words, are things that can be built.

This idea, which can be traced right back to the origins of western civilisation, is embedded not only in the machinations of religion, politics and society, but also in architecture. The obvious synthesis of all of these is *De architectura*, from around 15 BCE, in which the Roman architect and engineer Vitruvius sets out an ideal of human proportion as a prelude to perfect architectural proportion. He describes a human body as if it were a harmonic embodiment of ratios and geometry – the body as a mathematical object. Later, of course, he talks of the same principles in architecture, describing how 'in the members of a temple there ought to be the greatest harmony in the symmetrical relations of the different parts to the general magnitude of the whole'. But most radically he conflates the two in his description of what has come to be known as Vitruvian Man.

For if a man be placed flat on his back, with his hands and feet

the he
are pe
W
of all
ing *L*
from
to giv
Vitruv
figure
diagr

gio Martini's rather foppish
more calculated, geometric
recently, the signature squar
has lent itself to the depicti
stoner manhood, from a *Sta*
son to a generic fat guy in his
vian Man remains the one cr
image that quickly became th
ism. For it was the graphic cla
Vitruvian ideal as a convincir
that it had taken so long for
And the reason it took so long
alter the human form to mal
gravity of the circle and squa
metric idealism meant redesi

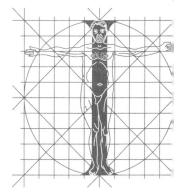

when I did my curling exerc
Leonardo image can also be a
ideas of cosmic resonance ar
'What? know ye not that your
preaches Corinthians 6:19–20
bore tut-tutting at your unhea

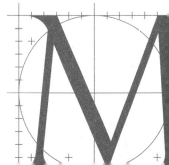

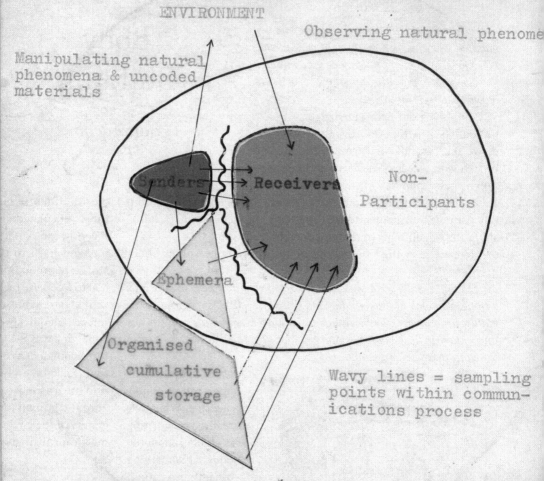

ENVIRONMENT

Observing natural phenome

Manipulating natural
phenomena & uncoded
materials

Senders → Receivers

Non-
Participants

Ephemera

Organised
cumulative
storage

Wavy lines = sampling
points within commun-
ications process

RELATIONS WITH THE ENVIRONMENT FOR A GROWING SOCIO-
CULTURAL SYSTEM

Shumon
Emily Ki
Jim Stoc

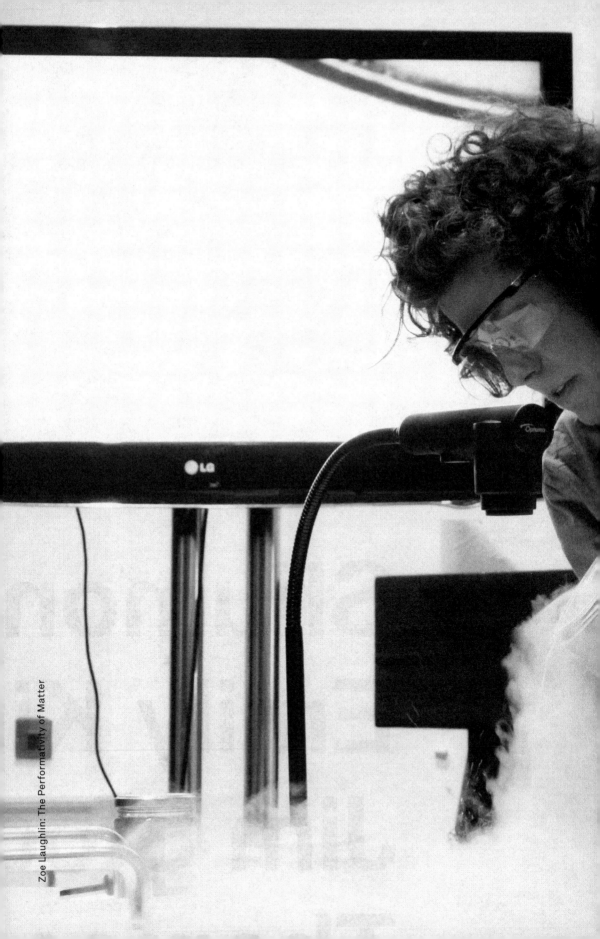

Zoe Laughlin: The Performativity of Matter

MAKING SPACE

Biomass Boiler House, Hooke Park

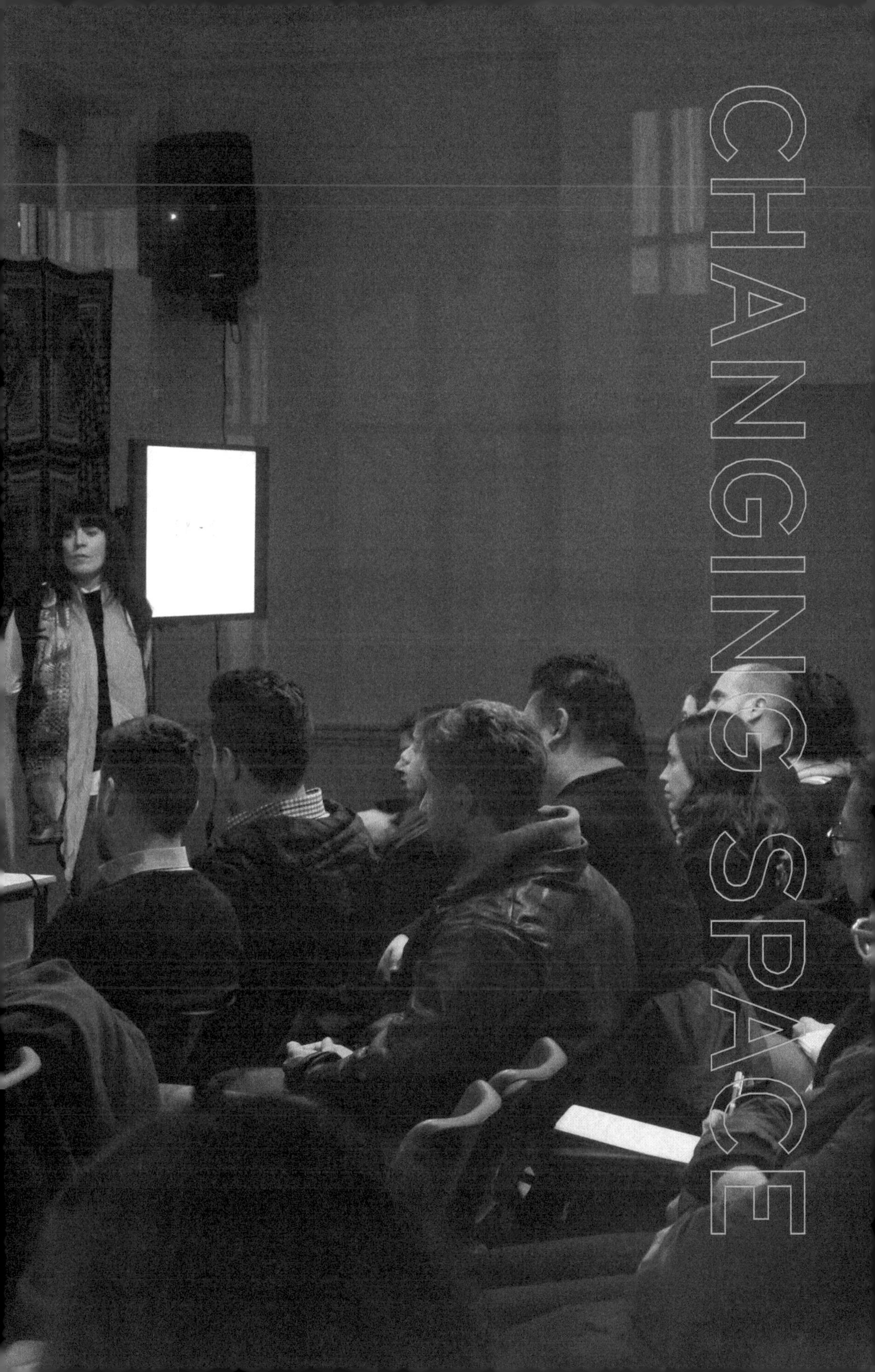
CHANGINGSPACE

CONCRETE
PICTURESQU

WORK
SALeM

...y about how history, science
...t to imagine new visions of Britain
...ver these new landscapes became

...lake's Jerusalem, through Arts and
...enities. Ebenezer Howard's radical
...alism of the postwar New Towns

...low story, for architecture and planning
...ation to build our own New Jerusalem
...rently asking questions like:

...ay disrupt traditional ideas of cities

...rerscend the economics of growth
...sustainability?

...e the place of public planning in re-visi
...al?

...al Britain and for eternal heritage
...rary planning?

...er Howard's question from 1902

Installation view, A Clockwork Jerusalem

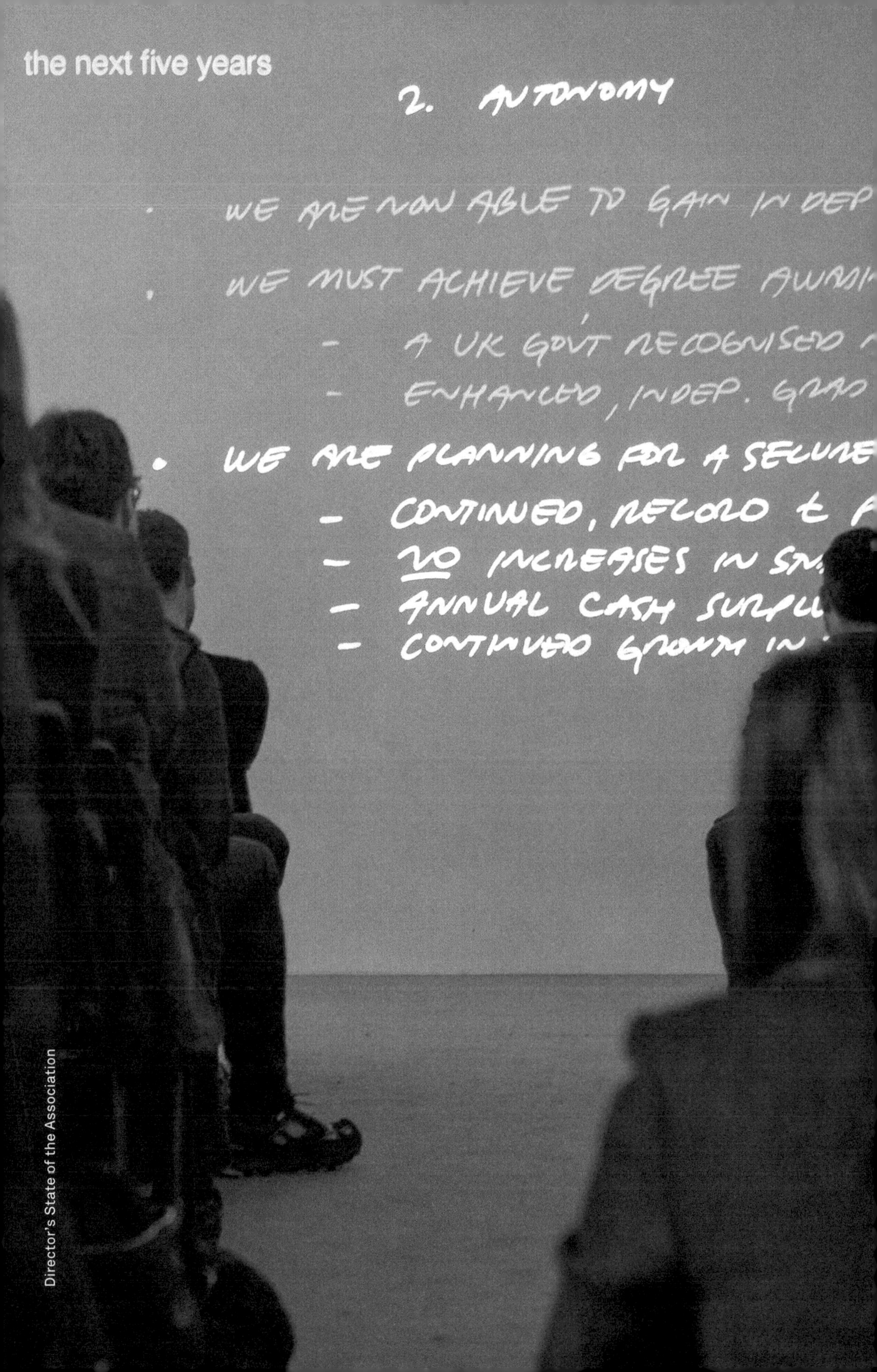

the next five years

2. AUTONOMY

- WE ARE NOW ABLE TO GAIN INDEP
- WE MUST ACHIEVE DEGREE AWARD
  - A UK GOV'T RECOGNISED
  - ENHANCED, INDEP. GRAD

- WE ARE PLANNING FOR A SECURE
  - CONTINUED, RECORD &
  - NO INCREASES IN SM
  - ANNUAL CASH SURPL
  - CONTINUED GROWTH IN

SHARED SPACE
Exploring the reactive, interactive and animated nature of spatial practice
semblyUnit

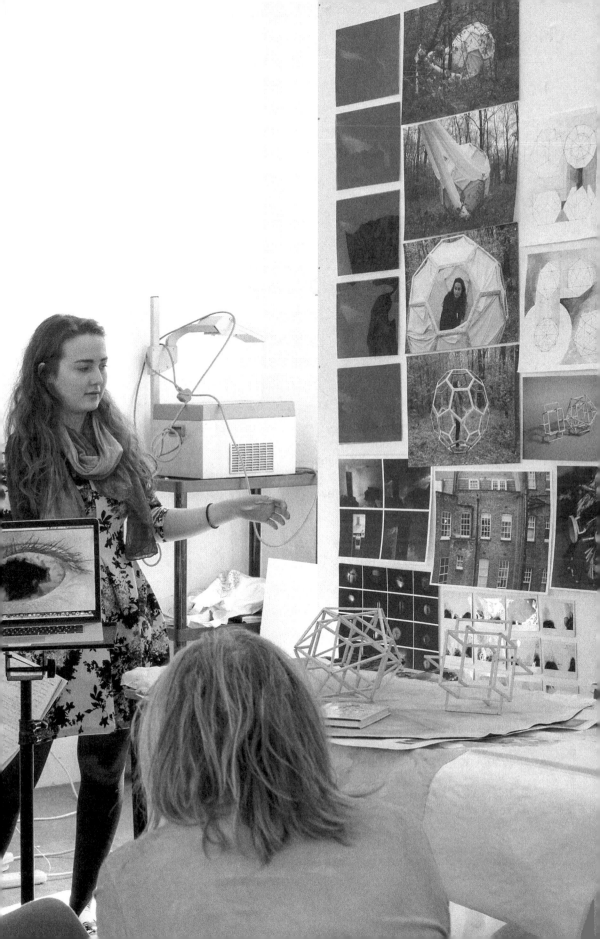

Colophon

Editor: Sarah Handelman
Art Director: Zak Kyes
Design: Claire Lyon, Wayne Daly
Renders: Eyal Amsili Giovannetti

Printed in Germany by
Printmanagement Plitt

ISBN 978-1-907896-76-7
ISSN 2053-7611

AA Publications are initiated by the
Director of the AA School, Brett Steele,
and produced through the AA Print Studio.

AA Book 2015 and back issues are
available from:

AA Publications, 36 Bedford Square,
London, WC1B 3ES

T + 44 (0)20 7887 4021
F + 44 (0)20 7414 0783
publications@aaschool.ac.uk

www.aaschool.ac.uk/publications

Download last year's AA Book 2014 ebook
edition exclusively on iBookstore. Search
'AA Book 2014'.

Space photos Sue Barr, Valerie Bennett
and Eduardo Andreu Gonzalez.